To Dana

THE YOGA STORE
MURDER

THE SHOCKING TRUE ACCOUNT OF
THE LULULEMON ATHLETICA KILLING

DAN MORSE

BERKLEY BOOKS, NEW YORK

THE BERKLEY PUBLISHING GROUP
Published by the Penguin Group
Penguin Group (USA) LLC
375 Hudson Street, New York, New York 10014

USA • Canada • UK • Ireland • Australia • New Zealand • India • South Africa • China

penguin.com

A Penguin Random House Company

THE YOGA STORE MURDER

A Berkley Book / published by arrangement with the author

For information, address: The Berkley Publishing Group,
a division of Penguin Group (USA) LLC,
375 Hudson Street, New York, New York 10014.

ISBN: 978-0-425-26364-8

PUBLISHING HISTORY
Berkley premium edition / November 2013

PRINTED IN THE UNITED STATES OF AMERICA

10 9 8 7 6 5 4 3 2 1

Cover art of *Yoga Mat* © discpicture/shutterstock; *Footprints* © Igor
Kovalchuk/shutterstock; *Abstact Grunge Texture* © Ursa Major/shutterstock; and
Detailed View of Yoga Mat Texture © Ambient Ideas/shutterstock.
Cover design by Jane Hammer.

Most Berkley Books are available at special quantity discounts for bulk purchases for sales
promotions, premiums, fund-raising, or educational use. Special books, or book excerpts, can
also be created to fit specific needs. For details, write: Special.Markets@us.penguingroup.com.

Contents

BETHESDA

CHAPTER ONE

It Couldn't Happen Here

The sounds—were they screams?—reached Jana Svrzo as she walked across the sales floor of the Apple Store, now closed for the night. Jana (pronounced "Yah-nah") was twenty-nine years old and wore funky black sneakers and a ready smile—an easy fit among Apple's hip, young sales army. It was just after 10:00 P.M. on Friday, March 11, 2011, in downtown Bethesda, an affluent area just north of the nation's capital, and Jana, the store's manager, had about an hour's worth of record-keeping ahead of her, following the opening day sales for Apple's hot new product, the iPad 2, which had created a nearly four-hundred-foot line of eager buyers down the sidewalk.

Now, though, she looked to her right and listened. The sounds were high-pitched yelps and squeals, and low-pitched grunts, thuds, a dragging noise, as if something heavy was being moved. Jana thought they might be coming from a room near the back exit or a room upstairs, where technicians were still on duty. She asked one of the two security guards to help her search.

Jana and the guard split up, meeting two minutes later upstairs, where they spoke to another young manager, Ricardo Rios, who wore a dark baseball cap and a bright blue Apple employee shirt.

"Screaming," the guard said. "It sounded like some lady was screaming."

They checked out the technicians' room. All clear. They walked downstairs to the sales floor and heard more yelling. Suddenly, Jana felt sure of the origin. "It's coming from next door," she said—from lululemon athletica, the luxury yoga store with which Apple shared a wall.

She and Ricardo walked closer to the wall. Jana now could hear someone saying: "Talk to me. Don't do this. Talk to me. What's going on?"

Then she heard what sounded like a different voice, maybe the one that had just been screaming. Now it was quieter: "God help me. Please help me."

Ricardo also could hear that first voice, the one saying "Talk to me," but couldn't make out the words of the second one. They were muffled, covered by crying and panting, as if a woman was trying to catch her breath. Ricardo kept staring at the wall, walked away from it, returned, then knocked on it, trying to get the attention of whoever was on the other side. "What's going on?" he asked, his voice raised.

No response.

"Maybe I should just call the cops," Jana said.

"That's up to you," Ricardo answered. He thought it was a private matter, and told Jana it sounded as if one person had just heard tragic news and the other was trying to get her to talk about it. "I think it's just drama."

Ricardo said he was going back upstairs and did so. It

was 10:19, eight minutes after Jana had first heard the noises.

Wilbert Hawkins, the second of the two security guards, had been observing the commotion without feeling overly concerned. The crashing sounds, he figured, could have been a merchandise display falling over, the yelling some kind of horsing around. It didn't seem threatening. Maybe if they were somewhere in nearby D.C., where, even in a high-end area like Georgetown, danger could erupt without warning—but not here, Wilbert thought, not along the tony, walkable streets in the middle of Bethesda.

Jana sensed the noises growing fainter. To her left, outside the glass front doors, the sidewalks were slowing down but still active. People huddled in coats against the chilly March air, walking to and from restaurants and bars. In the few months Jana had worked at the store, she'd come to see how safe the area was. Jana shared Wilbert's view: surely the noise was something explainable. She went upstairs. For the next half hour, she and Ricardo went through their closing duties, typing away on computers, adding up receipts for the day.

Ricardo left at 10:56 P.M. Jana finished ten minutes later. She walked downstairs again, across the sales floor to the front door. A new security guard on duty let her out. The restaurant to her left was still open. To her right, the yoga store and the store beyond it were dark and closed. It was March 11, 2011, and all seemed normal.

CHAPTER TWO

"Is She Going to Make It?"

The morning of Saturday, March 12, twenty-six-year-old Ryan Haugh walked up to the Apple Store in Bethesda. He'd tried to buy an iPad 2 the night before and waited in the long line outside for more than two hours, but the prized computer tablets were sold out by the time he got to the door. Ryan didn't want to make the same mistake again, so he'd thrown on some jeans and a bright red Philadelphia Phillies baseball cap and dashed out of his home that morning without a shower.

It was now 7:45 A.M., more than two hours before the store would open at 10:00. The skies were cloudy, the temperature 41 degrees. No other customers had yet arrived, so Ryan took a seat on a solid teak bench near the Apple Store, whipped out his iPhone and began reading the *New York Times*. Ryan didn't typically spend much time in this five-block area, called Bethesda Row, finding the prices a bit high and jokingly comparing it to elements of the 1998 movie *Pleasantville*, which captured safe and perfectly ordered streets. But the biotechnology-industry salesman certainly enjoyed the place when he did come. In the carefully developed retail blocks around him, stores offered serenity, luxury, and virtue—sometimes rolled into a single product. Spas served up $130 facials. An eco-friendly toy store sold $73 toxin-free, German-made fire trucks. A furniture place called Urban Country had a distressed-wood dinner table for sale at $2,513. Chic restaurants and bars stayed open late and gave patrons a sense of urban energy without the danger.

Others started to join Ryan in the line. Shortly after 8:00 A.M., he saw a woman approach, her orange running shoes bright against the gray morning, and go into the store next to Apple, clearly an employee about to start her day. Moments later, Ryan heard a voice.

"Hello? Hello?!"

There was an edge to it. The woman in the orange shoes came back out and was talking on her phone. "I hear someone moaning in the back," she was saying, "and it looks like it's been vandalized and I'm just really scared to go in."

To Ryan it was clear she had called 911. The woman's panic was growing. She answered a few more questions, giving her name, Rachel, and the address of the store. The police were coming. She ended the call and turned toward Ryan. "Have you seen anyone go in or out of this store this morning?" she asked him.

"No," Ryan said, leaving his spot in line to go to her.

"Do you want me to go in?" he asked her.

"Would you mind?" Rachel answered.

The two walked in. Ahead of them was a long narrow space with wooden floors and high ceilings. Ryan had never been inside a lululemon shop. He thought it looked kind of like a Gap, with lots of low racks and tables full of bright-colored clothes. He walked to the back as Rachel waited up front. "Anybody here?" Ryan called out. "Anybody here?" No response.

On the floor, Ryan saw scattered bloodstains, which grew more concentrated as he advanced to a back corner, near a five-foot chalkboard inscribed with colored chalk: "May each of us equally enjoy happiness and the root of happiness." He noticed even more blood at the base of a purple door, as if it had seeped from the other side. He gently pushed the purple door. It stopped, hitting the side of a body.

Ryan saw a pair of legs extending from a body facedown surrounded by more blood. He reached down. No movement. "There's somebody back here!" he shouted back to Rachel. "It looks like they're dead!"

He headed back toward the front of the store, for the first time noticing two bathrooms to his right. Their doors were both open, and he saw another pair of legs, bound at the ankles and extending from one of the doorways. "There's somebody else in here!" Ryan called out.

He approached the second woman, noting that her hands were bound over her head, and her face was bloody. "Are you okay?" he asked. She moaned, barely.

Rachel rushed outside and called 911 again. The other Apple customers waiting in line overheard her. "One person seems dead," she was saying, her voice shaking, "and the other person is breathing . . . Someone tied her up."

Seconds later a police car zoomed down Bethesda Avenue, stopping in front of the crowd. The officer jumped out and told the crowd to get back. The Apple customers retreated toward the Apple Store, still keeping some semblance of a line. The officer drew her gun and went into the store.

Then, silence. No shots. No screams. More cops arrived and rushed into the store, then paramedics, who rolled a stretcher into the store. Minutes later, they wheeled it out. There was a woman on top, covered in a blanket, writhing in pain. The customers could see blood on her face. "Is she going to make it?" one of them asked.

CHAPTER THREE

Evil Unleashed

Bethesda, Maryland, is a classic "inner-ring" suburb, close enough to a major city for quick commutes but just far enough out to boast great schools and little crime. Home to economists, lawyers, lobbyists, and biochemists, Bethesda ranks as the most educated place in the nation as measured by recent U.S. Census Bureau figures of graduate degrees per adult. It's part of Montgomery County, which itself spreads out for another twenty-five miles and has nearly one million people. Among that population, there are about twenty murders a year—far fewer than in Washington, D.C., but certainly enough to warrant an on-call homicide detective. The morning of March 12, 2011, that detective was sixty-year-old Jim Drewry.

Drewry had gotten up early inside his two-story home in Silver Spring, where he and his ex-wife had raised three kids, now grown. Drewry was ready to go when his cell phone rang at 9:05. Minutes later, he was driving his unmarked, county-issued Dodge Intrepid west toward the yoga store.

To his younger colleagues, Drewry was a real-life version of Lester Freamon, the cerebral African American detective from the TV series *The Wire*. A gray-haired grandfather with a bushy mustache, Drewry wore wire-rimmed glasses, sweater vests, and loafers, and spoke with a cadence that harkened back to the 1960s. Something suspicious was "funky." A house was a "joint." He refused to carry a BlackBerry, believing e-mail was robbing people of their ability to think, and didn't socialize much with his colleagues. At his redbrick house, he relaxed by reading fiction and listening to John Coltrane, Miles Davis, and other jazz legends.

He'd grown up in Cleveland, the son of a schoolteacher and funeral-home director. In summer, he would eat lunch with his dad in the embalming room, where as a thirteen-year-old he watched his dad work on a body marked by several large-caliber bullet holes. "The man was tapped lightly four times with a .45," Drewry's father told him.

Drewry's older brother, who went on to Harvard University, was the first African American to serve as president of his high school's student council. Drewry was elected vice president of his own class, before going to Howard University to study pre-med. He eventually dropped out and took a full-time job delivering mail for the U.S. Postal Service. He began having nightmares about towering stacks of mail surrounding him, so he left that job and, partially on the advice of his father-in-law, who was the director of the D.C. Department of Corrections, became a cop in 1979. He joined the major crimes unit eight years later.

Over the years, Drewry had developed a relaxed interrogation style that prompted suspects to do the last thing they should do: talk. What came out of their mouths was rarely the full story, but that was often just as good. "Lie to me. Please lie to me," Drewry liked to say, repeating a mantra he'd picked up years earlier. "Sometimes a provable lie is just as good as the truth."

He also saw firsthand how some murders came out of the blue—not the sadly predictable inner-city killings tied to drugs and turf, but the sudden ones fueled by passion and rage that Montgomery County's relatively well-off environs often specialized in. And of those, some of the most violent murders Drewry had worked involved female victims: the mother of two young boys hacked more than sixty-five times with a knife and machete; a molecular biologist dragged off her doorstep to a side yard, beaten, strangled, and raped; an artist killed in her studio by a man who rammed a pair of scissors into her ear canal.

Drewry's work included countless rape cases and death investigations (suicides, drownings, workplace accidents), and the long hours had taken their toll. He was weighing a move to the cold-case squad, which would afford him set hours and weekends off. A little time there to reach the thirty-four-year mark to boost his retirement benefits, and then—he liked to joke—he'd open a hot-dog vending truck on the National Mall near the Washington Monument.

As Drewry drove toward the yoga store crime scene, he called his boss, Sergeant Craig Wittenberger, who'd been around almost as long as Drewry. Drewry gave him the initial reports he'd received—two victims found in a store in downtown Bethesda, one killed and the other unconscious and possibly raped—and Drewry and Wittenberger didn't even have to discuss how the case would unfold.

They knew there'd be TV trucks, daily newspaper reports, elected officials asking questions, top brass needing updates.

Drewry pulled up to the store at 9:25 A.M., seeing yellow crime-scene tape outside the front door. He asked the patrolmen to extend the tape farther out from the store to keep passersby from walking across possible evidence. The expansion pushed into the line of Apple customers, who dutifully rerouted their line to head in the opposite direction from Apple's front door. Drewry saw no reason to rush in—not before more detectives and crime-scene investigators arrived—and turned his attention to a sergeant on the scene, Evan Thompson, who brought him up to speed. One store employee had been found dead in a rear hallway of the store, and the other had been taken to Suburban Hospital. The responding cops had searched the store, found no suspects, and were guarding the front and back entrances.

Sergeant Thompson had been inside the store himself, the fourth cop that morning. As he'd waited for the paramedics to arrive, he was able to take five photos of the survivor. He'd also given his digital camera to another officer, who took four photos of the victim in the rear hallway. Thompson now handed the camera to Drewry, who scrolled through the images.

The surviving victim, a young African American woman, was bound around her ankles and wrists. It appeared the assailants had used plastic zip-ties, which stores and other businesses use to cinch packaging, and cops and soldiers use as handcuffs when they have to make group detentions. The victim wore white footie-style socks stained with blood, black yoga pants that had been torn open at the crotch, and a bright, striped top that looked like a sports bra. Something was twisted around her neck. Several of the images zoomed in on her face, revealing how young she looked—maybe early twenties. Her face was caked with dried blood. On the tile floor next to her head was a white rock about the size of a flattened baseball, which sat in a wide streak of blood.

Those photos were disturbing enough, but the images of the murder victim in the narrow hallway looked like something out of a horror movie.

Two walls and a metal bookshelf were heavily spattered with blood, which ran in streaks to the floor. A Caucasian woman lay facedown in the middle of a blood pool so thick that it still had a wet sheen. Beneath her tangled and matted hair was what looked like a wide, open gash in the back of her head. Two ends of a rope extended from under her neck. A red metal toolbox rested on her shoulder. The back of her pants appeared to have been cut open.

Thompson told Drewry that word was starting to filter back from the hospital. The surviving victim had spoken briefly with an officer there, telling him that two masked men had slipped into the store after closing time the night before, and had attacked her and her coworker.

Drewry handed the camera back to the sergeant, and turned his attention to the two laypeople who'd been inside the store that morning. He started with Rachel Oertli, the yoga store manager with the orange sneakers. The detective introduced himself and, not wanting anyone to overhear their conversation, suggested they talk in the front seat of his car.

Rachel told him about the store, part of a nationwide chain. This one had twenty-two employees, and on Friday nights the place closed at 9:00 P.M., after which employees cleaned up and got the store ready for the next day. Drewry asked Rachel who had closed the night before, and wrote down her answer: Brittany Norwood, a twenty-eight-year-old saleswoman, and Jayna Murray, a thirty-year-old supervisor. The first name he'd just heard from the patrol sergeant. She was at the hospital. Therefore, Jayna Murray, Drewry figured, was probably the dead woman in the store.

Rachel told him that Jayna had called her shortly before 10:00 P.M. from her car. Their conversation had been about a store procedure typical in retail called bag checks, where workers check each other's bags and purses on the way out to make sure no one was stealing. As Drewry made notes, Rachel said she and Jayna "spoke briefly about suspecting Norwood of putting merchandise in her bag."

Drewry wasn't sure what to make of that. If Jayna and Brittany had gone through the bag checks and left, why had they been found in the store? But Rachel explained that, according to what she'd learned from other workers, Brittany had accidentally left her wallet behind when they'd closed, and called Jayna to let her back into the store. As a supervisor, Jayna had a key. As an entry-level saleswoman, Brittany did not. Drewry asked Rachel for the phone numbers of the other store employees who'd spoken to either Brittany or Jayna the night before. He would talk to them as soon as he could. For now, he didn't want to overreact to the bag check, not this early in the case, not before they'd even been in the store, and certainly not before they'd had a chance to speak with the survivor.

Drewry walked Rachel back to her coworkers, who had

huddled off to the left, hugging and crying on one another's shoulders, starting to figure out who was back in that hallway. Drewry could see lives starting to turn upside down, like he had countless times before.

The detective had barely arrived, and the story of what had happened here was already getting complicated: a series of phone calls that brought the victims back to the store, two masked men, a gruesome murder, a surviving witness at the hospital.

Next, Drewry spoke with Ryan Haugh, the Apple customer in the red Phillies cap who'd entered the yoga store. "He went in and saw stuff knocked over, blood on the floor and broken glass," Drewry wrote, summing up what Ryan told him. "He opened the purple door in the rear of the store and saw a body facedown on the floor. There was a girl on the bathroom floor."

As the two spoke, more Bethesda shoppers began arriving for the day, people who hadn't seen the stretcher wheeled out of the yoga store. To them, the police presence and yellow tape meant the possibility of vandalism, at worst a burglary. A woman carrying a cup of coffee approached the tape, casually lifted it, and continued walking toward Drewry. He was startled by her indifferent attitude to the police tape, but ultimately not surprised. He'd long ago concluded that for all their high-powered jobs and world travels, many Bethesda residents were clueless to the evil that humans could unleash on each other—any time, any place.

"Hey, hey, hey!" the detective said, raising his voice, holding up his hands and directing the woman back outside the yellow tape. "This is a crime scene."

CHAPTER FOUR

Auntie B and Tia T

Like so many people in the Washington, D.C. area, the two women found in the yoga store were transplants. Brittany Norwood, the survivor, had grown up in Washington State, just south of Seattle, with eight brothers and sisters. Her mother, Larkita, sixty-one years old, was a homemaker who did part-time advertising work. Her dad, Earl, sixty-five years old, ran a specialized upholstery shop. One of her sisters was a doctor, and three of her brothers were engineers. Brittany was particularly close with her sister Marissa, older by only seventeen months; growing up, they'd shared the same bedroom, the same hairbrush. When both ended up in Washington, D.C., it was only natural for Brittany to rent the basement apartment in the century-old, $555,000 renovated town house owned by Marissa, a business consultant, and her fiancé, an operations research analyst. But Brittany had her own outside door and a roommate she wasn't particularly close to, so when she hadn't come home the night before—Friday—it went unnoticed.

"Good morning! Are you awake?" Marissa had texted Brittany early Saturday morning. She sent another one thirty seconds later, indicating that Brittany's two young nephews—the sons of their sister Candace, who also lived nearby—had spent the night. One of the boys was eager to see Brittany. "A little person in striped pants is asking for you." No response. Brittany was probably sleeping.

To many people in her life, Brittany was a bubbly and caring presence—a former college soccer star with plans to one day open her own gym. A key first step to that goal was securing a personal-trainer spot at Equinox, the upscale health-club chain. Brittany had impressed the people at the Bethesda location so far, and a key interview was set for that Monday.

An hour after Marissa sent Brittany the text messages, she tried to call her sister but only got voice mail. Marissa handed the phone to their nephew, who, along with his brother, beamed whenever Brittany picked the two up from elementary school or took them out for pizza. "Call me back, Auntie B," he said. "I love you. Bye-bye."

As the morning progressed, those kinds of calls—greetings of affection, calling to discuss everyday matters—started to give way to calls of growing concern among those who knew both women.

In Texas, Jayna Murray's mother, Phyllis, a sixty-five-year-old retired flight attendant originally from Iowa, was finishing the dishes when the phone rang. It was Jayna's long-distance boyfriend, Fraser Bocell, who lived in Seattle. He told Phyllis that Jayna was supposed to work until about 9:30 P.M., but that she hadn't called him afterward, like she usually did every night. And there were other worrisome signs: Jayna was supposed to have met a friend that morning, but hadn't shown up. The friend drove by Jayna's parking spot outside the condo building where she lived, alone. No car.

Phyllis wrapped up the call and walked outside toward her husband, David, who at sixty-eight years old and with two titanium hips still ran oil-drilling projects around the world. He was pulling weeds from their flower garden. The two had married in 1969, and had three kids: thirty-nine-year-old Hugh, who'd spent ten years as a professional triathlete, gone on to law school and the U.S. Army's JAG Corps, and was now serving as a captain in Iraq; thirty-six-year-old Dirk, who'd competed in rodeo bull-riding as a kid, worked as a pilot, and had two young sons; and thirty-year-old Jayna, the girl who'd tagged along with Hugh and Dirk to Boy Scout campouts led by their dad, the teenager her parents shuttled to dance lessons, and the adult professional and world traveler fluent in Spanish. Jayna was now poised to take the next step in her career, just two months shy of getting two master's degrees, one in business administration and one in communication from Johns Hopkins University's campus in Washington, D.C. Like Brittany Norwood, she, too, was adored by her two young nephews, who called her "Tia T," a name derived from the Spanish word for *aunt* and the first initial of Jayna's middle name, Troxel, her grandmother's maiden name. That afternoon, in fact, David and Phyllis were due at one of the boys' fourth birthday party.

Phyllis made her way to the flower garden. She told David about the phone call with Jayna's boyfriend.

"Fraser feels that Jayna is missing."

CHAPTER FIVE

Successful People

Sergeant Craig Wittenberger, the homicide supervisor whom Detective Jim Drewry had called on his way to the yoga store, had quickly headed to the crime scene himself, calling in more detectives on the way. The sergeant selected "lead detectives" for cases based on a rotating system. On this Saturday, a relative newcomer to the homicide unit, Detective Dimitry Ruvin, thirty-one, was at the front of the queue. He'd only been working homicides for the past thirteen months, but he knew computers and cell-phone technology (an increasingly important skill in homicide work), had seemingly limitless energy, and meshed well with Drewry, whom Wittenberger wanted to keep on the case as well. By 10:15 A.M., Wittenberger, Drewry, and Ruvin were all gathered outside the store. They put together a plan for examining the place, and slipped on rubber gloves and rubber booties that looked like clown shoes. At 10:40 A.M., joined by crime-scene investigator Amanda Kraemer, they walked through the front door.

The detectives knew how critical the clues in front of them would be. Unlike convenience stores or banks, places where robberies were anticipated, the yoga store didn't have interior surveillance cameras. Also working against the detectives were the surviving witness's hazy recollections and the amount of time that had already passed, giving the attackers plenty of time to hit the road, dispose of evidence, or marshal alibis.

Documenting the crime scene was Ruvin's job. As new as he was to homicide, however, the detective was certainly no stranger to chaos, having grown up in the nation of Azerbaijan as it broke off from the Soviet Union. Violence there forced his parents, ethnic Russians, to seek political-refugee status in the United States in 1995, and the Ruvins settled outside Baltimore. Dimitry boned up on his English, enrolled in high school and later the University of Maryland's computer-science program, and secured an internship, designing websites at the prestigious National Institutes of Health, in Bethesda. His parents, who'd been chemical engineers back in the home country, couldn't have been more proud. As happens a lot in front of computers, though, Ruvin found himself surfing to other sites. He began reading about police work, and thought it sounded exciting. He secured a second internship, at the Montgomery County Police Department, and enjoyed it enough to apply for a slot in the academy. He was an appealing candidate. He seemed eager; his computer skills certainly were in demand; and in a county like Montgomery—peppered with foreign service workers, international economists, and new immigrants—how often did the academy get to produce a cop fluent in English, Russian, and Azeri? Ruvin was accepted right away,

went on to patrol, then burglary and robbery investigations, and now, homicides.

On one of his first murder cases, which he'd worked
with Drewry, Ruvin had learned both how critical small
details could be and how well he and the older detective
worked together. They'd been standing over a corpse of a
man who'd been cut and stabbed thirty-six times outside
an apartment building in Silver Spring. A lanyard holding
a key and three plastic cards rested on the victim's right
ankle. Ruvin figured the lanyard had been pulled from a
pocket while the killer rifled through it. Drewry had other
thoughts. He bagged the evidence, took it to the victim's
sister, and asked if she'd ever seen it. She had not. Nor did
the key fit in the victim's front-door lock. The detectives
started making calls based on the plastic cards on the key-
ring—one for a gym membership, one for a bookstore,
and another for purchases at CVS drugstores. Within
hours, they had their killer, Alexander Chambers, who—
during the confusion inherent in violently murdering
someone—had managed to leave the lanyard behind.
Chambers didn't say much to detectives when questioned,
but Drewry got this out of him: "I just need to pray.
Things didn't go real well."

Inside the yoga store, things up front looked largely
intact.

Like Apple customer Ryan Haugh, Ruvin was seeing
the inside of a lululemon athletica store for the first time,
and he noted the spotlit tables and racks of clothes; the
cubbyholes displaying yoga mats; the mannequins dressed
in yoga pants, thin tank tops, and, in some cases, running
gear. The feel was athletic and high-end. When Ruvin later
checked out some of the price tags, he saw just how

high-end: $25 for a water bottle, $98 for yoga pants, $148 for a running jacket. There was even a small men's section, with a pair of $64 shorts.

He was quickly picking up on the store's aspirational theme. On one shelf, he saw a series of framed photographs of staff members, with long-term goals well beyond their current jobs spelled out alongside their pictures. Ruvin had spoken minutes earlier with four store employees who had come down to the scene, and although they were rattled and scared, he'd found them poised as well. Now, as Ruvin stood behind the cash registers, he spotted a supply of bright red reusable shopping bags displayed so customers could see them. The bags showed the silhouette of a woman in a yoga pose and were covered with all kinds of sayings. Some advised taking a break, slowing down: "Breathe deeply and appreciate the moment." Others advised gearing up to succeed in today's competitive world. "Successful people replace the words 'wish,' 'should,' & 'try,' with 'I WILL.'"

The detective looked into the store ahead of him. From what he could see, and from what witnesses and employees had just told him, the place broke down into four main areas: this front section; a large fitting area beyond that; a rear stockroom; and—behind the purple door—a rear hallway leading to the emergency fire exit. Ruvin knew the body was in that hallway. He didn't want to rush to it, worried that doing so would impair his effort to document as much as he could in the other parts of the store.

Ruvin walked through the front section. For the most part things were in order, but two mannequins had toppled over, one with its hand dislodged and resting about eight feet away. There were blood drops scattered around the floor, and Ruvin could see faint bloody shoe prints that appeared to lead up to the front door. Where they went from there wasn't clear. By his count, at least a dozen people had crossed the tracks that morning, between the store manager, the Apple customer, the responding officers, and the medics. The shoe print was dry, though, and Ruvin hoped a shoe-print expert could later find more of them and re-create the exact movements of the person wearing them.

The detective gingerly stepped around the sales counter in his crime-scene booties, jotting down observations. "Safes behind front register opened. Receipts on the floor."

Ruvin moved on, and as he walked around a display rack, he could see trouble laid out before him. A flat-screen television rested on its back, having apparently tumbled off a table. A black athletic bag appeared to have been dropped suddenly, spilling out a white candle, a tube of lip balm, and a pair of headphones. Clothes and green water bottles were strewn about. "Visible signs of a struggle," Ruvin wrote.

Ruvin walked into the next part of the store, the fitting area, which was surrounded by full-length mirrors, changing rooms, and two bathrooms. He and Kraemer, the crime-scene investigator, looked at the walls and noted what looked to be a partial, bloody palm print in a corner. On the floor below them, red shoe prints crisscrossed each other. Kraemer measured the clearer ones, which stretched past twelve inches.

Ruvin stepped into the bathroom where the survivor had been found, noting blood and rocks on the floor. He looked at the sink, and saw drops of blood near the drain, a smudge of blood across the mirror. There was a severed zip-tie, presumably removed by the medics from the victim's wrists, and on the floor just outside the bathroom, a wooden coat hanger, a bottle of Windex, used paper towels, and a knocked-over, solid-looking Buddha statue, perhaps ten inches tall.

Ruvin walked up to the purple door. He pushed it forward until it bumped into a body, just as he'd been told it would. Ruvin eased off and let the door close. He knew he'd better take a different, less disruptive route to the body—but he'd check the other parts of the store and make sure he understood them first.

Ruvin walked into the rear stockroom. Shelves and racks stretched over his head, lined up in different directions and creating blind spots. He was thankful the patrol officers had come in here earlier, guns drawn, and made sure no one was squatting down, ready to strike. The floor here was also covered with bloody shoe tracks, but no real signs of trouble. Ruvin walked carefully to the side of the shoe prints, working his way to a back office, where a desktop computer was on and a white laptop sat closed atop a file cabinet.

Ruvin turned his attention back to the main stockroom. Near a wall, and to the side of a chair, he spotted a cream-colored woman's wallet. Kraemer carefully looked inside, finding the driver's license for Brittany Norwood. To the right, on the floor, the bloody tracks grew more concentrated in the far corner, where there was a little kitchenette—a sink, small refrigerator, and microwave. On the ground was another bottle of Windex, a bottle of Formula 409, and a lime-green scrub brush. Above the sink, Ruvin spotted a foot-long serrated knife, resting horizontally across two hooks. The blade was shiny and clean, the handle gray and shaped like a shark.

Ten feet away, back toward the entrance to the stock-room, Ruvin and Kraemer spotted a royal-blue lululemon athletica gym bag that did not appear to be part of the carefully grouped products on the shelves. They studied the contents: computer cords, a digital camera, a tangerine, a bottle of Argentinean wine, and a book, *The Leadership Pipeline: How to Build the Leadership Powered Company*. There was also a brown wallet, holding a Johns Hopkins University student ID and a Texas driver's license, both showing Jayna Murray's smiling face. Two things were noted by their absence. "No keys," Ruvin wrote. "No cash."

CHAPTER SIX

Starting to Talk

Less than two miles away, at Suburban Hospital, in Bethesda, Maryland, a uniformed police officer named Colin O'Brien had by chance been at the hospital that morning, and was told by a supervisor to meet the ambulance when it pulled up with Brittany Norwood. Officer O'Brien followed the gurney inside, stood near Brittany to protect her, and collected her garments as doctors and nurses removed them. "All of the victim's clothing was bloody and her pants were ripped/slashed in numerous places," O'Brien wrote in a three-page statement documenting his early involvement in the case. "When the victim was rolled onto her side, I observed several pieces of bloodstained glass on the victim's back."

One by one, O'Brien had placed the articles in evidence bags—pants, socks, a sports bra, a gray shirt that had been wrapped around Brittany's neck. The shirt was from lululemon's collection of running gear and was printed with motivational sayings: "Set your goals/Life is too short for the treadmill, get out and run!"

O'Brien watched the doctors and nurses treat Brittany's wounds, and he took particular note of an inch-long laceration between her thumb and her forefinger on her right palm. O'Brien had seen similar injuries repeatedly in his previous career in the U.S. Army, when he was a tactical medic on a Military Police SWAT team. In field exercises, when SWAT members used knives, the blades sometimes slipped and sliced into their own palms. O'Brien didn't say anything about his recollections to the doctors, and certainly not to Brittany—not even as he helped place large, loose fitting gloves over both of Brittany's hands to preserve any evidence on her skin.

All that had taken place about an hour earlier, before O'Brien started writing his statement. In the time since, any memories of SWAT team injuries had become overwhelmed by the broader picture of the tiny woman, a victim, shaking with fear, her face caked with blood. There could have been other explanations for the cut to her palm, such as fighting off an attacker—which was what O'Brien theorized in his report.

"There were numerous lacerations on the victim's chest, stomach, back and legs," O'Brien wrote, "as well as what appeared to be defensive wounds on the victim's right hand."

Brittany was wheeled into room 12, a private area in the emergency wing. When a detective named Deana Mackie walked in, she saw Brittany on her back, her face still caked in blood—the way it would stay until it could be swabbed for clues. Nurses had pulled a white blanket to just below Brittany's shoulders, leaving her arms and hands extending over the front of it. The young woman looked tired, dazed, and bloody, but nonetheless strikingly

pretty. Detective Mackie sat down next to Brittany, introduced herself, and turned on a digital recorder.

"We want to kind of figure out what's going on and
what we can do to help you," Mackie told her quietly. "I
know that you've been through a lot."

Brittany interjected, barely above a whisper. "Would
you mind just telling me how my friend is doing?"

"Well, I haven't been down to the scene yet," Mackie
said.

That much was true. Sergeant Craig Wittenberger had
sent Mackie straight to the hospital. But Mackie knew the
coworker was dead. She just didn't want to rattle Brittany,
and instead told her she'd check on her friend when they
were done speaking.

"Do I have to talk right now?" Brittany asked.

"You don't have to. We can't make you," Mackie said.
"But if it's something that you can tell us that will help us
find out who did this, you know, that's really important
to us, and to find these people."

The detective projected a natural compassion, which is
why Wittenberger had sent her to the hospital.

"If you want, you can just ask me questions," Brittany
said.

Mackie agreed, and the two spoke for forty-eight minutes. When they finished, Mackie headed to the yoga store
to tell the others the harrowing account Brittany had
shared with her.

CHAPTER SEVEN

Tension Mounts

Back at the crime scene on Bethesda Avenue, things were taking shape just as detectives had predicted. TV news trucks had quickly dug in for the day, their radio towers extending skyward for live coverage. Reporters and photographers crowded up to the yellow tape, gazing into the store's windows to try to figure out what was inside, until the detectives covered the inside of the windows with wide sheets of brown paper that had been brought in to pack up evidence.

Detectives Jim Drewry and Dimitry Ruvin and Sergeant Craig Wittenberger—the core team on the case—were joined by about ten detectives and commanders in the store. The whole crowd gathered in a semicircle to hear Detective Deana Mackie's report from surviving victim Brittany Norwood.

She and Jayna Murray had been the only two employees working late the night before, Brittany told Mackie. They had both left the store at 9:45 P.M., Brittany walking toward a nearby subway station and Jayna heading in the opposite direction, toward her car. Minutes later, Brittany realized she'd left her wallet behind, so she called Jayna's cell phone and asked that she return to let her back in. Jayna told Brittany she'd left her laptop in the store, too, so she didn't mind going back. The two met outside the store, then went in and deactivated the alarm, but didn't lock the front door behind them because they thought they'd be in and out quickly.

After they were inside, however, two men, covered head to toe in dark clothes—with gloves, ski masks with narrow slits cut out for the eyes, and hoodies over their heads— slipped in behind them. They unleashed a brutal attack on the women. One was about six feet tall, and he dragged Jayna by her hair as she yelled for help.

The shorter one—closer to Brittany's height of five feet three inches tall—threw Brittany to the ground, knocking her bag to the floor. "Where's the money?" he demanded, making her open three small safes at the front of the store, then forcing Brittany back to the rear of the store, where he tied her up and raped her, at one point also violating her with a wooden hanger. He struck her in the forehead, hard enough to make it difficult for her to remember much of what happened next. Brittany said she never saw the skin color of the assailants, but when pressed by Mackie, said they'd sounded young and white.

Mackie told the crowd around her that Brittany was a believable witness. If she couldn't remember something, she said so, and didn't seem to make things up to fill in voids. "I didn't doubt what she told me," Mackie told the other detectives.

*   *   *

With the core team focusing on the crime scene, assisting detectives fanned out to talk to nearby store workers, hoping one of them might have seen or heard something. At 12:25 P.M., Detective Mike Carin walked into the adjacent Apple Store. The place was about the size of a tennis court, filled with customers who'd come for second-day sales of the iPad 2. Everyone had noticed the yellow crime-scene tape on the way in, all the cop cars and the media trucks, but none of them knew what was unfolding on the other side of the wall. Shoppers examining software products along the wall near the back of the store and asking questions to the Apple sales staffers were unaware that they were only five feet from Jayna's body.

Detective Carin was five feet eight inches tall, and was nicknamed "Bucket" because of his large head. That he answered to the moniker, and was often the first to joke about it, was part of a disarming manner that had strangers easily opening up to him.

He said there'd been an "incident" next door, and asked to speak privately with anyone who had been working the night before. Carin was led to an upstairs office, and introduced to store manager Jana Svrzo. She told Carin that she'd started her shift the day before at 1:00 P.M., and that final customers hadn't left until around 9:30. Then she began closing up.

"Did you hear anything?" Carin asked.

"Yes, screaming," the manager said.

Carin tried not to change expression, though he could see the manager processing all that was going on—the hubbub outside, the detective asking questions. Still, she seemed intent on telling him exactly what she remembered, even if backpedaling at this point might've been in her own interest. The screams began sometime after 10:00 P.M., she said, and sounded like they were coming from the yoga store next door. And there were other sounds she could hear as well. "Dragging," Carin wrote in his notes. "Something heavy hitting."

Then, the manager said, she heard parts of what sounded like two women's voices. Again, Carin jotted the recollections down.

"Talk to me. Don't do this," one of the women said. "Stop. Oh God," said the other.

The voices would rise and fall, Jana said, and she couldn't make out everything. She didn't hear any male voices.

Carin could tell that the manager was getting more and more upset. She finally asked him what had happened. Someone had been killed, Carin told her.

At that, she started to sob.

Detective Carin walked back to the yoga store to tell his colleagues about the screams Jana Svrzo had heard. The screams' timing tracked with information the other detectives had just gotten from ADT Security Systems, the company that monitored the yoga store's burglar alarms. Someone had set the alarms the night before at 9:45 P.M., the same time Brittany and Jayna left. The alarms were then turned off at 10:05 P.M., when they would have returned. ADT said there was no further activity for the night, meaning people could have gone in and out unnoticed anytime after 10:05 P.M.

More clues flowed in. A patrolman found Jayna's car, a silver Pontiac, parked about three blocks from the yoga store in a lot behind the farmers market. That seemed a little strange. If Jayna had driven back around 10:00 P.M., wouldn't she have been able to get a closer spot?

Then the story of the parked car got really strange. A patrolman named Justin Tierney arrived at the front of the store and asked to see Drewry. Officer Tierney told Drewry that he had just heard about the recovered Pontiac and its connection to a murder, and realized he had seen that same car parked in the lot at 12:30 A.M. that morning—with someone sitting behind the wheel. Come again? Drewry asked, as he was quickly joined by others who wanted to hear the patrolman's story.

So Tierney went through his story from the beginning. He'd worked an overnight shift in Bethesda. Just after midnight, he eased his patrol car through the parking lot, looking for anything out of the ordinary. He took note of the silver Pontiac, parked headfirst into a spot, because it had its lights on. Tierney said he drove by the back of the car, going 5 to 10 mph, and saw the car's Texas plates.

"There was somebody in the car. Sitting in the car, in the driver's seat," he told the crowd.

Tierney added that he didn't know if the person was a man or a woman. He'd considered stopping his cruiser to talk to the driver, but at the time it hadn't seemed like a big deal. He was familiar with the county's restrictions about smoking inside bars and restaurants, and he figured it was someone grabbing a smoke on a cold night.

Two hours after spotting the car, Tierney continued, he drove through the lot again—and again saw the car with its lights on. He didn't notice if anyone was behind the wheel or not. About an hour later, Tierney said, he returned to the lot. The Pontiac was still there. Its lights were off. Tierney looked for occupants and didn't see any.

The account seemed weird and tantalizing and a near miss now, of course, but one part of Tierney's story also made a lot of sense: at the time, how could he have known it would matter?

CHAPTER EIGHT

Working the Scene

Hunches are tricky things for detectives. They can create tunnel vision, blinding detectives to unexpected leads, or lend focus and halt investigations from spiraling off into fruitless directions. By early afternoon inside the yoga store, Craig Wittenberger, the sergeant supervising the case, had a strong hunch. It was tied to his favorite motto: "Evidence doesn't lie. People do."

The fifty-year-old knew Montgomery County inside and out, having grown up in the county as the son of two PhD researchers at the National Institutes of Health. As a kid he considered pursuing architecture, but leaned toward police work at about the time he started at the University of Maryland, where he picked up a degree in criminal justice. With his closely cropped hair, slight paunch, and dead-serious expressions, Wittenberger projected a first impression right out of Hollywood central casting of a grizzled, blunt-force detective. But at home in the placid, northern Montgomery community of Damascus, where he and his wife had raised three kids,

Wittenberger liked nothing more than retreating to the woodworking equipment in his garage to build furniture. And at one point in his career, wanting a change of pace, he spent several years teaching constitutional law at Montgomery's police academy, becoming so well-versed in the Fourth and Fifth Amendments that prosecutors began calling him to discuss U.S. Supreme Court opinions.

Inside the yoga store, Brittany Norwood's story wasn't adding up for him. To begin with, Detective Jim Drewry had told him about the phone call between Rachel Oertli, the store manager, and Jayna Murray, the woman now dead—the one in which Jayna had told her she suspected Brittany of shoplifting. What did that portend about Brittany's character? And her descriptions of the attackers seemed too vague: ski masks generally exposed some amount of skin around the eyes, yet Brittany said she wasn't sure of their race. But what really troubled the sergeant were photographs he was now reviewing that had been taken at the hospital. Yes, the bloody cut to Brittany's forehead looked serious. But what about all those long, superficial cuts across her back, thighs, stomach, and breasts? They were straight, and appeared to be the same depth, as if Brittany hadn't moved or squirmed when they were inflicted.

Wittenberger's hunch was that whatever had happened the night before, Brittany might somehow have been in on it. He suspected that she knew the robbers, and had helped get them into the store. But then maybe things got way out of hand, and Brittany came up with a cover story that included injuring herself.

"I'm telling you. Something's not right," Wittenberger told Drewry and Captain David Gillespie, ticking off his troubles with Brittany's story, notably the massive injuries to Jayna compared to all the superficial ones to Brittany.

Gillespie, whose command included the homicide unit, was relatively new to the post. One of the first cases he oversaw, oddly enough, also involved yoga. Two miles from where they stood now, an American University accounting professor had been found beaten to death inside her home. Thirteen hours into the investigation, patrolmen in Washington, D.C., spotted the professor's stolen Jeep and tried to pull it over, prompting a wild chase, a crash, and the apprehension of the eighteen-year-old driver, who couldn't quite explain how he came to be driving the Jeep. But detectives were unable to tie him to the killing and held off on charging him with murder. That turned out to be the right move, since new evidence had pointed them to the professor's at-home yoga instructor—and the sole beneficiary of her half-million-dollar life-insurance policy—as the killer. The theory was that after killing the professor, staging a burglary, and ditching the Jeep (with keys inside for someone else to find), the yoga instructor had fled to Mexico, where detectives had established that he had settled into a life of teaching yoga, writing poetry, and trying to cash in the professor's life insurance. With a little more information, the detectives were almost ready to make their move on him.

In this latest case, Gillespie didn't discount what Wittenberger was saying. It was just that what he was saying was so potentially explosive. What if it got out that they were investigating a victim—a tiny, female rape victim—while the two madmen she described were on the loose? And what if the two struck again? Judging by the crime scene they'd evidently just created, they were crazy enough to do so, and soon. Nor did it escape Gillespie that this was Bethesda, home to many of the county's politically elite residents, who'd be closely watching any development.

"We aren't going down this route unless you are 100 percent, dead-on certain," Gillespie said.

Wittenberger said he wasn't anywhere near certain. Even with his doubts, he knew there could be another side that explained them. Rape victims can sometimes take days to sort through the trauma and remember exactly what happened. Maybe Brittany's story would start to make more sense. And he knew where Gillespie was coming from regarding the sensitivity of the case. If they got on the Brittany train and it derailed, there'd be hell to pay.

"Just work the scene," Gillespie told him.

The detectives did so, continuing to avoid a detailed study of the victim's body. They knew that once detectives started to focus on her injuries, the energy of the whole scene would naturally focus on that, and they could miss their best chance to pick up something critical twenty or thirty feet away. At 1:45 P.M., three hours after the detectives had entered the store, Detective Ruvin decided that the time had finally come to examine the rear hallway. Ruvin and an assisting detective, Randy Kucsan—a six feet two, forty-seven-year-old with a spiky hairdo and a goatee— walked out the front of the shop, past the Apple Store, and turned left down a narrow walkway to the rear parking lot. It was secluded, bordered by bushy pine trees, a fence, and, now, yellow police tape.

Patrol officers guarded the store's rear-door, emergency exit. Ruvin and Kucsan examined the bloodstained push-bar inside. On the right side of the bar, they saw a key inserted into the lock, indicating that the fire alarm had been deactivated. Had the assailants slipped out this way? That ran counter to what the detectives saw when they looked down the store's rear hallway. There were dried, bloody shoe tracks coming at them, but the tracks stopped at the doorway. The detectives couldn't pick up a track on the pavement outside. "The blood stops," Kucsan said.

They discussed possible explanations. Maybe the assailants had gone out the front, though that seemed risky. Maybe they came out this door, but just before doing so, put their bloody shoes in an athletic bag—there were certainly plenty available in the store. This would have allowed them to get to a car without tracking blood. Criminals often tried a lot of things to cover up evidence these days, having watched just enough *CSI* episodes to believe they might work. The detectives stepped into the hallway. They had a clear sight line to the body, fifteen feet away, and the blood-spattered walls surrounding her. Could Jayna have tracked the blood to the rear emergency door, even touched the push-bar, trying to escape? Then gotten dragged back? Whatever the case, the killer was able to trap her in that far end. The detectives stuck with their methodical, inch-by-inch observations.

This part of the hallway was cluttered. Full trash bags sat ready to be taken to the Dumpster. The bags were transparent, another common antitheft practice in retail that kept employees from hiding goods and sneaking them out. Columns of cardboard boxes, filled with clothing, and stamped "lululemon," were stacked to the ceiling. On the floor next to one of them, detectives saw a turned-off or disabled BlackBerry—likely the latter since its center scroller button was missing. Ruvin hoped it belonged to the killer, but it was almost certainly Jayna's, likely swatted away during the attack. Nearly ten minutes had passed since they entered the hallway. Kucsan now noticed a box that had been obscured by the clutter. "These are the fucking zip-ties," he said. The detectives pulled one out. Kucsan asked Ruvin, if two guys rushed into the store and attacked both saleswomen, how would they know to come all the way back here to find these things? It was possible that the men had brought their own zip-ties, or had forced Brittany or Jayna to tell them where they could find restraints. But both scenarios seemed like a stretch.

Kucsan and Ruvin finally arrived at the victim. They saw the red, open wound to the back of her head, the one that had been so visible in the photographs taken earlier by the patrol officer. The wound seemed to be about four inches across, and the product of repeated blows. Up close, the volume of blood spatter on the walls was stunning. And the detectives knew it could have gotten there one of two ways: as the killer drew back a blood-drenched weapon, flinging blood onto the walls, or as the killer pounded a weapon into a surface already covered in blood.

Looking directly down at Jayna's body, the detectives could see that her right arm was actually crossed under her body, coming out on the left side—an indication she had been faceup at some point during the attack and may have been rolled over. Resting on her left hand was a Buddha statue similar to the green one they'd seen hours earlier near the bathroom. "Maybe she was hit with that," Ruvin said to Kucsan. "Maybe she tried to defend herself." The detectives noted other weapons near Jayna's head: rope, a claw hammer with blood on the handle, a wrench, and three box cutters: essentially, razor blades with handles. Also lying across the victim's left arm and shoulder were a blood-spattered, orange Dyson vacuum cleaner and a red metal box labeled with masking tape: "Everyday Tools." The detectives didn't want to open it, fearing disruption to any trace evidence on the body. Other items were scattered near her head—two paintbrushes, a roll of duct tape, a bicycle reflector. Some of the items, the detectives and crime-scene investigators figured, might have spilled out of the toolbox.

The body still hadn't been formally identified, though there was little doubt this was Jayna Murray. Detective Ruvin tried to make the match with Jayna's photo from her driver's license and student ID, but all he could really see was matted and bloodstained hair on the back of her head. That was as far as Ruvin wanted to go until a forensic investigator from the state autopsy lab arrived.

CHAPTER NINE

Hoping Against Hope

As detectives continued to comb through the store, the Montgomery County Police Department's media-affairs captain, Paul Starks, had begun talking to the gaggle of reporters parked outside. The hope was to give out information that could draw in potential witnesses. Starks gave reporters the basics: two male suspects, last seen wearing dark clothes, gloves, and masks, had managed to slip into the lululemon athletica store after closing time. They had killed one of the workers and sexually assaulted the other, who'd survived and was at a local hospital. "We only have one eyewitness, and she's been through a lot," Starks said.

As a news story, it had all the elements that the media and public craved: innocent female victims, madmen on the loose, an unfolding mystery in a place that was supposed to be so perfect. Reporters stopped people walking down Bethesda Avenue and interviewed them. "It's just shocking that it could happen here in this neighborhood at a time when seemingly there's a lot of people around," a man told the local NBC television station. "It's really just scary."

For Brittany Norwood's family, it was all that and much more, of course. At the hospital, she'd given nurses a phone number for her sister Marissa, her upstairs neighbor in the town house. Marissa had rushed over to see her, and the two were soon joined by their sister Candace, an obstetrician whose sons were so fond of Brittany. She spoke with Brittany's treating physician about administering drugs and vaccines to combat possible exposure to HIV or hepatitis B. Candace was able to help explain the risks of the drugs to her sister. Everyone agreed it was the prudent course. Out in Washington State, Brittany's parents made plans to fly across the country the next day. They wondered if they would have to put their daughter back together. And they thought about Brittany's poor coworker's family, knowing her parents would never get the chance.

Back at the store, Detective Jim Drewry already had spoken once with Brittany's mother, Larkita, and Jayna Murray's mother, Phyllis. With Larkita, he could stress the positives: her daughter was safe, under doctors' care at the hospital, and being protected by police officers there. With Jayna's mother, however, he'd had nothing positive to tell her, and instead was forced to dodge her questions. At the time of that call, the detectives hadn't even been inside the back hallway. Drewry was pretty sure the body there was Jayna, but certainly not sure enough to tell her mother.

That horrible dance had started after a police dispatcher called Drewry to tell him that Phyllis Murray had called to report her daughter missing. The dispatcher passed along Phyllis's phone number, which had been confirmed as legitimate. Drewry called, and Phyllis answered, speaking with the quiet confidence of someone telling herself it would still work out. "I understand that my daughter is missing, that she was closing the store," she'd told Drewry in her decidedly Midwestern accent. Phyllis said she'd heard there was a robbery at the store, with a survivor, maybe a kidnapping, maybe someone who was dead. She gave Drewry her daughter's driver's license number, passport number, and the VIN to her 2009 two-door Pontiac. She told him about Jayna's nervous habit of chewing her fingernails. "She has no fingernails," Phyllis said. "Another thing is, she will have an orange sapphire earring in one ear." Drewry knew what she wanted to hear—that somehow the information she was giving him would rule her daughter out as dead. Since he couldn't give her that, he assured her they were working hard on the case, and wrapped up the call quickly. "I will call when I know more," Drewry said.

Hours passed, until finally, at 5:30 P.M., Drewry's phone rang. It was a Houston area code, but a different number than Jayna's mother. Drewry answered it, and listened as a man with a slight Texas twang introduced himself as David Murray, Jayna's father. Drewry was stuck. This number hadn't been confirmed by the dispatchers. There were sensible rules to follow in times like this, since anyone could be calling him, claiming to be Jayna's father. Drewry politely said he had to go, hung up, and considered what to do. There really was no more doubt about who was in the rear hallway. Brittany had said Jayna was attacked there; Jayna's wallet had been found in the store; her car was discovered three blocks away; no one—Jayna's coworkers, her friends, her family—could reach her.

Drewry didn't want Jayna's parents to hear it from

anyone else, but despite his decades in police work, death notifications never got easier. In fact, Drewry had noticed them getting more difficult. Maybe it was the compound effect of having delivered them so many times. Maybe it was the fact that each time made him think of his own kids, now grown and probably about the same age as the Murrays' children. Drewry picked up the phone and called Jayna's mother. Phyllis answered. Drewry said he had just heard from David Murray.

"Yes, he's my husband. He's sitting right here." The detective apologized for not being there in person to say this. "I'm so sorry to tell you," he said, "that your daughter is deceased."

CHAPTER TEN

Caught on Video

By late afternoon, Dale Giampetroni, a forensic investigator from the state autopsy lab, had arrived and was led to the rear hallway. She took photographs of Jayna Murray's body and slowly pulled away items resting against her shoulder and head. Giampetroni unfolded a white plastic body bag and laid it on the floor near Jayna's feet. For now, the bag would serve as sort of a plastic gurney—a way to move the body into the main part of the store, where they'd have more room to examine it. Giampetroni and Detective Dimitry Ruvin lifted Jayna's body, placed it on the bag, grabbed the bag's corners, and carried it out of the hallway.

Behind them, two crime-scene investigators collected the items that had been near Jayna's head. The red toolbox, as it turned out, was empty, so the investigators placed some of the bloodstained items inside it: the box cutters, paintbrushes, a bicycle reflector, and something that had been obscured by several items resting atop it—a foot-long metal bar. The crime-scene investigators closed the tool-box, assigned it a crime-scene number (CS-35), and placed the toolbox inside its own evidence box.

The main part of the store, where Jayna's body now was, became the center of attention. The store's stylish lights offered a flood of bright light under which to work. The brown-paper shields over the front windows offered privacy. Giampetroni and about ten detectives, supervisors and crime-scene investigators went to work, bending over Jayna's body, still facedown on the plastic bag.

They looked at Jayna's fingers, at the chewed-down nails her mother had mentioned. Detective Jim Drewry saw clumps of hair, which she must have pulled from some-where, in Jayna's clenched fingers. On the backs of her hands were cuts and bruises, but the dried blood made it hard to figure out too much about them. At the base of her neck, they noted two significant stab wounds, the depths of which would be measured the next day during the autopsy. Giampetroni lifted Jayna's shirt and saw another wound in the middle of her back.

Their work was accompanied by constant chatter—notes to be compared, pictures to be snapped, cop wise-cracks to be made. The time came to turn Jayna over.

What they saw shut them up fast.

Her face, Ruvin thought, was destroyed. Deep gashes and gouges—too many to count—crisscrossed Jayna's forehead, cheeks, lips, and chin. Beyond all the wounds, Jayna's face was bruised and bloodied into a grotesque shade of purple. It didn't seem human anymore. Ruvin thought back to Jayna's smiling image on her driver's license. He couldn't recognize her.

Ruvin tried to break the silence. "Someone say something."

"Oh my God," Giampetroni said.

She and the others bent closer. Their thoughts turned to weapons. Which ones had done this? The hammer found in the rear hallway was a good possibility. The box cutters seemed too small. What about the serrated knife hanging in the kitchen? It was in pristine condition, and didn't have the look of something that had been jabbed into a skull.

Conversation slowly picked up again around such topics. Giampetroni took photographs from every angle. She could see how the rope had fallen away from Jayna's face. She pulled it away and told Ruvin to take it with him to the autopsy the next day so the doctor could compare it with the wounds to Jayna's neck.

Brown paper bags were placed over Jayna's hands to contain any evidence, though her chewed-off nails may have limited her ability to scratch skin cells off her assailant. Clear tape was wrapped around Jayna's forearms, sealing the top of the bags. Several people lifted the corners of the body bag, now bloodied from Jayna's body, into a second, clean bag, and the sounds of closing zippers could be heard inside the quiet store.

Everyone weighed what to do next. Jayna's body needed to be loaded into a van and driven to the forensics lab in Baltimore, thirty-five miles away. Taking Jayna out via the front door would pass over the least amount of blood tracks. And the detectives could use a wheeled gurney. But reporters, cameramen, and photographers were all waiting to catch that very image—producing footage and pictures Jayna's parents would inevitably see. Going out the back meant having to carry the body bag down the narrow rear hallway, across the bloodiest footprints. But the investigators were all wearing their booties, and knew to step over the thick pools of blood that were finally drying. The entire back parking lot was still taped off, and shielded by the bushes and fences. So that's the direction they chose.

Detective Ruvin walked around to check in with the patrol officers who were guarding the front of the store along Bethesda Avenue. A woman approached, and told Ruvin she'd been outside the store walking her dog at 11:15 the night before and heard a woman shouting. She'd thought the sounds were coming from the street, though, not the store. The woman went on to say that at the end of the block, outside the Barnes & Noble, she saw a parked 1965 Dodge convertible with windows down and keys in the ignition. Near the car was a dark-skinned black man in a gray jacket. Anything remarkable about him? Ruvin asked. No, she said. The young detective went back into the store, shaking his head—as he knew, the police description of the suspects released to the public hours earlier had said nothing about race, because Brittany said she wasn't sure herself. What stood out to Ruvin about the woman's story was how it apparently exemplified her own fears.

At 8:00 P.M. Drewry and others were still in the store looking for clues, as they would for the next several weeks. Lululemon had given them "control" over the place, along with a set of keys, and not too surprisingly didn't seem to be in a hurry to try to reopen for business. But Ruvin was anxious to do one more thing before he went home for the night: study surveillance video given to him earlier in the day by an Apple manager. It captured images from the night before in the parking lot behind their store, and with any luck, it also captured something behind the yoga shop.

Ruvin grabbed the taped-up, brown-paper evidence bag that held the bloody rope, walked to his car, and drove ten miles north to Montgomery's police headquarters, a glass and brick structure nestled among a series of gleaming office parks along Research Boulevard, a name befitting all the biotech firms stationed there. Inside headquarters, though, the place was dingy and dated, the result of the department having moved in thirty-three years earlier in what was supposed to be a temporary stay. As the department grew, the building's layout became ever more dysfunctional—carved up, partitioned off, overcrowded. Ruvin went in through a side door, wound around a kitchenette, and took a left down a hallway toward his cubicle with its four-foot high walls. He sat at a desk adorned with photos of his wife, Yasra, a native of Morocco, and their six-month-old son—and one of his favorite dumb criminals, a teenager who'd snapped his own picture in front of a bathroom mirror, which Ruvin had captioned: "Mohawk Haircut: $10. Shower Curtain with Sea Creatures: $40. Taking a photo of yourself with the victim's stolen phone: $$$ Priceless $$$."

For the most part, the young detective enjoyed his work. But it involved a staggering amount of "death calls"—not necessarily murders, but any passings that had to be checked out for signs of foul play: drug overdoses, suicides, drownings, healthy people not waking up in the morning. Talking about all the gloom with his wife the previous year, Ruvin had come up with an idea to create some balance in his life by starting a side business as a wedding videographer. He'd discovered a talent for the work when editing the lousy footage from their own wedding a friend had taken, which Ruvin had been able to salvage by editing with a program that allowed for cuts, fade-ins, background music, and other effects. It had been relatively easy for him to do, and all their friends thought the video had been done professionally. The side business shooting and editing wedding videos might not make him rich, but being around the happy gatherings—with their dancing, drinking, and laughing—seemed about as far from death as you could get. So the couple bought two cameras, placed an advertisement on Craigslist, spread the word, and launched their business, doing a handful of weddings a year.

Ruvin popped the surveillance DVD into his computer and scrolled to shortly before 10:00 P.M. For more than an hour he saw nothing helpful, just cars, couples, individuals in light-colored clothing. Just after 11 P.M., two men suddenly appeared from the left, walking right. One looked to be about six feet tall. The other was shorter. Both were dressed head to toe in black clothing. One wore a knit cap, similar to the way robbers were known to roll up their ski masks after leaving a crime scene. Ruvin scrolled the DVD backward, slowed it down, kept repeating the images. He couldn't see the men's faces, but he could see one of them talking on a cell phone. Tremendous, Ruvin thought: if they found the guy, they could use exact cell-phone call logs and GPS tracking technology to further tie him to the area. Ruvin called Wittenberger. "I think I see these two guys," he said.

The sergeant was about to leave the store anyway.

Twenty minutes later, he stood over Ruvin's shoulder, watching the video snippet over and over. Wittenberger strained his neck to look to the far left of the image, trying to make out a piece of lululemon athletica's back door. He couldn't. But the men were moving quickly. One had a backpack.

If Brittany had been in on it, Wittenberger thought, surely she wouldn't have described the guys so exactly; she would have at least come up with different heights and different colored clothes for these guys. And why say it was a pair of assailants? Why not one, or three? "Well, my fucking theory's out the window," he told Ruvin. "I guess it is two masked men."

CHAPTER ELEVEN

Hundreds of Wounds

Early on Sunday, March 13, 2011, Detective Dimitry Ruvin had two things to pick up before driving to Jayna Murray's autopsy in Baltimore: the rope at Montgomery County Police headquarters and Detective Mike "Bucket" Carin at his home. By 8:00 A.M. the skyline of downtown Baltimore appeared, burnished by new office buildings and high-rise hotels. But off to the left and right, as the detectives knew, were the low-slung, row-house neighborhoods that served up more killings in a given month than Montgomery County might see in a year.

The detectives drove into an area just west of downtown, parking in a garage across from the state's five-story, brand-spanking-new, $43 million Forensic Medical Center. Ruvin grabbed his paper bag and notebook. The two detectives eventually were led into one of the building's two cavernous autopsy rooms—fifty feet long, thirty feet wide. The gurney holding Jayna's body had already been wheeled into position, next to a stainless-steel table that held knives, scalpels, clamps, and other dissection tools.

The body bag was zipped open. Jayna was still on her back, just how they'd last seen her in the store.

A thirty-one-year-old autopsy technician in a white coat introduced himself as Mario Alston. "What happened?" he asked.

Ruvin explained about the crime scene at the yoga shop in Bethesda. He told him about the suspects they were looking for—two guys in masks, and how they'd attacked two workers inside the shop. "These two assholes go into the store, kill this girl, rape this other girl. It's crazy."

Alston was shocked. Moments before, when he'd unzipped the bag and seen Jayna's distorted face and the athletic clothes she was wearing, he'd thought maybe she'd been hit by a car while riding a bicycle, maybe even slammed headfirst into a tree.

"Are you kidding me?" Alston asked Ruvin, who said he wasn't, and handed over the brown paper bag.

Two doctors joined them: Mary Ripple and Kristin Johnson. They cut open the bag and looked at the rope, noting its dark-red stains and coarse fibers. A lab photographer started taking pictures. Ripple bent down to look at Jayna's hands and forearms, quickly noting what the detectives had seen the night before: dozens of defensive wounds. Entangled in Jayna's bloodstained fingers were fibers similar to those on the rope, and hairs similar to her own.

Dr. Ripple knew this autopsy would take all day. "Uh-oh," the forty-eight-year-old Ripple had said to herself as she'd looked through pictures from the scene in her office earlier that morning. She was one of the agency's deputy directors, and supervised the work of other doctors. For cases like the Montgomery one—numerous injuries, unknown weapons—she often took part herself. Twelve bodies had arrived from around the state over the previous twenty-four hours. Eleven of the cases seemed fairly straightforward, including a gunshot victim from Baltimore, a traffic fatality from a rural part of the state, and several drug overdoses. But the murder case from Montgomery County was something else.

Ripple, Johnson, and Alston removed Jayna's blood-soaked clothes, putting them in individual evidence bags. They looked over Jayna's body and took swab samples that later could be tested for DNA. Ripple stared at Jayna's long hair, and wondered aloud if they could get away without shaving it off. It wasn't a question so much as a remark of frustration. If they didn't, how else could they evaluate, let alone count, the injuries? And Jayna's face was so distorted, Ripple knew her family wouldn't want an open-casket funeral. "We have to," she told the others.

Everyone paused to watch Alston delicately go to work with a pair of scissors, antibacterial soap that acted like shaving cream, and an orange disposable razor. He tried to collect as much of Jayna's long hair as he could so it could be returned to her family. Maybe they would want it washed and sewn back in before she was buried. Every inch or so, he came across a red gouge in Jayna's skull that he had to work around. Some were circular—as small as the tip of a ballpoint pen or as large as a quarter. Others were straight, stretching for two inches and in some cases turning at right angles. Alston carefully worked his way to the four-inch wide, open wound on the back of Jayna's head. As he cut and shaved, everyone could clearly see how the wound corresponded to a section of skin on Jayna's scalp that flapped open.

After he'd shaved her head, Alston washed down Jayna's face, head, and body with a narrow hose, as the red outflow ran down little canals on the edges of the exam table and into a collection sink.

It was time for the two medical examiners, Ripple and Johnson, to begin individually documenting each injury. They typically did so by mapping each wound on relatively simple forms—one that was an outline of the body, another that was an outline of the head—but the doctors quickly realized that their simple head outline was too small for them to list the extent of Jayna's injuries. They instead went to plan B: printing out color photographs of different portions of Jayna's head and drawing wound diagrams directly on those printouts. The doctors also had to measure the length and depth of each injury. They sorted through wounds on top of wounds, and tried to determine whether each injury was caused by something sharp that cut into the skin or by something blunt that had caused the skin to burst open. The injuries were extraordinary, but their notes reflected the dry medical nature of it all: "Irregular curvilinear lacerations . . . subcutaneous tissue of the right frontal scalp . . . helix and the antitragus of the right ear . . . outer table of the skull oriented on the 10 to 4 o'clock axis with the convex aspect of the fracture."

Ripple could envision broad outlines of the murder. With the first blows, Jayna probably reached for her head reflexively, which is how what appeared to be her own hairs ended up in her hands. She tried to shield herself as the blows kept coming. The killer, or killers, probably used the rope late in the attack, maybe after Jayna had fallen to the ground. Those fibers in her fingers, Ripple figured, meant that Jayna had been able to get her hands under the rope and loosen it even as she was dying.

Ripple could feel anger swelling. Such an immediate, emotional reaction was unusual, but she couldn't help identifying with the victim. Ripple had always been strong-minded, growing up on a small dairy farm in western Maryland and playing all kinds of high school sports. In college, she taught volleyball to help pay tuition. And now, on the table was a younger version of herself—someone who'd tried to fight off the attack even after becoming dazed and disoriented. Ripple knew she'd have done so as well.

She and Johnson examined in detail the open wound on the back of Jayna's head. Within its borders, they counted thirteen fractures, which had caused that portion of the skull to cave into Jayna's brain. The doctors compared the area with Jayna's forehead, which was gouged with similar patterns that hadn't caused fractures. The doctors noted that the front of Jayna's skull was unusually thick. "Maybe that's why the front of her head didn't break," Johnson told Ripple.

As the autopsy entered its second hour, the detectives moved to a second-floor observation deck where they could sit down, talk on their phones, and still watch. They knew the autopsy was their best chance to connect Jayna's injuries to the various tools they'd found in the store. From there, they hoped to connect the tools to her killers.

Ripple eventually came up to visit. She said they hadn't totaled the wounds yet, and that she couldn't tell if Jayna had been raped, but based on bloodstains they'd seen early in the exam, it appeared that she had been. The doctor went back downstairs to continue her work.

Ruvin's phone beeped. It was his sergeant, Craig Wittenberger. Ruvin told him about the possible rape. "They beat this girl down," he said. Wittenberger let out a long, slow sigh. Then he got to his point: he needed Ruvin and Carin's help researching a suspect. "Come on back in," Wittenberger said.

By 3:00 P.M., Ripple and her physician colleague Johnson were inside Ripple's fifth-floor office, having finished the main exam downstairs. Of particular difficulty was analyzing all the wounds to Jayna's face and head. The doctors laid out the printed photographs, now diagramed with little marks that mapped out all the injuries. Johnson used a red pen to circle the slashing and stabbing injuries, and a black to circle the pounding injuries. The doctors tried to be conservative in their totals. The wounds atop wounds were difficult to measure, so each one was counted as a single wound. Ripple knew it could be weeks before she had a precise total, after they'd had a chance to study their notes and all thirty-seven autopsy photos. Preliminarily, though, the doctors had found more than two hundred injuries to Jayna's face, head, and neck, and more than one hundred to her hands, arms, and shoulders.

Ripple and Johnson also counted at least five different wound patterns, meaning at least five different weapons had been used. Ripple noted quarter-inch-wide circles that surrounded smaller circles on Jayna's hands and skull. "I bet that's the back end of a wrench," she told Johnson.

The kind of wrench she had in mind was one she'd seen in two previous homicides—an adjustable, crescent-shaped tool, which the killer would rotate 90 degrees to deliver the most forceful blow. The resulting mark mirrored part of the wrench's adjusting mechanism. Ripple headed downstairs, found a maintenance worker's tool cart and borrowed a wrench to compare with the photographs. Perfect match.

The medical examiners had also found two rope-burn injuries on Jayna, one to her throat, the second to her chin, perhaps made after she'd been able to loosen the rope. And another horrific pattern emerged from all the injuries: blood in the wound paths. That meant Jayna's heart was still beating, that she had still been alive for all of them. Ripple hoped that, even as Jayna's heart was still pumping blood, she was unconscious toward the end.

Of all the injuries, the worst wasn't the four-inch long gash; it was a stabbing wound at the base of her skull. The opening measured one inch long and only one-sixteenth of an inch wide. But a thin knife of some kind had gone deep enough to chip off a piece of vertebra, pierce her skull, and cut the base of her brain. She couldn't have survived for another ninety seconds after that. That wound path also showed blood, indicating it was probably the fatal blow. *Jayna's murderer finally figured out a way to kill her*, Ripple thought.

As 5:00 P.M. approached, the case weighed on the doctor in a way that only a handful of cases ever had before. Ripple dwelled on the dozens of wounds to Jayna's hands and arms. Most, if not all, appeared to come from Jayna defending herself, not from her trying to deliver blows herself. In Ripple's mind, that meant Jayna likely received a powerful strike early in the assault that dazed her. *Goddammit*, Ripple said to herself. *I wish she could have been able to fight back.*

Mario Alston, the autopsy technician, was also affected by the case. Maybe it was in part because of Jayna's age, so close to his and his wife's own. When he went home that evening to the town house in downtown Baltimore he shared with his wife and two young sons, he found himself telling his wife about the case, something he rarely did.

There wasn't a whole lot the thirty-one-year-old hadn't seen. One of his first jobs out of college had been helping FEMA identify the bloated bodies of drowning victims in the aftermath of Hurricane Katrina. Since joining the Baltimore state lab, he'd helped perform more than 3,000 autopsies. But he couldn't remember another murder so horrific.

What he kept going over in his head was how Jayna Murray's killer or killers had had time to watch her suffer, time to watch any emotion she had fade away, time to think about what they were doing. Eventually, though, Alston walked to the refrigerator, pulled out a cold Guinness, sat down, and tried to put it out of his mind.

CHAPTER TWELVE

Locked In

The Montgomery County detectives discussed what kind of men could have invaded the yoga store and unleashed such an attack. It seemed unlikely they were experienced robbers, who preferred to hit cash-heavy businesses and dash out with their money. What fit better, unfortunately, was a pair of crazed men, or at least one crazy man who had convinced a buddy to go along with him. One of them murdered Jayna while the other assaulted Brittany; then they both dashed off. Maybe they were locals, familiar enough with Bethesda to know about the yoga store and its staff of pretty young women?

Already, the initial wave of what would become more than 300 telephone calls and e-mails had poured into the department's tip lines. Most were too vague and unrelated to pursue. Others centered on the same person, a forty-year-old character named Keith Lockett. "All of Bethesda has called on this guy," Detective Randy Kucsan, the investigator who'd found the box of zip-ties in the rear hallway, told Detective Dimitry Ruvin when he'd returned from Baltimore.

The investigators were skeptical, wondering if Keith Lockett stood out in the area simply because he was a tall, black homeless man with a tendency to get drunk and obnoxious. In a way they were right; homeless people largely went unseen in Bethesda, even as they were being helped. Bethesda Cares, a local nonprofit where Keith was a regular, operated from a nondescript storefront a half-mile north of the yoga store. One of its staff members made regular rounds to homeless people to invite them to come inside the Bethesda Cares building during the daytime. There, they could receive counseling, send and get mail, shower, shave, drink coffee, eat lunch, and get help finding a shelter or a subsidized apartment. Bethesda Cares also ran a "Clothing Closet," much of it designer stuff donated by Bethesda residents. Once cleaned up and outfitted in nice, if not perfectly fitting, clothes, Bethesda Cares's clients filtered back into the streets, some making their way to the library or the second-floor café at Barnes & Noble. Keith could be inconspicuous as well, having recently held a job stocking produce at a grocery store. But among some Bethesda merchants and beat cops, he was also known to drink too much beer and uncork sexually charged comments to women. "I'm terrified of him," one of the callers had told Kucsan.

It was all pretty squishy. None of the callers put Keith near the store at the time of the murder. And Brittany had said the assailants sounded white. But other callers noted that Keith hung out with a short guy and hadn't been seen at the store where he bought his beer since the afternoon of the murder. The detectives printed out his ten-page, single-spaced rap sheet and talked to Bethesda patrolmen who knew Keith. A portrait of instability emerged. Born in Washington, D.C., he'd graduated from high school and had a long career as an amateur boxer. The arrests started by the time he was nineteen years old: cocaine possession, assault and battery, robbery, carrying a loaded gun, disorderly conduct, beating someone with a stick. Not all the charges stuck, but it seemed clear that Keith Lockett was no stranger to trouble. The detectives found an active warrant charging Keith with furnishing alcohol to a fifteen-year-old. That was relatively small-scale stuff but would allow them to bring Keith in for questioning if they found him. He was definitely someone they wanted to speak with.

The detectives headed to Bethesda to visit the shops and try to find more outdoor surveillance video. They arrived to find reporters staking out the yoga store, asking for interviews. The detectives declined and called their media-affairs colleague, Captain Paul Starks, who hustled down to Bethesda, then stood outside the yoga store in front of the cameras and announced that detectives were canvassing the neighborhood.

Around the corner, Ruvin found himself inside a store, speaking with a manager and asking if he knew anyone suspicious in the area.

"Yeah, there's this guy, Keith Lockett," the manager answered. On the morning of the murder, the manager continued, he'd seen Keith and two white guys walking toward the street where the yoga store was, Bethesda Avenue. "He had a backpack, and I've never seen him with a backpack before."

Ruvin immediately thought of the video images from behind the store: two men, one tall with a backpack, the other short. He walked back to the yoga store, where his colleagues were searching for more clues, and told them about the backpack witness. Sergeant Craig Wittenberger was intrigued.

More than that, though, the sergeant had a sneaking feeling there was more to be learned right around them. He kept looking, walking up to a table in the fitting area. There were drawers underneath it. The table slid easily and was rotated slightly off center. Wittenberger kicked himself, realizing the table had probably gotten pushed against the wall during the melee. Yet no one had examined the backside, underneath the table, facing the wall.

With the table now pushed away from the wall, Wittenberger bent down and looked at items on the shelves. He saw two pairs of running shoes without laces. A women's pair rested on a large men's pair. What were they doing in a store that didn't sell shoes? With his gloved hands, Wittenberger placed them on the wooden floor. Both pairs showed traces of small red stains, as if someone had cleaned off blood but not gotten it all. Wittenberger picked up one of the size-14 Reeboks, and turned it over. His eyebrows rose toward his nearly bald head. He carried the shoe to the back stockroom, where the bloody shoe prints were particularly clear. Ruvin followed him. Wittenberger compared the sole to one of the prints. All of the wavy, waffle patterns lined up perfectly.

You gotta be kidding me, Wittenberger thought.

"These are the shoes," Ruvin said.

The two talked about Keith Lockett and his backpack. Homeless guys carry extra clothes around. That kind of fit. But why leave the shoes in the store? Why not toss them in a Dumpster? Then again, some of the behavior in Keith's police file didn't make sense either.

They decided to amp up the search for Keith, calling in a team of undercover officers to try to find him. It didn't take long. In short order, the undercover officers called in a report that perked up the detectives. Keith had turned up six miles away, at Washington Adventist Hospital, with bloody clothes and a swollen eye, and the undercover officers were heading there quickly. "Maybe Jayna put up a good fight," Ruvin said.

The undercover officers called the detectives back at the store, recounting the conversation. Excitement grew. Maybe Jayna's DNA would show up in blood on Keith's clothes. Ruvin speculated that Keith had avoided a closer hospital in Bethesda because he didn't want to be recognized. "I think this is our guy," he said.

The officers found Keith in a hallway of the emergency room, lying down on a bed with an ice pack over his left eye, a swollen jaw, and a bloody nose. Keith recognized one of the officers, Curtis Jacobs. "I know you," the patient said. "We go way back, man."

Jacobs asked Keith what had happened to his eye and nose. His first account: a black guy in dreadlocks hit him the night before at a club. It was a lucky shot, the former boxer said, and had caught him off guard. Keith didn't know the guy's name, but said he was in his thirties. Keith repeated the story, but this time said the assailant punched him on a street outside of Bethesda Cares—and tried to rob him. Keith said the man hung out with a short "Spanish dude," the pair had robbed stores in Bethesda recently, and they had cut "that girl." Jacobs asked Keith how he knew this. By hanging out on the streets, Keith said. Then he got teary eyed, and said he was across the street when the woman got hurt. "The black dude and the Spanish dude robbed the lady and cut her. I seen it with my two eyes."

Detective Jim Drewry hurried over to Washington Adventist Hospital to get Keith before he was discharged. The detective arrived at 7:20 P.M., and found the suspect still wearing a hospital gown. The undercover officers gave Drewry Keith's bloody clothes, which had been placed in evidence bags. Drewry took them to his car, came back, and waited for Keith to be discharged. At 9:30 P.M., the two walked out of the hospital, Drewry in a leather jacket and steadying his handcuffed prisoner, who was wearing socks, undershorts, and the gown. Drewry laid a white bedsheet on his front passenger seat, which he found to be a safer way to transport someone, particularly when he didn't have a partner with him. The suspect asked Drewry about his clothes, and allowed that the man who hit him was named Ricky. Drewry stayed away from direct questions about the yoga store, wanting to first get Keith to the station, where he could advise him of his rights to remain silent and contact a lawyer.

Just before 10:00 P.M., the pair arrived at the police station. Drewry led his gowned suspect through the side door, past the detectives' cubicles, and into a gray, dank interview room—nine feet long, seven feet wide, outfitted with a black metal table, three black chairs, and a secret audio and video recording system that had been activated upon their arrival.

"In here, Keith, you can sit down in here," Drewry said.

"I gotta pee, man," Keith said.

"Okay, we're going to let you do that."

"I can't pee with two handcuffs on me."

"I'm going to get those off, okay. Trust me dude."

The two left, returning several minutes later. Drewry guided Keith to a seat and handcuffed his left wrist to a metal ring on one of the table legs. Keith looked around. "Where are my clothes at?"

Drewry assured Keith he had his clothes. "I'll be back witcha' in a minute," he said, and left the room.

Left by himself, Keith quickly dozed off. Out in the squad room, Drewry, Ruvin, and Wittenberger slowly started going through Keith's clothes. There were dried blood drops on his Lakers cap, sweatshirt, jeans, and white-leather Air Jordans. All intriguing signs. Keith's black Nike jacket was also streaked with blood. But it seemed too fresh to have been left Friday night. The detectives felt no real hurry to go back into the interview room. They wanted Keith sober enough to answer yes to question 6 of the "Advice of Rights" form: "Do you understand what I just said?"

At 11:15 P.M., Drewry went back into the interview room and offered Keith something to drink.

"I want cappuccino," he said.

"Well, that one we don't do," Drewry said, "because this ain't the Ritz."

Keith laughed. He said he'd take some water.

Drewry left, eventually returning with Ruvin.

"How you doing, Mr. Lockett?" Ruvin asked.

"I wish I had some clothes on," Keith said.

Ruvin retrieved a dark-green prison jumpsuit, which Keith declined to wear, saying they were trying to make him look like a criminal. "How about a blanket instead?"

Keith nodded, and Ruvin helped tuck in the suspect, his left wrist still handcuffed to the table leg.

Drewry started going through some basic biographical questions. Keith spoke of his boxing career. "Five-time Golden Gloves champion of the world! No joke! No joke!" He grew quiet when telling Drewry that both of his parents had died young. "I went off the hook and started drinking and stuff."

Drewry began to read Keith his constitutional rights. But the suspect kept interrupting him, careening from one subject to the other: "I was drinking and he hit me . . . Guys I know killed somebody in front of my face; they're trying to kill me . . . I need protection . . . I'm schizophrenic affective . . . I need to be on my medication . . . I gotta hang out on the street and watch my back . . ."

Drewry got nowhere. "Let's take a break."

"Don't leave me here," Keith said. "I can't stay by myself."

Ruvin stayed behind. The detective unlocked Keith's handcuffs, hoping that might put him at ease. Keith poured ice cubes out of a red plastic cup, placed them on a paper towel, folded over its corners, and held the cold compress up to his swollen eye. Ruvin moved one chair closer to him, again trying to establish a bond. Every time Keith said something bizarre, Ruvin thought, it showed that he might be off-kilter enough to have attacked both women. Finally, at 1:15 A.M., after the two had been alone for more than an hour, Ruvin brought Keith to the cusp of talking about a recent robbery he had seen in Bethesda. The detective leaned back in his chair, allowing the suspect to describe it in his own words.

"I just seen them young kids run away," Keith said,

lifting his hand and making a fluttering-away motion. "That's the only thing I seen, the young kids just run away. Them young kids be on their skateboards who hang out at the Metro station. You need to be talking to them."

Out in the squad room, Drewry watched part of the interview on a monitor, confirming the feeling he'd had since meeting Keith at the hospital: the man seemed too addled to partner up with another assailant, to use the zip-ties, to clean off evidence, as suggested by the Formula 409 bottle and scrub brush found in the back stockroom. Yes, Keith appeared to know something about the yoga store murder, but at this point who in Bethesda didn't? Wittenberger shared Drewry's views, and Drewry decided he would go back in, act like he thought Keith killed Jayna, and see what happened. It went against Drewry's nature to confront someone without having any good evidence. But it was also 1:30 in the morning, and Keith had started going in circles again.

Drewry walked back into the interview room, sat down, and told Keith he was going to check the blood on his clothes to see if it matched the blood of the murdered woman.

"You think I had something to do with that?" Keith asked.

"Yup."

"Check my blood!" Keith yelled. "Check my blood! And you're going to be wrong!"

More ramblings, more assertions about the skateboard kids. Drewry tried again.

"This woman that got killed inside the store. Did you do it?"

"No. No. Hell no! Nah. Nah."

"And this woman that got raped inside the store, did you do it?"

"No, no, no. I swear to God no!"

"Because that's what people are thinking: that you're playing all these silly games because you killed this woman and raped this woman inside this store."

"Why would I do that? I would never do no shit like that, man. I got a woman," Keith said. "The blood on my jacket came from me. The guy hit me in my nose."

Drewry and Ruvin wanted to get a sample of Keith's DNA by drawing a cotton swab from the inside of his cheeks. Legally, they could do so if they asked him and he said yes, but the two worried the evidence wouldn't be allowed into court because Keith hadn't understood their request. They decided that they had better do this the more deliberate way, by getting a court order. Drewry retrieved the jumpsuit and told Keith he was taking him to jail. "Put this on. That way you'll stay good and warm."

This time Keith accepted the garment. But he was concerned about how he'd get to the jail.

"I can't be in the back of no paddy wagon."

"You're not going to be in the back of a paddy wagon. You're going to be in the front seat of my car like you were when we came up here."

As they walked out, Wittenberger approached, still hoping to garner something from Keith. "I think you could have helped us out. Because I think you know who killed that woman."

"I don't know," Keith said. "I am being straight up on my mother's grave and my father's grave, man. I don't know who done that."

Drewry drove Keith to the county's jail in Rockville, three miles away. Ruvin followed. They booked Keith on the relatively minor alcohol charge, hardly what they were hoping for. It was 2:45 A.M. If the detectives were lucky, they could get three hours of sleep before starting up again on the case.

CHAPTER THIRTEEN

A Bit of Magic

By Monday morning, residents in and around Bethesda were growing alarmed. The masked killer-rapists were still on the loose. And they hadn't struck in a distant ghetto or the closed-off home of a nearby neighborhood. They'd invaded a carefully designed "Urban Village," where thousands gathered daily to decompress a little from the hectic, high-pressure lives they led in the shadow of the nation's capital.

The five-block area hadn't always been such a draw. Until the 1990s, it was home to car-repair shops, drab government buildings, and a concrete plant, where drivers who lined up to get their trucks loaded were known to put the truck in park and run into a nearby tavern for a quick cold one. Detective Jim Drewry knew the area well; it had been part of his route when he'd been a mailman, and he'd enjoyed the laid-back feel of the place, even if it had fallen further behind the ever-more-prosperous neighborhoods stretching for miles in other directions.

But a smart local company named Federal Realty
Investment Trust had smelled opportunity. Its planners
studied the neighborhoods, whose residents were described
in adjective-laden and affirmative terms: *I look at the work
I do as a career, not just a job . . . It's important to continue
learning new things . . . I am interested in other cultures . . .
I make a conscious effort to recycle . . . It's important to feel
respected by my peers . . . Store environment makes a difference where I shop . . . I prefer food presented as an art form.*
They had a lot of money, were eager to spend it, and they
wanted to do so in a safe, walkable area.

Federal Realty began buying up the aging properties,
pouring more than $190 million into a project designed
around principles called "placemaking." Buildings were
leveled, and new ones constructed, as was a large but con-
cealed parking garage, wider sidewalks, attractive land-
scaping, a community fountain. Soon enough, there was
what Federal Realty called Bethesda Row, a five-block area
lined with popular branded stores like Apple and Barnes
& Noble, as well as clothing boutiques, specialty shops,
and restaurants that stayed open late into the night offering food from around the world on tables that opened
onto those new, wider sidewalks. There was even a
pedestrian-only, cobblestone avenue called Bethesda Lane,
bordered by fetching little stores below a chic five-story
apartment building. A canopy of lights stretched across
Bethesda Lane, evoking a lazy evening in the plaza of an
old European town, albeit one that offered lemon-ricotta
gelato for $5.30 a serving.

The whole thing was a bit of magic. People drove to
Bethesda Row, parked, and walked around. They joined

forces with the people who lived in Bethesda Row or close enough to walk there. It created a critical mass of humans who kind of appeared to all be living there. And placemaking adherents loved it. "A vibrant urban gathering place," said the Urban Land Institute, which gave Federal Realty an Award of Excellence. "A retail icon," was the title of a presentation at a conference of the American Institute of Architects.

Of the more than seventy-five stores and restaurants, few businesses understood the aspirations of their customers better than the one with a funny name, lululemon athletica, a wildly successful chain of yoga-gear stores that announced its 2008 arrival in Bethesda with a press release describing its planned immersion into the community. "Guests are invited to kick off the opening weekend with a complimentary yoga class on Saturday, June 7, at 9:00 A.M. The celebration continues throughout the day with yoga demos, a live DJ and kids' face painting." The store targeted educated, professional family women. "By creating products that help keep people active and stress free," the company said in its press release, "lululemon believes that the world will be a better place." A year later, in a presentation to Wall Street investors, the company described target customers of its own: *Affluent . . . Confident . . . At the top of her game . . . Looks for quality . . . Shops organic.*

What businesses like lululemon and Apple understood— really, really understood—was how a growing segment of consumers had begun to question the belief that consumption would bring happiness . . . but they still liked to shop. It led down a path of virtuous consumption, or what retail guru Martin Lindstrom, who wrote a book called *Buyology*, described as the subconscious answer to a subconscious question: "How do I still accumulate my way to happiness?"

Beyond that core Bethesda shopper, of course, the place offered a broader experience: families strolling down sidewalks, people stopping to pet dogs, the whole notion that they were more apt to meet a guest from *Meet the Press* than anyone out to do harm. The idea of mayhem, to say nothing of murder, erupting inside a yoga store was unimaginable. At Ginger, an upscale women's boutique two hundred feet from lululemon athletica, the owner gave her saleswomen panic buttons and had them close the store early, before dark. Customers talked almost exclusively of the murder and masked men. "Oh my God, are you guys afraid?" they'd ask. Workers walked to their cars together, passing white ribbons tied on doors in honor of the two victims from the yoga store, and reported their progress with text messages: "In the car . . . Made it home." The nearest place people knew to buy pepper spray, Ranger Surplus, saw sales of the product triple in the days after the murder. Business at nearby restaurants dropped by as much as 50 percent. Even patrons who still came to Bethesda at night moved more quickly, eyes peeled for a tall man and a short man, walking together.

For years, Bethesda Row had been safe, comfortable, and cozy. All of a sudden it wasn't, and wouldn't be again until the men were caught. "Is Bethesda going to get hit again?" people wondered.

CHAPTER FOURTEEN

Storming the Walls

All weekend, reporters barraged the phones of officials with questions about the case, and the wave was still cresting Monday morning. Leads? Suspects? Bethesda still safe? Responsibility for the answers, or deflections, fell to Captain Paul Starks, the police department spokesman. He asked Captain David Gillespie, the major crimes commander, who had a simple message for his longtime friend: *I've got nothing for you Paul, and tell the press to quit calling down here.* Starks went to see his boss, Montgomery Police Chief Tom Manger.

A onetime journalism major before switching to criminal justice, Manger was well seasoned in media. Between his six years as police chief of Fairfax County, in northern Virginia (another large, prosperous area outside D.C.), and his seven years at the Montgomery post, it amounted to thirteen years of navigating the kinds of public and political fallout that came from someone getting killed in a wealthy enclave where such things weren't supposed to happen. Manger knew he had to stand in front of news cameras, flanked by his commanders, with a clear, two-part message: that he understood how scared people felt and that his detectives were working tirelessly. Absent such declarations, residents would start calling their elected officials, who'd start calling him. Or they'd light up their neighborhood e-mail discussion lists and write letters to the editor, raising a stink.

Until then, Gillespie had kept his updates to Manger and Starks limited—the parking-lot video of the two men, the homeless suspect. But he had not mentioned Sergeant Craig Wittenberger's early suspicions of Brittany, for instance. "We haven't yet been able to get a full story from the rape victim," Gillespie told the chief. Now the idea of having a press conference made him nervous, but he liked the idea of drawing more attention to the case, if that was possible, to scare up possible witnesses—and he figured that playing up a mounting reward fund couldn't hurt.

In addition to his media background, Manger was also a polished public speaker who'd performed in community theater and musicals. The three decided he would do the talking. And they thought it would be good to hold the press conference outside the store. That's where all the reporters were camped out anyway.

Down in their squad room, the detectives didn't have to be in the meeting to know what a high-octane story this had become. To work murders in a large county like Montgomery—which was generally affluent but had sections of middle- and lower-class areas as well—was to inherently understand a weakness in American society. Statistics bore out what they knew: in the United States, nearly 5 of every 100,000 residents are killed every year, a markedly higher rate than most all of the developed world, and yet many pockets of America go along just fine. Residents rarely dwell on the possibility of murder—until a killer strikes, and there's the sudden sense that danger is storming the walls. It was a phenomenon that Detective Jim Drewry, Sergeant Craig Wittenberger, and other longtime Montgomery detectives always groused about as a simple matter of class and race: how people viewed victims from places like Bethesda as innocents, while those murdered in Montgomery's less ritzy areas—the Wheatons, the White Oaks, the Germantowns—they, well, somehow, someway, must've been doing something they weren't supposed to.

At the moment, it was background noise the detectives tried to ignore. They had to figure out what to do about suspect Keith Lockett, who'd been booked in the jail just six hours earlier. Detective Dimitry Ruvin was still hopeful, citing the comments Keith had made at the hospital, and at least some of the bloodstains—the dry ones—found on his clothes. "He might still be our guy," he told Drewry. "Or maybe he's not the guy in the store. Maybe he's the lookout. But what a big, freaking coincidence if he's not."

"I'm just not feeling this guy," Drewry replied.

Still, Drewry wanted to get a sample of Keith's DNA. To do so, he and Ruvin had to convince a judge to essentially allow them to swab the inside of the suspect's mouth. As Ruvin started typing up the affidavit request, however, he quickly came to the challenging part: building his argument that Keith was a viable suspect. He summarized the homeless man's criminal record and what tipsters had said about him. Ruvin studied his notes from their 1:00 A.M. interview. He watched portions of the video. Neither added much to his argument.

Keith's alcohol charge was so minor he wouldn't be

locked up long. And, sure enough, Drewry heard from the jail that Keith had just been released on his own recognizance and climbed into a taxi headed for Suburban Hospital. Over at Ruvin's cubicle, others hovered over his shoulder, offering suggestions on what he should say. "Everyone leave him the fuck alone," Drewry said, "and let him type the search warrant."

Drewry wanted to talk to people who knew Keith. He headed to Bethesda Cares, the homeless day center that provided the free lunches and donated clothes. Pulling up to the place, a half mile from Bethesda Row, Drewry could see how the nonprofit had smartly blended itself into the streetscape, just 100 feet from a restaurant that offered $40 rib eyes and nightly jazz. It was set back from the street, recessed under a five-level parking garage. Drewry walked into Bethesda Cares and spoke with people who knew Keith. He learned more about his boxing career, and the lasting effect that might have had on his ability to stay on task. Yes, Keith could be rude. But from everything Drewry was hearing, he wasn't a cold-blooded killer either. Drewry asked for some clothes he could give to Keith, which he received, figuring it was the least he could do after seizing the bloody ones the night before.

Outside the yoga store, police officials and county prosecutors gathered for the press conference, set to begin at 3:00 P.M. Manger, the chief, wanted to confer with others about exactly what he'd say. But he couldn't do so amid the reporters, so the officials ducked inside the yoga store, where crime-scene investigators were still at work in the back. Manger knew how serious the whole situation was, but once he saw the luxury athletic garb, he couldn't help thinking—his wife would probably love this stuff.

Starks, the media-affairs captain, reviewed for the group that lululemon athletica and its founder were pledging $125,000 in reward money. Federal Realty had chipped in another $10,000. Manger went over what he was going to say with Gillespie, the major crimes commander. Seemed safe enough, Gillespie told him.

The contingent walked back outside. Starks made a few opening remarks, stumbling over the store's name: "lululemon athleta athletica." He introduced Manger, who provided the more exact timeline from three nights prior: how at 9:45 P.M. two employees had left the store; a short time later, one realized she left something behind; at 10:05 P.M. they went back in. "We believe that the two suspects in this case followed them in just seconds after the two victims entered the store," Manger said, describing the suspects as two men wearing dark clothing, gloves, and ski masks. "What occurred next was that the two victims were beaten, sexually assaulted. One of the victims was beaten to death."

In past high-profile murder cases, if Manger knew the killing wasn't random, he didn't hesitate to tell the public, knowing how instantly calming that could be. But he couldn't do so here. Still, in front of the bank of TV cameras, Manger tried to at least let the public know his department was on the case. A team of detectives was working around the clock, he said, and they hoped to solve the case as quickly as possible. "We have good solid leads that we're following up on," he said.

As Manger spoke to the reporters, Ruvin was making his way to a courthouse eight miles away, carrying an affidavit laying out why a judge should let them get Keith Lockett's DNA. Ruvin tracked down the judge on duty to review such matters, got his signature, and hustled

down two floors to see a prosecutor who'd let him use a
fax machine. Ruvin zapped the document to a number
Drewry had given him for a machine at the emergency
room, where Drewry grabbed it. And for the second time
inside of twenty-four hours, he found himself waiting for
Keith Lockett to finish up with a doctor. At 4:55 P.M.,
the detective was allowed in to see him. Drewry handed
him the clothes, and Keith willingly opened his mouth to
let Drewry scrape the inside of his cheek for DNA. Drewry
had no doubt in his mind: the guy didn't do it.

Five minutes later, WUSA, a CBS affiliate, led its evening broadcast with an update on the case, one of a series
of reports on TV, online, and in print from the news conference. "Tonight, police hope a six-figure reward will help
lead them to the masked men who killed a store employee
and sexually assaulted her coworker," anchorwoman Anita
Brikman said. "A huge reward tonight for the arrest and
conviction of the Bethesda yoga store killers."

The report flashed to a striking, smiling photo of Jayna,
dressed in a baby-blue tank top. She, too, had been sexually
assaulted, coanchor Lesli Foster said, before the report cut
to footage of Manger outside the yoga store. "We have no
indication at this point," the chief said, "that this was
anything but a random crime of opportunity."

BRITTANY AND JAYNA

CHAPTER FIFTEEN

The Soccer Star

Brittany Norwood's stay at the hospital turned out to be relatively brief. Doctors stitched the cuts to her forehead and right hand. The CT scans and other tests came back negative. On Sunday night, thirty-six hours after she arrived, a policeman walked Brittany and her family members to their car. The twenty-eight-year-old's identity remained shielded from a growing national audience following the story, but among Brittany's friends, word had quickly spread that she was the survivor.

"I've been freaking out all day," one of them said by text message. "Tell me when you're ready for a visit."

"I thank the goodness of God that you weren't killed," another said by voice mail. "I just hope you are somewhere safe. Send me a sign or give me a call, okay?"

"I just want you to know how much I love you, chica!" a coworker texted. "You are AMAZING!!!"

Liking Brittany was easy—she was quick-witted, self-effacing, and energetic. She liked to round up friends for 7:00 A.M. "Boot Camp" exercise workouts, or 6:00 P.M.

happy hours, and she encouraged their efforts to build careers in high-pressure Washington. And she attracted a string of accomplished boyfriends and lovers: a U.S. Secret Service agent, a college professor, a political pundit who regularly spoke on TV news programs, a dentist. To her large family, she was a conduit of good humor, the one who made sure everyone was coming in for the holidays.

Brittany was born outside Seattle on May 19, 1982, the sixth of nine children to Earl and Larkita Norwood. The family lived twenty miles south of Seattle, and went to Catholic mass. The Norwoods worked hard to surround their kids with middle-class comforts like a two-story house in a safe suburban neighborhood, soccer camps, or even private schools when they could afford them. They paid $1,170 a month to rent a 2,400-square foot home in Federal Way's planned community of Twin Lakes, with curved streets, parks, and private security patrols.

Brittany's dad, Earl, scratched out a living as a furniture upholsterer. The shop he managed sat amid other small business: auto-body garages, sign makers, steel fabricators, and the like. He worked long hours—lights on by 7:00 A.M., still on after 7:00 P.M.—and would take on just about any project. Don Brown, the owner of a nearby machine shop, recalled Earl showing up with a battered chair that he'd just received from a customer.

"This thing is beyond hope," Don told him.

Nevertheless, Earl asked him to fabricate metal support bars for the chair's interior. Don did so, relatively easily, and brought them to the upholstery shop. "You owe me a sandwich," he told Earl, who insisted on paying him $25. Don stopped by later to see the rebuilt, reupholstered chair. "That's gorgeous," he said. Years later, after the two became close friends, Don walked into a breakfast place fifteen miles away and found Earl inside, finishing a night's worth of booth reupholstering.

"Little far from home," Don said.

"I'll take my trade anywhere," Earl told him.

One customer, Mary Jo Reintsma, got to know Earl well enough to talk about their families. "When he talks about his kids," she remembers thinking, "he glows."

But at $33,000 a year, all of his hard work didn't keep pace with the cost of raising nine kids. During the 1990s, as Brittany became a teenager, her parents went through two personal bankruptcy proceedings, at one point listing $91,513 in debts that included money owed on prep school and university tuition, plus doctor and hospital bills. The couple also listed just $7,800 worth of personal property, including a 1985 Audi sedan and a 1986 Ford van.

The hardships seemed to have little effect on how the Norwood kids were cared for. One neighbor, Lesley Rogers, who had three kids of her own, took full notice of the Norwood kids when they stood outside her front window at the school bus stop. They were always on time, backpacks full, and dressed in the right jackets, hats, and gloves for the sometimes tricky Pacific Northwest weather. "Well-scrubbed," was her first thought.

In time, one of the Norwood daughters asked Lesley if she needed a babysitter, a question Lesley and her husband didn't take lightly because their ten-year-old son had epilepsy. In front of her was a girl who smiled and looked directly in her eyes, like a kid raised well. By then Lesley also had met her parents. Sure, she said.

For a while, it worked out well. Then a younger Norwood girl started coming over also. She seemed different, not only from her older sister but her other siblings as well. Brittany seemed to always be tagging along, and looked down when she spoke. Maybe it was shyness. A few baby-sitting sessions later, Lesley feared it was something else.

Her husband kept a bowl of change on his nightstand, a pile of coins that would slowly grow until it overflowed and finally needed attention. Now, though, the pile was getting smaller. Even more concerning was what happened inside their walk-in closet in the bedroom. There, hidden behind clothes on a shelf, Lesley kept a purple bag filled with jewelry. It was inexpensive, costume stuff, but had belonged to Lesley's late mother, and she liked to take the bag out periodically, look at the jewelry, and remember her mom. When she did so, about half of it appeared to be gone.

Nothing had happened when it was only Brittany's older sister coming over. Now? Lesley thought about it. Maybe Lesley had just misplaced some of the jewelry and her husband had grabbed change without thinking about it. Neither seemed at all likely. But the lack of proof out-weighed bringing the matter up with Brittany's parents. Who am I to do that? Lesley thought, knowing the strug-gles she had just raising three kids, and knowing how respectful the other Norwood children had always been. Lesley felt she had only one choice: she simply quit asking Brittany's older sister to babysit.

Brittany attended Saint Vincent de Paul, a private ele-mentary school, but for high school, she enrolled in Deca-tur High School, a public school with about 1,400 students, including two of her older siblings. Her brother Chris served as vice president of his senior class, and went on to graduate with a degree in electrical engineering at Seattle University. Her sister Marissa was a brilliant soccer player before blowing out her knee, but impressed her coaches even more by still coming out to cheer for the team. She was a member of two high school volunteer organizations. "I love to give back to those less fortunate!" she wrote in a yearbook, where she was also voted her class's "Next Oprah Winfrey" before going on to graduate from the University of Maryland.

Brittany was also a stellar soccer player, making the varsity soccer team as a freshman, and playing in games immediately. In class, she was rarely the first to raise her hand, but almost always knew the right answer. She developed an outgoing personality that attracted friends, and had a signature style: chic T-shirt, designer jeans, and a sharp pair of Nikes, all touched off by lavender-scented, Johnson & Johnson baby lotion. "She was beautiful," a close friend remembers.

Not much seemed to bother Brittany, particularly the high school social dramas around boyfriends and breakups. She could just let things go, seeing little need for students she considered "fakes." Many times she found herself the only African American in a group of students, but plenty of other races and ethnicities were present, and Brittany and one of her friends joked about being "Ebony and Ivory," a tribute to the Stevie Wonder–Paul McCartney song.

Her friends came to see Brittany's house as one of smiling welcome. "Hi sweetheart, how are you?" her mom would ask, walking up with a big hug. The place was decorated with furniture that was more comfortable than fancy. The kids shared rooms, and always seemed to be looking out for each other. To one friend, whose parents had split up at the time, "It was what a family was supposed to be."

Others shared that impression. Brian vanBlommestein, Brittany's coach at a high-end soccer club, the F.C. Royals, had come to expect a certain set of questions from parents: What practice drills will you use? How good will the team be? Why isn't my kid playing more? With the Norwoods, it was always simple and more personal: "Hi, Brian. How are you doing?" They showed up to all of Brittany's games, often with three or four of their other children.

Brittany was slight, topping out at five feet three inches tall and 120 pounds. But she never complained at practice, could run extremely fast, and preferred playing defense to scoring goals. Brittany fearlessly tackled anyone, the result of growing up playing the game around older brothers. She helped lead the F.C. Royals to the state title, and played for her high school team.

"I think that this is the year we're going to go all the way!" Brittany wrote in a paragraph for that squad's program when she was a junior. "I hope to play soccer throughout my college years, and someday play on the U.S. Women's National Team."

The only time Brittany ever did anything that gave her coaches pause was after the final game of the season in her junior year.

It happened on the way home from a game 140 miles away on the border of Oregon. The game had been a big deal, with the winner advancing closer to the state finals, played before hundreds of her fellow students who had made the trip to watch. And for the first time all season, Brittany hadn't been the fastest player on the field—an honor that went to twin sisters on the opposing team who zipped by Brittany all game while leading their squad to a 2–1 win. Brittany and her teammates boarded a bus for the trip home. A short time later, they pulled off Interstate 5 to an exit filled with fast-food places. Their coaches gave them each $6 and told them to be back in fifteen minutes. Everyone returned except Brittany and a teammate. Head coach Brandon Frederick asked the other players where they were, couldn't get an answer, and began searching the fast-food restaurants with his assistant coach. After ninety minutes, the coaches felt they had no choice but to continue the trip home.

It was only after returning that the coaches learned Brittany and her teammate were safe: they'd jumped into the car of other students who'd pulled into the same fast-food area. The coaches called both players' parents in for a meeting. Earl and Larkita Norwood were serious and apologetic, reflecting the anxiety their daughter had put everyone through. Afterward, Frederick's assistant coach spoke to Brittany.

"What were you thinking?" she asked.

"We felt bad because we lost," Brittany said nonchalantly.

Brittany did well her senior year, finishing high school with a B average and a soccer career that attracted attention from coaches at large universities in Washington State, Oregon, Nevada, North Carolina, and New York. She visited the New York school—Stony Brook University on Long Island—during a snowstorm, loved the place, and enrolled there.

The choice, so far from home, surprised her parents. But on Long Island, Brittany stood out on campus with a big smile and a decidedly non-northeastern accent that pronounced "Hi" and "How are you?" as if exclamation points were needed. She studied sociology but struggled, winding up on academic probation by the end of her freshman year and putting her soccer scholarship in danger. She practiced with the soccer team but didn't play games, a common practice for first-year college athletes called redshirting, which allows them to extend college to five years. By her sophomore year, though, Brittany picked up her grades and exploded on the soccer field—starting all nineteen games and earning an award as the best rookie among the nine teams in Stony Brook's athletic conference. Her coach, Sue Ryan, said in a news release that Brittany had the mental makeup of all great defenders: "Brittany hates losing more than she likes winning."

Teammates were initially drawn to her. Brittany showed up on the team bus with snacks and would do things like give out her blanket if it was cold or bring a friend a favorite sandwich. The friendships extended off the field. One of her teammates recalled telephoning Brittany at 8:00 A.M. because she was having a meltdown over a boyfriend. Brittany walked across the snow-covered campus to hang out with her. The two would go shopping at a nearby mall, or eat out at restaurants, with Brittany often picking up the tab.

But her friend's wallet kept disappearing, something she first chalked up to misplacing it. She told several teammates, who stunned her with a warning: it was probably Brittany. They suspected Brittany of going into lockers, stealing textbooks, and reselling them. Her friend also couldn't track down a Versace shirt. She and her teammates finally confronted Brittany, who broke down and admitted it, but said she wouldn't do it again. They warned other students about her.

"Brittany's really fun to hang with," they would say. "But be careful: she steals and she lies."

Joanna Katz, who played on the school's lacrosse team, received one such warning. She was cautious, but enjoyed Brittany's company and liked how Brittany didn't seem to take herself and events in life too seriously. "Joanna, get real," was one of Brittany's favorite phrases. During a summer break, Katz got a job tending bar and carried a lot of cash from her tips. She found herself clutching her purse around Brittany, even as she enjoyed her company. At one point, she couldn't find $60 after Brittany had been at her place. It was all so strange—the relatively small-value items, the insistence from Brittany that everything was fine. "She would look you dead in the face and say she didn't know where it was," Katz would later say.

In 2003, Brittany's fourth year at Stony Brook and third season on the field, she played in only twelve of nineteen soccer games. By then, teammates had taken their complaints to their coach. Brittany and the team parted ways, with accounts differing over how it happened. But the result was clear, and it quickly punctured everything: not only her dreams of playing for the U.S. national team, but her identity on campus and, even more importantly, the scholarship that paid for her classes. By the fall of 2004 Brittany was out of school completely, just eleven credits shy of graduating.

Leaving school, Brittany moved to the Washington, D.C., area, where her two sisters Marissa and Candace already lived, and soon were joined by a third, Heather. To many who asked, even family members, Brittany claimed to have graduated from Stony Brook but that a hang-up over tuition loans had kept her from being allowed to attend the graduation ceremony.

But, of course, she didn't really have a degree, certainly not one that an employer could verify, and her work experience was limited. Brittany got a job as a teller for Bank of America at a branch in the city. One day, a dentist with offices down the street, Dr. Maury Branch, walked in and the two struck up a conversation. They hit it off, and by 2006, the two were not only dating, but Brittany was working in the dental practice as an office manager. But, over time, Maury found things not adding up—like whether or not Brittany had her degree—and he broke up with her, and she left the practice in 2007.

It was not an easy breakup. Indeed, it prompted what Maury described as a series of bizarre events that prompted him and his new girlfriend, Marjorie Noel, to go to the D.C. Superior Court to file restraining orders against Brittany. In sworn statements given to the court, they made several assertions.

Brittany had called weekly after the breakup. Maury said he just wanted to be friends. One Sunday afternoon, Brittany texted him to say she was coming over. He ignored the message and left the house. A short time later, when he and Marjorie returned, they discovered a number of Marjorie's belongings missing: a Movado watch, a pair of diamond earrings, a bottle of Vera Wang perfume, a Lacoste polo shirt, checks from her checkbook, her house keys, her car keys, and her cell phone. It had been Brittany, they asserted, who still had a key to the place and must have also learned the burglar-alarm code by watching Maury punch it in. Later, Marjorie found her cell phone in her car, and by then Brittany must have figured out the number. She called, Marjorie picked up and said hello, and Brittany hung up.

In statements filed with the court, Marjorie alleged she was in "immediate danger," and asked that Brittany be ordered to return all her stuff and undergo psychological testing. Maury made a similar request, saying that Brittany had stolen from him as well, and that when they were together, Brittany would push and punch him and throw things at him. He told the court Brittany needed a psychiatric evaluation and "anger management" counseling. The judge ordered Brittany to stay away from Maury and Marjorie for two weeks, a standard move pending a hearing on their allegations. Brittany showed up at court and signed a consent order, agreeing to stay away from the couple for a year but without admitting to the accusations.

Brittany admitted to a close friend that she'd "gone off" on the dentist and had thrown things at him, but she said it was because he'd started to date Marjorie while they were still together, something Brittany found out by following him one day. In Brittany's view, Maury had filed the restraining order to show his new girlfriend how serious he was about moving on.

The whole matter seemed to be quietly going away until Marjorie returned to the courthouse accusing Brittany of having violated the restraining order six weeks earlier. Marjorie claimed that Brittany had driven a dark-blue Honda Accord to an alley next to Maury's house, then tailed the couple to an Office Depot store in Silver Spring. The court set a new hearing on whether to file criminal contempt charges against Brittany for violating the restraining order.

At the time, Brittany was working a new job at the front desk of the Willard InterContinental, a four-star luxury hotel two blocks from the White House. She asked the court to postpone the hearing, saying she'd only been given two days' notice and couldn't get off from work. "This matter is very serious to me," she wrote. A delay was granted.

Her bosses at the Willard hotel had no reason to know about the proceedings—a good thing because things seemed to be going well there. Brittany was an ideal presence to greet hotel guests—petite, striking, smiling, smartly appointed in a dark business suit over a white blouse. Her coworkers began to rely on her to deal with the rudest of guests—those exhausted after travel, those expecting perfect service for the Willard's high rates, those whom Brittany seemed to be able to sense as they walked across the lobby. "I got it, guys," she'd tell them. "Don't worry."

Her colleagues, like Whitney Osborne, never saw Brittany get ruffled. "She had this invisible shield, where she was always happy, always smiling," Whitney would later recall. Brittany started filling in at the Guest Services unit, which combed through reservation lists to flag celebrity guests and those paying $700 or more a night. Brittany made sure their rooms and suites were stocked with fruit baskets, fresh-cut flowers, and—for the really high-enders—a Montblanc pen. Brittany gave them tours of their rooms, her smiling, confident bearing on full display. Outside of work, as some of her coworkers knew, Brittany had also settled into an apartment inside a chic building overlooking D.C.'s trendy Columbia Heights neighborhood. She could have people over for cocktails, then take them out to a host of bars and restaurants just steps away.

But, privately, she was making trips to the D.C. Superior Court, first for the stalking allegations and then a whole new matter. On April 25, 2008, the management company of the sleek apartment building filed a claim to evict Brittany and her roommate because they were two months late on their $2,565 monthly rent. After a brief legal proceeding, the roommates were evicted, and Brittany moved in with one of her sisters. As for the stalking claims, Brittany managed to make them go away quietly by simply not showing up for a hearing, prompting the judge to issue a standard "bench warrant" for such matters. But in a city full of crime, cops didn't have time to serve bench warrants. They only enforced them when they picked up someone for something else. The warrants often automatically expire after a year if they're not served, which is what happened for Brittany.

At the Willard, work demands and long hours mounted. "I spent the WHOLE weekend at work, literally," she texted to a friend. "Even had to stay over because I had Johnny Depp and Tim Burton in house. Didn't get home until 11:45 last night."

But Brittany's bosses took notice. "You won employee of the quarter and didn't tell me?!?!," a colleague and friend texted her in late 2008.

"Oops. Sorry! You didn't ask," replied Brittany, who friends knew was quicker to talk them up than herself. "I am truly blessed to have friends like you!!!!" she wrote in one such text.

Outside of work, much of Brittany's social life revolved around her three sisters who lived in the area, Marissa, Heather, and Candace, and Candace's two young sons. They got together for dinners, or took the boys to movies and sleepovers.

"Thank you so much for making this day SO special," Candace wrote to her sisters after a long birthday celebration. "I love you guys VERY much!!"

"We LOVE you too," Brittany wrote back a minute later. "Glad you had a good time."

Brittany also kept in touch with her siblings who lived outside the area: older brothers Jay and Chris, who lived in the Seattle area; younger sister Lauren, who lived there as well; and younger brothers Zach and Josh, who lived in Indiana and North Carolina, respectively. Indeed, a day after she gathered with her local sisters for the birthday celebration, Brittany learned that Josh, who was still in college, was low on funds to fly home for Thanksgiving. She reported it to her siblings in a group text message. "Hey Everyone, I just spoke with Joshy and he wasn't going to come because he said he didn't have the money," Brittany wrote. "I was wondering if we could all pitch in and get his tic. I'm gonna look now and see how much we're looking at. I will keep you posted. No phone calls until 10 please. My shows are on :)."

It prompted immediate responses.

"Let me know. I'll donate to that cause," one brother wrote.

"Of course, let us know!" another sister added. "What's his schedule? I will also search for tickets."

Brittany texted them back about two hours later.

"OK, so after a little research, if everyone can, we will probably be looking at about $65-$75/person. I will do more research tomorrow and finalize things then. Love Ya."

They quickly thanked her.

"Of course," Brittany wrote back. "Turkey Day wouldn't be the same."

Brittany had a taste for nice things: designer clothes, $35 crab cakes, Maker's Mark bourbon, close-in seats to Washington Redskins games, a well-known hairstylist.

Brittany was known for always having great hair. It was hardly an accident. She went to one of Washington's top stylists, who charged $275 for hairstyles. And he was the kind of professional you didn't cancel on at the last minute without good reason.

So on December 28, 2009, Brittany gave him one. "I went home for Xmas and my grandmother is sick and in the hospital. She had a heart attack yesterday. Instead of flying back tonight, I am leaving Wednesday morning," she texted from Washington—D.C., not Seattle. A month later, she had to cancel again, this time using the shifting schedule of a VIP guest at the Willard as her excuse. "I've got the Jonas Brothers coming on late now today at 7 instead of 3, so once again will have to reschedule," she wrote the stylist.

"OK, no prob," the stylist wrote back.

Brittany looked into buying a boutique condo or loft in downtown Washington, some going for close to a half million dollars. "I just wish I was rich so I could be like 'I'll take one of those and two of those!'" she wrote to a friend who worked at a nearby hotel. "I'm going to have to get a second job."

Brittany struggled to find a steady boyfriend to replace the dentist, but certainly didn't lack for companionship. On a trip to Miami with a friend, she met a guy from the United Arab Emirates. "When am I going to see you again?" Brittany wrote afterward. "I'm thinking Dubai in two weeks. What's your work schedule like?"

"Naw, that's not going to work," he wrote back, suggesting she visit him after relatives cleared out and an upcoming religious observation concluded. "I have my parents there the exact same time. How about end of September? That would be a good time because Ramadan is coming in three weeks, so the entire country will be shut down for that month."

Brittany proposed they stay in touch. "You enjoy the time you have with the fam."

In Washington, Brittany carried on a longtime casual relationship with a Democratic Party operative that seemed to involve just two features—him telling her when he'd be appearing on TV and the two of them getting together for sex. Brittany seemed to always squeeze in time, often on a moment's notice. Only a few things got in the way. "Baby, I need to get my nails done," Brittany wrote him in the summer of 2009. "If I cancel they'll charge me. I can do tomorrow at lunch."

With her family scattered in different states, Brittany kept in touch with them with a running stream of wisecracks and well-wishing. But everything wasn't perfect between the siblings. After returning from a family gathering in

Seattle, Brittany learned that her sister Heather was accusing her of swiping $300 cash out of her purse.

Brittany fired off a quick missive. "I have never done anything to you to give you the impression that I would ever steal from you, especially money. Anytime I've ever needed it, I've always asked you straight up," she wrote. "At least have the decency and respect to ask me yourself, instead of going around telling people I stole money from you!"

"If you didn't take it," her sister wrote back, "then sorry for accusing you. I don't know what to think!"

"At this point I can care less you didn't know what to think. What have I ever done to make you think I would steal from you?" Brittany replied. "You don't just accuse someone of doing something and throw false allegations out there before even speaking to them."

The two sisters soon seemed to patch things up, returning to concern over each other's lives.

Away from work, away from happy hours with friends, Brittany would fall into social isolation. She'd go through bouts of poor concentration, of trouble sleeping. In the spring of 2010, Brittany took a vacation but stayed in town. "At the gym twice a day," she texted to a friend.

It was high-octane stuff: kickboxing classes, ab classes, "Boot Camp" classes. And it seemed to help revive the great athlete that Brittany had been. She started thinking about moving on to a new career—as a personal trainer, perhaps even owning a gym. And Brittany knew a place she thought might help her get there.

CHAPTER SIXTEEN

Mediocre Lives Are Lousy Lives

Of all the stores in America, the ones considered the most successful generally fall into two camps: luxury retailers, like Tiffany jewelers, or volume ones, like Costco. Rarely mentioned but squarely in the first camp is lululemon athletica, which in 2011 ranked fourth highest in sales per square foot of floor space—trailing only Apple, Tiffany, and Coach, according to the research firm RetailSails. Lululemon owed its quiet success to its limited but intensely loyal set of customers.

To customers, lululemon hit all the right buttons. The store's roots were in yoga, offering stylish tights and tops made of moisture-wicking fabric, chafe-resistant seams, and hidden pockets for cards and keys. But the stores sold plenty of other workout gear as well, and its vibe wasn't completely Zen and serenity. They targeted customers with high-paced lives, women who wanted to succeed on all fronts—as professionals, as mothers, as people.

Lululemon espoused their ethos in a thirty-one-part manifesto printed on its shopping bags, water bottles, and various merchandise. Number 11: "The world is changing at such a rapid rate that waiting to implement changes will leave you 2 steps behind. DO IT NOW, DO IT NOW, DO IT NOW!" Number 25: "Nature wants us to be mediocre because we have a greater chance to survive and reproduce. Mediocrity is as close to the bottom as it is to the top, and will give you a lousy life."

Central to the company's success were its saleswomen, called "educators," whose mission it was to teach customers, called "guests," about the technical specifications and design elements of the apparel, and allow them to decide what to buy. The ideal educators were fit and high-achieving women themselves; guests wanted to see themselves reflected when they spoke with them.

So when Brittany first met the manager of lululemon athletica's store in Washington, D.C.'s Georgetown section, the manager saw a seemingly perfect employee. Brittany knew style. She knew high-end athletics. She had spent more than three years disarming the demanding guests of a luxury hotel. And with her petite but chiseled frame, Brittany clearly looked the part. She started the same day she filled out her application.

When she completed the forms, Brittany created a fictitious paper trail in keeping with this persona, indicating not only that she'd graduated from Stony Brook but that she'd posted a 3.4 GPA while there (considerably higher than her real one of 1.98). Brittany reported that she'd been making $55,000 a year at the Willard, quite a bit more than the lululemon job, which started at $11 an hour. With commissions, that could translate to about $30,000 a year. Brittany wrote that a desire for a "career change" was what prompted her to leave the Willard.

As she made the transition, a friend from high school caught up with her over the phone. Brittany was as encouraging as ever: "I'm so happy that you're doing well." Brittany told her friend that leaving the Willard reflected her attempts to appreciate life more. She talked about trying to get to Haiti to help the earthquake survivors. "Life is too short to miss opportunities," Brittany said, sounding content and happy, and signed off as always: "I miss you and I love you."

Brittany was a natural on the sales floor—spirited, energetic, fun to be around. Like her colleagues, she enjoyed benefits that for an hourly retail job were good. Lulu paid for health-care insurance, yoga classes, and fitness-club visits, and offered its employees the pricey merchandise at a steep discount—good news, since employees were expected to wear the form-fitting garb not just to work, but also out to yoga classes and fitness clubs, talking up its benefits as part of lulu's brilliant, grassroots marketing strategies. The Georgetown store also sent Brittany to help organize Sunday sessions of "Beach Bums & Bellinis" at the well-known W Washington hotel. For $39, participants got a workout followed by brunch overlooking the White House.

Lulu could be an unusual place to work—one that reflected the same Zen-to-attain message to its employees as it did to customers. Employees read a handbook called *pramana*, a Sanskrit term used for "obtaining knowledge," and were expected to follow *asteya*, another Sanskrit term used for "not stealing and not coveting." They were encouraged to watch DVDs by self-help guru Brian Tracy, be part of a mission to "elevate the world from mediocrity to greatness," and publically document their personal one-year, five-year, and ten-year goals for their lives and careers.

Brittany tried to lock in on becoming a personal trainer and opening her own gym. In December 2010, at her brother Jay's wedding, she spoke to her brother Chris about how during her childhood, she'd thought she was fat and hated the way people looked at her. Being a personal trainer was a way she could help people. To Chris, this was welcome news. He'd long felt Brittany lacked professional focus.

Meanwhile, back at the Georgetown store, employees were reporting incidents of missing cash, of money taken from wallets in the back room and registers coming up short. Brittany said that she, too, was missing money. Still, the store manager grew suspicious—no one ever accused Brittany of stealing, but she had worked all the shifts reporting problems.

It was around this time that lululemon ran its nationwide, employees-only "Shop Night," where workers could purchase apparel at 70 percent off, an even steeper discount than normal. To ward off depletion of inventory, the company set purchase limits at $1,000. At the Georgetown store, Brittany asked the manager on duty if she could go over the limit. The manager agreed, but would later say she thought Brittany was talking about a relatively minor amount. Yet Brittany more than doubled the purchase limit, racking up $2,196 worth of purchases—which, with the discount, cost her only $659.

The manager felt her goodwill had been taken advantage of. And her suspicions about Brittany only grew. By now, she more strongly suspected Brittany of the thefts. On December 29, 2010, she brought Brittany in for a meeting and asked her about going over the $1,000 "Shop Night" limit. Brittany questioned why the rules were suddenly so strict. The manager fired her on the spot, citing "discount abuse" on her termination letter.

For Brittany, it was a big blow. Lululemon wasn't just a paycheck; it was a pathway to success—a ticket into high-end health clubs, a way to make valuable connections—that could make up for stumbles in her life and match the accomplishments of those around her. Brittany called a friend who also worked at lulu, and learned workers at other stores had likely gone over the limit, too. She complained and a regional manager got involved.

The company's handling of her firing was, to some extent, a product of its success. Just like other fast-growth retailers, lulu had expanded quickly and profitably by granting autonomy to the store managers. It made for creative and energetic places to work. But the fast growth meant the company didn't always have time-tested systems in place. In this case, the company didn't follow a structured process for handling the trickiest of personnel matters—suspecting thievery but lacking proof—and had carried out a termination citing different reasons, one that had created more problems than it solved.

The company's regional office launched an internal investigation. It turned out that across North America, twenty-seven other lululemon workers had topped the $1,000 limit on the end-of-year discounts. Brittany talked to friends about hiring a lawyer. It was never clear if she told people at lululemon that she was considering legal action, but perhaps she didn't have to—given the issues with other employees from "Shop Night," and given lululemon's relentless attention to its corporate image.

The store manager's decision was overturned. Within two weeks, Brittany met with a regional manager who told her she would be reinstated, and gave her a choice of stores to work at. But rather than appreciate the company's gesture, Brittany groused about how the whole thing had played out in texts to another lulu worker: "It totally went how I expected and I swear the apology wasn't even genuine!"

"Jeeze! I'm so sorry! Are you ok? What do you want to do?"

"I will prolly end up at Bethesda, but haven't fully made up my mind yet . . . It's definitely unfortunate, but now all I can do is try and make the best of it!"

Brittany had a couple more weeks off, and fell back on the enjoyable parts in her life—friends, family, and fitness. "Today, just doing the relaxing thing. Massage, manicure, then dinner w/the girls," she texted to a friend, laying out weekend plans that included watching her beloved Seattle Seahawks. "Tomorrow, yoga in the A.M. then football!!!!! Hopefully the Seahawks will kick some Bears Ass :)"

Brittany also reconnected with a U.S. Secret Service agent whom she'd dated six months earlier, joking with him about how she'd been playing with one of her nephews and her cell phone fell into a sewer. "Ahh the joys of kids," the agent replied. The two had lunch the next day and hung out at Brittany's place.

She was also hitting trendy bars and dance clubs with friends, and used the time to hang out with her young relatives. Brittany and her three sisters looked out for each other—texting and calling during snowstorms to make sure everyone made it home from work safely. Brittany organized a thirtieth birthday dinner for her sister Marissa.

The next morning, she heard by text from her mother in Washington State. "Good morning sweetie, How are you this morning? Did you go out to dinner yesterday for Missy's Birthday? I'm glad all of you have each other there, and you are there with the little people. Have a wonderful day. I love you very much, Mom."

Brittany responded, saying they'd all gone to the Carlyle. "I'm pretty sure you've been there with us too. Enjoy the Rest of your Day. Love You!"

Out in Washington, Brittany's parents talked proudly about their children. "All the kids are doing great," Earl Norwood told his friend Don Brown.

On January 18, 2011, Brittany met with Rachel Oertli, manager of the Bethesda lululemon athletica store. It couldn't have been an entirely comfortable talk. Several months earlier, she'd applied for a management job at Rachel's store—hoping that her years at the Willard would make up for her lack of retail experience—but Rachel had turned her down. Still, for Brittany, the new meeting went well, and she sent a text to one of her future coworkers: "You have such a solid team. I know it'll be a great experience."

CHAPTER SEVENTEEN

A Narrow Gray Zone

A key member of lululemon athletica's solid team in Bethesda, Maryland, was Jayna Murray, a gregarious thirty-year-old Texan poised to start a new chapter in her life.

As 2011 opened, she was closing in on dual master's degrees in business administration and communication, and looking for a corporate marketing job in the Pacific Northwest, where her longtime boyfriend, Fraser Bocell, was getting a PhD in educational statistics at the University of Washington. The two had started looking at engagement rings. One of the companies interested in hiring Jayna, at its corporate headquarters in Vancouver, Canada, was lululemon athletica.

As lulu executives knew, Jayna could fill a room with her personality—her laugh, her confidence, her penchant for asking thoughtful questions. She collected friends everywhere she went: people she'd met at college, on jobs, or during trips she'd taken to places around the world. She bungee jumped, scuba dived, skydived, drank margaritas, and danced salsa until 3:00 in the morning. "If you're afraid to do something," Jayna liked to say, "go do it."

But she had her struggles, too. As a senior in high school, Jayna drifted away from clear ambitions, and refused to fill out college applications. As she got older and moved from city to city, she'd often go through months of private sadness before forming new friendships.

Her father, David Murray, grew up the son of a military officer and earned a scholarship to play linebacker at what was then a full-time military school, Texas A&M University. Her mother, Phyllis, was raised in Manly, Iowa, population 1,500, and eventually attended Texas Lutheran University, which is how she and David met. In 1966, he went to the U.S. Army's Airborne and Ranger schools. He learned a relatively new style of combat: flying aboard helicopters into hot spots and either jumping out or sliding down zip lines. David shipped off to Vietnam and led a platoon of soldiers into battle. As they hacked through the jungle one day, a booby-trapped land mine erupted, killing three of his men and badly injuring David's legs. He recovered in a military hospital and charged back into battle, this time leading a Special Forces unit. When David came home, in 1969, he and Phyllis married.

Both went on to pick up postgraduate degrees, Phyllis in family and child development, with a specialty in family counseling, and David in geological engineering and international affairs. Phyllis worked briefly as a therapist before pursuing a career as a flight attendant for TWA. David went to work for Phillips Petroleum, even as Vietnam continued to weigh on his mind. He struggled with anger and vivid flashbacks of friends killed next to him, often having trouble sleeping. David tried talking to counselors, but that didn't do much.

What did, and what kept his rage in check, was to smile at all he had. A big part of that was his wife, Phyllis; their two sons; and, as of November 22, 1980, their daughter, Jayna. Jayna was strong-willed from the get-go. At age two, she already hated their weekly family ritual of splitting up sections of the Sunday newspaper for everyone to go through. Jayna knew the other four were reading but couldn't understand why she wasn't able to do so—a contradiction that sent her off crying to her room. A couple of years later, she tried to escape a spanking by hiding every wooden spoon in the house.

"With guidance, she'll set the world on fire," a swimming instructor once told her mother. "Without guidance, she'll destroy herself."

Phyllis and David took that advice to heart. Her father began taking Jayna along on Boy Scout campouts for the troop he led. Jayna carried her own backpack, helped her dad pitch their tent, and rolled out their sleeping bags. She learned to tie knots and start campfires—the same activities that the older boys, including Jayna's two brothers, did to collect merit badges. Jayna also went to Boy Scout meetings, said the Pledge of Allegiance alongside them, and watched the boys receive their badges. David told Jayna the rules said she couldn't officially receive badges— but he gave them to her at home, away from the troop.

Phyllis's degree in family and child development also played a role in Jayna's upbringing. If Jayna or her brothers wanted to try a sport or a musical instrument, they had to agree to commit to it for a certain amount of time, such as six months or a year. Their parents didn't want them to quit before they understood if they really liked something. "Always moving forward" was the way David thought about it. "And the only way to do that was through self-awareness and self-improvement."

He had worked his way up at Phillips and began managing drilling sites around the world. Phyllis, too, of course, traveled a lot for her flight-attendant job. The result: heavy rotations of single-parent duty. But they found ways to make their schedules work with the kids' interests. For example, one of them would take Jayna to dance class at the Houston Metropolitan Dance Company, where for three hours, six days a week, she eagerly worked through the paces. Her teachers started telling her she had a good chance to make it on Broadway.

For her parents—with the family home more than an hour away—it made little sense to drive back and return for pickup. David spent much of his three hours outside in their Ford Aerostar, reading technical journals, writing drilling plans, or watching ball games on a portable television. One night, on the way home, Jayna, about thirteen at the time, looked up from the homework she was doing under the dome light and asked him about it.

"Dad, why don't you come inside?"

"Well, sometimes I do."

"You don't come inside all the time."

"I'm just more comfortable out in the car."

"What do you mean you're more comfortable out in the car? It's dark out in the car."

"The car's got lights. I read. I watch baseball."

"Well, you need to come inside the studio."

As Jayna kept pushing, David realized his daughter had figured out the real reason behind his reluctance. He felt uncomfortable around Jayna's dance instructors, at least two of whom he thought were gay.

"Dad, they're not interested in you," Jayna continued. "They don't care about you. You're married."

David didn't have a comeback. He talked to his wife about it. She told him his daughter was right. He began spending the full three hours inside the studio. As he got to know the instructors, he saw how much they cared for his daughter, how athletic they were, how foolish he'd been, how lucky he was to have a daughter who would speak her mind and teach him things.

Jayna did well academically—low As—but had trouble finding the right school. By the time she was in her senior year, Jayna had been to four different high schools, including one year spent in Norway, when her father was transferred there. About the same time, she realized that dancing, even on Broadway, was a tough way to make a living. Her parents took her to two days of aptitude testing, which revealed she seemed built for a career in sales or marketing. "I don't want to do that," she told them. Phyllis and David took her to visit nearly ten colleges. Many had dance programs. But Jayna always put off filling out the applications.

Her parents had long ago figured the best way for them to parent a strong-willed daughter with ambitions was to suggest this, talk about that, nudge this. But now they had a daughter exerting her will to not really do anything. They decided to meet force with force. The night before her high school graduation, Phyllis told Jayna she had six weeks to either get accepted to a college or secure a full-time job. "If not, you're going to be out of this house," Phyllis said.

Jayna stormed out, passing a brother's girlfriend in the driveway. "Mom and Dad are kicking me out!" she cried.

She quickly applied to two colleges: the University of Central Florida, where she thought she could get a job dancing at Walt Disney World, and Saint Louis University, which appealed for two reasons: it was in the city of TWA's hub, from which Jayna could use family benefit miles to travel around the world, and it had a study-abroad program. Jayna flew to Saint Louis for a student orientation and convinced the administrators to let her start right away—in Madrid. Suddenly, she had a plan.

Jayna and her classmates took an orientation trip to the Pyrenees mountains, on the border of Spain and France. Things got off to a tense start, with students either too shy or homesick to say much. On their first night, they all went to sleep on the floor in one room. Jayna had a trick up her sleeve. She knew how to throw her voice.

"Help, I'm trapped in the closet," she said softly. "I'm trapped in the closet."

Another student jumped up and flipped the lights on. "Did you hear that?!"

Jayna and the student next to her started to laugh. Soon the whole room was cracking up.

Jayna studied in Madrid for two years, then enrolled in a Semester at Sea program, studying with hundreds of other students aboard a converted cruise ship that made stops all over the world. One night she went to a salsa dance class taught by a fellow student, Rudy Colberg, a native of Puerto Rico who'd taken seven years of Latin dance lessons while growing up. As the class got under way and Rudy walked among the students, he saw Jayna's dance skills and asked if she wanted to help him teach. She agreed. Afterward, she and Rudy ended up dancing by themselves for two hours and trading moves they knew. Rudy was stunned. This blue-eyed blonde was by far the best salsa partner he'd ever had. The two became close friends.

Rudy was with Jayna on the deck of the ship when it reached Vietnam. As they sailed up the Mekong River toward Ho Chi Minh City, the big cruise ship towering over groves and swamps, Jayna thought about her father— how he'd been here three decades earlier, how many friends he'd lost, how he'd struggled with harrowing memories. She started to cry. "My dad was here during the war," she told Rudy. The students spent six days in Vietnam. "I wish he could come back one day and see the country." After the Semester at Sea program, Jayna came home and talked to her dad about going back to Vietnam. He was skeptical, but slowly started to make plans to do so.

Jayna finished up her bachelor's degree at George Washington University, in Washington, D.C. Just before her senior year there, she walked into her dorm room to find a new roommate, Marisa Connaughton, sitting on the floor and crying. Marisa said she and her boyfriend had just broken up. Her phone beeped. "Oh my God, it's him," she told Jayna. "What should I do?"

"You've got to answer it! Tell him you're out having a great time!"

As Marisa answered, Jayna immediately started whooping and laughing, and got a friend she was with to do the same thing. The guy on the other end of the line could hear them. "Where are you?" he asked.

"I'm out with my friends," Marisa said, and quickly hung up. She tried to cry but found herself laughing instead. Jayna tended to have that effect on people.

Despite her exuberant attitude, Jayna was resolute about some things, like loyalty and limits and values. "Jayna's gray zone," Rudy would later say, "was very well-defined and very narrow." But with anything outside the zone, Jayna generally tried to laugh her way through. One of her favorite things to do was teach five-year-olds how to dance. "They don't care about how they look," she'd say.

By 2006, Jayna had graduated from George Washington with a degree in international business and marketing, and was back in Houston, Texas, working in marketing at Halliburton, the energy and engineering giant.

She became good friends with her office neighbor, Chasity Wilson, despite their outward differences: Jayna, a twenty-five-year-old white girl with an undergraduate degree in international business and marketing, who put her career plans ahead of any intentions to marry or have children, and Chasity, a thirty-one-year-old African American mother of two going through a divorce, who had joined Halliburton as an administrative assistant and worked her way up. Jayna invited Chasity to her desk for early morning sessions of "cube therapy" with two other female colleagues, where they spent ten minutes discussing various personal issues or cutting up before getting to work. Jayna would sit atop her desk or a filing cabinet. Back in their seats one morning, Jayna used instant messaging to tell Chasity she could hear the music quietly coming out of her computer.

"I love that song," Jayna typed. "Give me one of your speakers."

The two looped one of Chasity's speakers into Jayna's cubicle, and went on to spend their days listening to Chasity's iPod collection of top 40 and hip-hop. "Play that one again," Jayna would type.

The two began traveling together overseas for the company. And outside of work, the two hit bars, laughed loudly, and danced. But things weren't all roses. About eighteen months earlier, Jayna's condo had been destroyed by a fire, and she'd lost everything inside: photographs, traveling mementos, letters, a twenty-one-year-old cat named Sally. Jayna needed more than a year of counseling to recover, but did so with a renewed appreciation of the value of all her relationships with family and friends. Chasity was having a hard time dealing with splitting up with her husband of thirteen years. She and her husband were rotating in and out of the house, so that the kids could stay put. Jayna let Chasity stay with her. They'd sit on the floor, drink wine, and talk themselves to sleep, with Chasity often in tears. Jayna never wavered in her message: Chasity and her husband were doing right by their kids. "You're doing everything right," Jayna told her. "The kids don't have to go anywhere."

Chasity had never met anyone like Jayna, who could impart such insightful advice, despite being six years younger and having no personal experience with marriage or kids. Jayna got her friend to take college classes again, something she'd halted. "You can't stop," Jayna told her. "You have to keep going."

*   *   *

Jayna's professional interests lay outside the oil industry and more with companies that lived and breathed marketing and branding—the Coca-Colas, the Nikes. She applied to MBA programs, was accepted to Johns Hopkins University, and ended up back in the Washington, D.C. area. A short time later, she noticed a bag her friend Marisa was using to carry her lunch. It was red and white and had writings all over it.

"What's this bag?"

"That's lululemon," Marisa said, "where I buy my stuff to work out in."

Jayna read the writing on it. " 'Friends are more important than money . . . A daily hit of athletic-induced endorphins gives you the power to make better decisions, helps you be at peace with yourself, and offsets stress . . . Jealousy works the opposite way you want it to.' "

She'd never heard of the store and asked her friend about it, shocked to hear that running shorts there cost $54. "I know," Marisa said. "But the clothes fit and make me feel good when I go to the gym and it makes me go more often."

That the company could develop such loyalty intrigued Jayna. It related to both degrees she was pursuing: a master's in business administration with an emphasis on marketing and a master's in communication that looked at the confluence of companies, brands, and the media. Teachers asked students to study specific companies, and Jayna found herself delving more and more into lululemon athletica, her analyses honing in on how the company used grassroots marketing to help customers feel good about themselves, even as they dropped $98 for a pair of yoga pants. "Lululemon athletica helps you develop the look and lifestyle that you self-inspire," Jayna wrote when asked to define a company's core message.

Jayna's interest in the company led to a job at the Bethesda store. She needed spending money, but she also wanted to see its creative marketing in action. In time, she found the Bethesda staff offered something else: a social circle she'd been lacking since returning to Washington. The women who worked there talked about their goals and ambitions. They trusted each other enough to pile all their bags and wallets on the same two chairs in the back stockroom. They went out together for drinks, and covered one another's shifts on short notice. And, as an inside joke, they all called each other some variant of the same name: Jim, Jimbo, Jimmy, James. It was a tight bunch.

But Jayna wouldn't be there forever. By late 2010, she and her longtime boyfriend, Fraser, had committed to having Jayna move to the Seattle area. About this time, a coworker who Jayna supervised, Eila Rab, asked Jayna to write her a recommendation for a position Eila had just learned about—in the marketing department of lululemon's headquarters in Vancouver, Canada, near Seattle. Jayna was immediately intrigued by the job as well. But she didn't want to apply behind Eila's back. The two were close friends, and Eila had found out about the job first. That mattered to Jayna. She brought Eila into the store's small office and shut the door. "If you don't want me to apply, I won't," Jayna said. "It's not worth it to me." Eila told Jayna that she should apply as well.

* * *

In the wake of American corporate scandals at Enron, WorldCom, and Lehman Brothers, business schools like Johns Hopkins pushed ethics discussions in their classes. Jayna was asked to write about her broad, moral values. She reflected on her travels around the world, both with Semester at Sea and with Halliburton, when she tried to take extra days to seek out the most interesting, if not the safest, places in countries like India, Nigeria, and Brazil— the orphanages, the slums, the tiny villages. For years, she had been thinking about people living among violence and strife. In the essay, she described herself as a pacifist, asserting how it ultimately would make the world safer. "Is it possible that growing up with a family full of military veterans, with three family members having served in wars, that I might have this moral judgment? Yes, it is true," she wrote.

By January 2011, Jayna's brother Hugh, a U.S. Army captain, was preparing to deploy to Iraq. Her views on war hadn't dimmed her admiration for what he was about to do—try to help the government there prosecute terrorists. Jayna climbed into her Pontiac and drove to Fort Bragg, North Carolina, to see him off. Her parents and Hugh's wife, Kate, were also there. As Jayna hugged him good-bye, she let her emotions fly, and when Hugh boarded a bus to take him to the plane, a buddy next to him tried to lighten the mood by joking, "Jayna was more upset to see you leave than Kate."

Jayna's dad, David, who by then was working for Halliburton, took the occasion to spend more time with her. He drove back with her to Washington—just the two of them, talking in her car while driving north. Subjects swung from politics to pacifism to David's questions about the principles of marketing as they applied to specific business projects. "Why do you say it that way?" he'd ask. David could sense Jayna's fears for her brother Hugh. They were well-placed: Iraq was chaotic, even if it was no longer at war. And her brother would be moving around, the most dangerous thing to do there. David, of course, knew all about combat. "Hugh is going to be fine," David told his daughter.

Time was ticking on their visit. As they got into Washington, David drove Jayna by a friend's house so she could pick up a bridesmaid dress. The two planned to get a few hours of sleep before their flights the next morning—David back home to Houston and Jayna to Minnesota, for the wedding. But when it was clear Jayna needed more time to finish packing that morning, David said he didn't need a ride to the airport. He hugged his daughter good-bye. "I love you," they said to each other.

David walked out of the condo and two blocks to a subway stop. It was January 20, 2011, and the last time he'd see his daughter.

CHAPTER EIGHTEEN

Coming Together

The first morning of February 2011, Brittany Norwood woke by 6:00 A.M. It was her first day at the new store. She wanted to get in a workout before her shift began, at 11:00 A.M., and had agreed to meet three friends for a 7:00 A.M. "Boot Camp" training class at a health club. Later, after her shift, she was scheduled to meet another friend for a high-octane "spinning" class atop exercise bikes.

Top physical fitness was key to Brittany's goals. She exercised with personal trainers, lifted weights, took boxing lessons, and unwound with yoga. She read books on nutrition, and fought food cravings by eating fruit and small meals throughout the day.

"Are you a ripped up superwoman yet?" the Secret Service agent asked in early February.

"I wish I was already ripped! But that's my goal," Brittany wrote back.

She studied human anatomy, exercise physiology, kinesiology, and other disciplines for the personal-trainer exam given by the National Academy of Sports Medicine. If all went well, she'd have her certification by March. Having a clear goal helped Brittany try to fit in with her accomplished colleagues at the new store, which included a recent MBA graduate and a part-timer who worked as an immigration attorney. In addition to Jayna Murray, two months shy of her business and communication master's degrees, other staff members held degrees in mathematics from DePaul, Spanish from Tulane, and biology from the University of Maryland.

Their ambitious, smart personalities also helped fuel sales. That was another reason everyone worked as a team: commissions were doled out for a shift's total sales, not individual ones.

As a saleswoman in the Bethesda lululemon, Brittany picked up where she'd left off in the Georgetown store. She jokingly engaged in a push-up competition with a customer, jumping down and ripping off more than twenty. "That woman is a hoss," colleague Courtney Kelly stood there thinking.

Courtney and others found Brittany easy to get along with. After Brittany learned Courtney ordered the same sandwich she did from the place across the street—plain bagel, tuna salad, lettuce, cucumbers—Brittany sought her out. "Do you want one of our sandwiches?"

Courtney said yes and handed Brittany her bank card to pay for her sandwich.

Brittany returned ten minutes later with the sandwiches. "Hey asshole, you gave me an expired card," she said—not in a mean way, but in a funny, we're-in-this-together way.

"Oh my God, I'm sorry," Courtney said.

"Don't worry about it," Brittany told her. "You can get me next time."

Like previous times in her life, though, others who got close to Brittany saw glimpses into darkness. Months earlier, when Brittany had agreed to rent the basement apartment from her sister, she'd also sought a roommate by posting an online classified advertisement. A religious woman named Lisa[1] in the education field responded, met Brittany, found her cheerful and likable, so she moved in. A short time later, however, she arrived home to find her dishes taken out of a kitchen cabinet and stacked on the counter—a signal that "common" areas weren't actually communal. Likewise, Brittany would have friends over at midnight and rattle around in the kitchen to fix them food, with no consideration that she was waking her roommate.

As for the utility bills, they were all in Brittany's name. She told Lisa how much to give her. "Every month, it's going up," Lisa told Brittany. "I want to see if we're doing something wrong. Can you put my name on the bills so I can open them?" Brittany did, only for the roommate to discover that Brittany hadn't paid the gas or electric bills in months. Even more concerning was that Lisa began noticing things going missing: perfume and toiletries missing from her room; a box of checks she was expecting from her bank never appearing, and then a forged one ending up at a bank twenty miles away in Laurel, Maryland, cashed for $1,600. The two women quit talking, and the roommate started making plans to move out.

Debt collectors hounded Brittany. So did her bank,

---

[1] Denotes pseudonym.

about an overdrawn account. And she faced an outstanding judgment of $19,953 in unpaid student loans from the State of New York. The night of February 18, 2011, Brittany reviewed a series of Craigslist postings offering quick money, including those from men holding themselves out as "Sugar Daddies," a term often applied to men who had sex with women whom they gave money and gifts.

"Sugar daddy looking to help," offered one man. "Seeking a sweet sugar baby," read another. Over the next few days, she visited dozens of similar posts: "Seeking a cute girl/student. Friendship and financial help you need . . . Biz traveler in town next week. Need spending money? . . . Rape Fantasy? . . . Are You A 'Princess Girl' In Distress In These Tougher Times?"

The morning of February 24, Brittany texted one of the men. "It's 'Your Princess' from CL," she wrote.

"Does my precious princess have a name?"

"Brittany."

"I'm Bobby."

After a few more exchanges, Brittany cut to the chase. "So tell me what you're looking for, expect, etc."

"Something like a relationship. Weekends together," Bobby responded, "and all that goes with being a man and a woman."

"So it'd only be weekends?" Brittany asked. "And explain to me the weekly allowance. Do you live in D.C.?"

"Well I would want you as much as possible," Bobby said. "It's just hard because of work. And do you have an amount weekly in mind?"

"Ummm no amount in mind," Brittany said. "I guess we can discuss later."

The two continued exchanging messages. Brittany's

sales skills came to the fore. "Excited to see you," she wrote him late one night.

It was a life kept secret from her successful and caring friends, a group of whom met the next night to drink wine at a bar in Washington's trendy Dupont Circle area. As Brittany was on her way to meet them, one delivered the good news: "Waiting for you with new bottle!!!!!"

Brittany worked occasional shifts with Jayna Murray, whom she learned was planning to move to the Pacific Northwest to be near her boyfriend. "You know, I'm from Seattle," Brittany told her, starting a conversation about their backgrounds.

Jayna had been at the store for two years by that time and had served as a mentor to several younger coworkers, including Courtney Kelly, who spoke to Jayna about how she felt their store manager wasn't complimenting her enough. Jayna gave Courtney the simplest of advice: the fact you're not being criticized means you're doing your job, and your need for affirmation probably speaks more about your attitude than the store manager's. "Let it go. She's not thinking about you as much as you think she is. Be confident."

As Jayna built her résumé for lulu's corporate office, she knew there was one ticket she still needed to punch. The company firmly believed in the self-improvement seminars taught around the country by a firm called Landmark Education, and offered to foot the bill for employees who'd worked for them for a certain amount of time. "You'll either love it or you'll hate it," a coworker said, referring to the way the seminar forced participants to break into small groups and share personal details about their lives. Jayna began her Landmark seminar the last weekend of February. One of the group discussions delved into how choices made years prior shape your thought processes today. They were told to record their thoughts at night, and Jayna found herself writing a letter to her parents, thanking them for steering her in certain directions. She called them in Houston and read it to them, crying as she did. David and Phyllis Murray started to cry, too. "Jayna, you've always honored us," her dad told her.

On February 25, 2011, Brittany was working in the store's fitting-room area, called "Fits" by the staff. A coworker was ending her shift, and showed Brittany a new $80 bottle of perfume, pulling it from her lululemon bag.

"Oh, that's Vera Wang. I love that scent," Brittany said.

Her friend sprayed some on herself and on Brittany, then returned it to her bag, placed the bag on a hook and asked Brittany to watch it while she went into the bathroom to change her clothes. Several minutes later, she came out, grabbed her bag, left the store, and headed to her boyfriend's house. Two days later she couldn't find the perfume. She texted Brittany.

"Brit, did I leave my Vera Wang perfume in the store on Friday?" she asked.

"I don't think so," Brittany responded two minutes later. "After I used it, I know you definitely picked it up from Fits. Oh No, can you not find it?"

"I have NO clue where it is," her coworker responded. "I never used it after the store. I'll have to check the store tomorrow."

"Then it's gotta be at the store. You'll find it."

Brittany always seemed one step ahead of what most people could learn about her. Low on funds, she came up with outrageous explanations for last minute cancellations with personal trainers, stories that also engendered their sympathy. "I had to go to NY last minute yesterday because one of my best friends was in a really bad car accident," she wrote to one of them from Washington on February 28. "Not completely sure when I'll be back in D.C., just depends on her condition. I'll keep u updated."

"OK," the trainer responded. "I hope all will go well with your friend."

Two hours later, she took a Budokon Flow & Flexibility yoga class in Bethesda and met a guy she was dating for coffee.

Brittany was burning candles at every end—work, exercise, barhopping, debts, babysitting her nephews, responding to Craigslist ads. She managed to communicate with at least five men interested in her, juggling those she met in person and had a romantic interest in with those she met online.

"How's your rainy day off going?" asked a man named Rick. "Not too bad," Brittany answered. "Definitely didn't get much done. Didn't want to be out in this weather. How's your day?"

"Yeah, also a bit lazy at work," Rick said. "I need to hit the gym after taking the weekend off. Maybe you can give me a personal training session!"

"I would love to," she texted back to Rick.

The two talked logistics for that night. "Unfortunately I do have a roommate so could only host if it's during the day," Brittany wrote. The two made tentative plans for

Brittany to take the subway to a bar where they'd meet for a drink. Rick would then drive her to his home in Potomac, a suburb farther out from the city beyond Bethesda, and take Brittany back to the subway station.

"That works for me," Brittany said. "What time do you typically get off?"

Seven minutes later Brittany received a text from her mom, who signed off with a family nickname. "Hey! Where Are You? I'm missing you. Just call, e-mail, g-mail, text, fax, Western Union, or just plain write a letter. Love You, Sparky."

Brittany didn't text her mother back, instead typing out a question to Rick: "Well, how do you want to do this?"

Three hours later they met at a bar called Clyde's in the upscale Friendship Heights area just south of Bethesda, touching off a night that had Rick checking in the next day. "Fun time last night. Getting distracted thinking about it at work."

By then Brittany was back in the store and didn't text him back. Instead, she wrote to two close friends, saying she was feeling down. "It's been such a long day." One of them offered to drop by the store. "Yah! I'm here 'til 5."

Four days later, Brittany made plans to meet up with Bobby from Craigslist, asserting she was interested in a long-term relationship. "To be completely honest, I'm a normal girl. Can't believe I answered an ad on CL, but seems like something really good can come out of it. I can definitely have a freaky side, so am pretty sure you won't be disappointed in that area. But also really hope that we connect even in a nonsexual way. I don't have any hidden agendas. Am just a younger woman with goals/dreams and could use financial assistance."

Bobby appeared smitten. "I can tell you have a great heart. You make mine pitter patter."

"I really hope I have the pleasure of meeting you," Brittany wrote. "Kind of giving me butterflies."

Brittany's fitness regimen continued at full speed. With lulu freighting the cost of health-club visits, she avoided the personal trainers. "Still in NY," she wrote from D.C., continuing that saga of the car accident. "My girlfriend went into a coma two days ago. Not looking good. Just trying to stick around for any changes."

"Sorry to hear about condition of your friend. Stay strong and I'll send a few prayers for her."

Two hours later, Brittany was out with a friend, club hopping into the morning hours.

On March 4, 2011, Courtney Kelly worked a shift at lulu, placing her bag next to Brittany Norwood's on one of the big orange chairs in the stockroom. Inside was her wallet, with $13. That night, at a friend's house, Courtney took out her wallet for the first time all day and found just $3. The only thing that made sense was that a coworker had stolen the $10. Yet that made no sense. Why slip into someone's bag for such a meaningless amount? Some kind of thrill? And who among her coworkers would have done so? She reviewed everyone she'd worked with on Friday. They'd all been in and out of the stockroom. None of them seemed capable of it.

Courtney's next shift was on Monday. She approached an assistant store manager. "This is going to sound strange, but I have money missing," Courtney said.

"Tell me you're kidding," the manager said.

"I'm not kidding."

"You're the third person to report something."

The manager called up a computer screen in front of her that showed who'd been working that Friday. "Shit," she said, turning to Courtney and pausing. "I can't tell you."

Later, another manager called up the same screen for Courtney to see, pointing to Brittany's name. The same Brittany who knocked out push-ups with customers, who joked about their shared taste in bagel sandwiches?

"Really?" Courtney said. "No. Really?"

The next day, one of the store's assistant managers had Brittany sign her "pramana lululemon U.S. Employee Handbook Acknowledgment" form, something she'd been late in doing. The form bound her to lululemon's Code of Business Conduct and its Ethics and Integrity Program. While the company used the yoga term *pramana*, which loosely translated to "obtaining knowledge," the form Brittany signed was standard fare in the world of retail: "I acknowledge that lululemon has the right to end my employment with or without cause or without notice."

On Wednesday, March 9, the store's management team held its regularly scheduled meeting. Six people attended, including Courtney, who had recently been promoted, and Jayna Murray. The store manager walked the group through a number of housekeeping matters. Then she brought up three separate incidents: the missing perfume, the missing $10, and $60 previously reported missing from the wallet of another worker. Brittany Norwood had worked all the shifts where items had gone missing. There was one more telling clue, which one of the supervisors spoke up about: just days before, she had looked inside Brittany's bag after a shift as per standard procedure—lulu workers employed bag checks, as was typical retail practice—but what was noteworthy was that she'd seen a bottle of Vera Wang perfume in Brittany's bag. It meant little to the supervisor at the time, but now, hearing about the missing bottle, she thought the two could be connected.

The whole thing was bizarre. Why would Brittany steal items of relatively small value? And why would she bring one of them back into the store, knowing about bag checks? It was as if she got a thrill out of it. As a store manager, Rachel was one of the few people outside the Georgetown lulu store who knew about Brittany's dustup over "Shop Night" there, and told the group about the backstory. "The reason why Brittany left Georgetown was because she closed two nights in a row and money was missing," she said.

The group's conclusion was that they had among them a petty thief willing to destroy the trust everyone had with each other, not a dangerous criminal. But what if Brittany was stealing merchandise as well? That would make the whole store look bad, since they were ultimately judged for keeping track of inventory.

With no interior security cameras, and no eyewitnesses, the managers didn't feel that they could go to the police. Besides, it was their store, their problem, and they were going to figure out a way to solve it. They discussed ways to catch Brittany. Maybe they could buy a nanny-cam, one of them suggested, only half kidding.

That same week, things had picked up for Brittany. Equinox, a high-end health club two blocks from the store, granted her an initial interview to be a fitness trainer. It'd be a foot in the door ahead of the official personal-trainer certification she was expecting soon. The first interview went well, and Brittany looked forward to being called in for a second one.

On Thursday, March 10, she walked up from her base-ment apartment to house-sit for her sister Marissa while a serviceman installed windows. Their sister Candace called to say she expected a long day in the operating room, and asked Brittany if she could pick up her two boys at school. Brittany agreed, looking forward to seeing her nephews after not having done so for two weeks. Brittany sent a text to Marissa, saying she would bring Candace's sons back to her house: "Your friends will be here when you get home tonight."

Brittany remained close with her older sisters. Just four days earlier, they had eaten brunch and looked for a wed-ding dress for Marissa, whose marriage was set for the end of the year. Now, alone in Marissa's town house, Brittany checked her e-mail. The Equinox fitness manager had just sent one: he wanted Brittany to meet with the health club's general manager on Monday. Elated, Brittany dashed off a text to the friend who worked at the club and had helped set up the initial visit.

"I have an interview Monday!!!!!!!" Brittany wrote. "I'm sooooooo excited and just as equally nervous!"

"Ha, you shouldn't be nervous. You killed it yesterday and have such a great personality."

"I owe you big time."

"Oh please you did it all yourself."

Brittany headed out from Marissa's place to pick up her nephews, walking to catch a bus in the driving rain. She again texted her health-club friend, offering to buy the friend's sister something from lulu with her store discount. "Find out what your sis' wants and let me know."

When Brittany got off the bus, it was still raining as she walked to the school. She got the boys, and the three left in a taxicab. Brittany took them to an Italian place for dinner. Checking her phone, she could see a text from a guy she liked, who wanted to see if they were still getting together on Sunday. Yes, Brittany said, adding that she was out with her nephews. "My food was horrible, but I knew my nephews would eat pizza and pasta."

"Pizza always saves the day with kids," the guy said.

"Who're you telling!" Brittany fired back.

That same Thursday night, Jayna had dinner inside her condo with her friend from undergraduate days, Marisa Connaughton, the woman she'd prompted to answer the phone when her ex-boyfriend called so soon after their breakup and who'd first shown her a lululemon bag. The two normally ate together on Friday nights, but Jayna had swapped shifts with a coworker who wanted to leave town for the weekend to go see her boyfriend. Dining on left-overs and a $5 bottle of Merlot, the longtime friends talked about their dwindling days in Washington. Marisa was moving with her fiancé to Atlanta, and Jayna would soon join her boyfriend in the Seattle area. They talked about the remaining places in Washington they wanted to see and cross off their list. But both felt good about where they were headed. Jayna spoke a little bit about work, how the store was currently understaffed. Indeed, instead of the normal three people working late the next night, there would be only two.

When Brittany woke up the next morning, Friday, March 11, the warm and fuzzy feelings she always got from spending time with her nephews gave way to something else. At 6:53 A.M., she visited the first of seven Craigslist offerings. "Spring Breakers where are you?" the listing read. "I need some fun and am generous." Brittany sent a message to Bobby, the man who earlier had called her his Craigslist princess. "Are we still on for this weekend?" Brittany asked.

Wanting to exercise before her shift started at 3:00 that afternoon, Brittany left her apartment for Crunch Fitness, a gym with the industrial decor of a stylish dance club. She walked to the rear classroom, with its wooden floors, cement columns, exposed ductwork, and mirrors on three walls. Brittany wiggled into a hammock-like sling hanging from the ceiling for an "aerial yoga" class. The suspended positions allowed everyone to twist and move into all kinds of contortions. After the class, Brittany sent a text to coworker Eila Rab, who was supposed to have met her there. "Urrggh, I can't believe u stood me up!!!!" But Eila was waiting for her in the health club's lobby. "Since I missed class, why don't we go to lunch?" she said.

They headed off to the Rock Bottom Restaurant and Brewery in Bethesda, about seven blocks away from lululemon. Brittany ordered a beer with her food, and spoke about wedding-dress shopping with her engaged sister— and how she was enjoying living the experience vicariously.

"It's so much fun," Brittany said. As for lululemon, she said she didn't feel she had much chance for advancement there. "If I get this job at Equinox, I want to cut back my hours at lulu."

"That seems like what you want to do," Eila agreed.

The two finished lunch and walked six blocks to get manicures and pedicures at Blue Zen, a salon one block from the yoga store.

Jayna also was scheduled to start her shift at 3:00 P.M., but she left her apartment around noon, wanting to get there early to help with what she figured to be a typical Friday afternoon surge of customers. On the drive over, she spoke by phone to her good friend Rudy Colberg, her salsa dance partner from the Semester at Sea college program. Rudy also was getting his MBA, at the University of Michigan, and had earlier passed his CPA exam. Jayna wanted to set up a time over the weekend to double-check her tax forms. "I want to make sure I am paying my fair share," Jayna said. As she got close to the store, she told him she'd call him on her way home.

In the store, Jayna and Courtney spoke privately about Jayna having to work alone with Brittany later. "I have to close with the thief tonight," Jayna said. "Do you think I will catch her?"

At Blue Zen, 3:00 P.M. was fast approaching as the beautician finished up Brittany's toes and fingers. Brittany asked her to spray them with a drying enhancer. She hustled out, flip-flops still on, walking down the cobblestoned Bethesda

Lane, lined with its boutique dress shops, a French bakery, and a restaurant that offered house-made duck prosciutto and $17 cheeseburgers. Brittany walked by a line already forming outside the Apple Store for the prized iPad 2, set to go on sale that night at 5:00 P.M.

Once inside lululemon, she walked about with her fingers outstretched because the polish was still drying, then changed into a pair of running shoes. Four other saleswomen were working, though soon they started clocking out for the day. One of them, DePaul mathematics graduate Chioma Nwakibu, lingered a bit, speaking with Jayna about how her parents didn't understand why she was working retail. To Chioma, lululemon was much more than a store: it was a place that encouraged self-development and a chance to advance up into a corporation. Jayna agreed, and told her she was impressing all the managers. "Thank you for listening to me," Chioma told Jayna by text after leaving.

About 6:00 P.M., a regular customer named Janay Carlson walked in. Jayna and another saleswoman, named Rachel LaMarca, helped her look through running shorts and jackets. Janay spent nearly an hour in the store, at times the only customer. Brittany approached her and complimented the lulu top she already was wearing, one purchased previously from the shop. "When that shirt first came out, I wasn't sure about it. You're changing my mind," Brittany told her.

To Janay, the three lulu employees were the same typically polite, energetic women she always encountered at the store. She walked out with more than $200 worth of garb: running pants, a running jacket, a shirt, and a headband. As Rachel got ready to leave at 7:00 P.M., Jayna was replenishing displays with new apparel and Brittany was standing over a table in the fitting area, taping up a box of items that needed to be shipped to another store. They both seemed happy as Rachel said good-bye.

Courtney was working her second job at a bakery several miles away, and sent a text message to Jayna. "If I get out of work before you, do you want me to stop by?" Jayna didn't respond, which wasn't unusual. Lulu workers were not allowed to use their phones on the sales floor. Courtney tried again at 8:36 P.M., making reference to having to work alone with someone who—if she really had taken the items—seemed above all to be completely strange. "Hey just got done with work. I'm exhausted and have to be back at 7. I'm headed home. :(Sorry. Hope you survived!"

Inside lululemon, two more customers walked through the doors at 8:45 P.M., fifteen minutes before closing. Paul Rodriguez and Elizabeth Schlappal were making their second stop of the night in Bethesda. They'd started at Sweetgreen for a couple of organic salads, then Paul offered to buy Elizabeth a pair of running shorts. They were greeted by Jayna, who made an immediate impression—at once bubbly and laid-back. Jayna helped Elizabeth pick out a pair of shorts and walked her toward a fitting room. By the time she came out, it was Brittany who was in the fitting area, folding a garment on a table, and also friendly. "Those look good on you," Brittany said.

Elizabeth tried on another pair as well, eventually made her choice, and walked toward the cash registers at the front of the store. Brittany followed and passed her, walked behind the counter next to Jayna, and rang up the sale. One pair of black "Speed" shorts, $57.24, including tax.

It was 8:57 P.M. The two saleswomen pleasantly said their good-byes to the couple. Brittany led them to the door and locked it behind them—an indication to Paul and Elizabeth that the saleswomen were eager to shut things down before another customer came in. The store now closed for business, Brittany and Jayna counted money, finished reports, made sure the displays and racks were lined up, swept the floors, and shut down the computer-ized cash registers. Around 9:30, they performed a final duty: checking each other's bags. Both had plenty of items inside. Jayna's held a digital camera, battery charger, black leather datebook, a leadership book, and a bottle of red Argentinean wine her coworker had left for her for agree-ing to switch shifts. Brittany's had a black makeup pouch, workout clothes, the flip-flops, a candle, and a curling iron.

As Jayna looked through Brittany's bag, though, she also spotted a pair of "crops"-style workout pants with a price tag still on them. She asked Brittany if she had a receipt. Brittany said she'd thrown the slip away, some-thing employees often did because they couldn't return the merchandise they purchased at a discount anyway. But Jayna had more questions. "Who rang you out?"

"Chioma," Brittany said, referring to the floor supervi-sor and mathematics graduate who'd spoken with Jayna earlier in the day.

Jayna wanted to check Brittany's explanation. "I can just go into the computer," Jayna said. But she couldn't boot up the system; it was programmed to stay off once it was shut down for the night. "It's no big deal," Jayna said. "We'll deal with it later."

She set the burglar alarm at 9:45 P.M., and the two dashed out before the sensors engaged. Jayna locked the door from the outside. She and Brittany said their good-byes and walked in opposite directions—Jayna toward her parked car, Brittany toward the subway station.

It took Jayna less than three minutes to turn the corner, cross Arlington Road, and descend seventeen steps into a parking garage. By then, she'd taken out her BlackBerry and called Chioma. Jayna asked if she'd sold Brittany anything that day. "Nope, I sure didn't," her colleague said.

"I didn't think you did," Jayna said, "because when I bag-checked Brittany, I found a pair of crops in there that still had the tag on." Jayna wrapped up her call, saying she needed to get in touch with the store manager, Rachel. Seven seconds later, she did.

The two were very close. Rachel considered Jayna smart, sassy, and honest. Brittany, on the other hand, was someone Rachel hadn't had a good feeling about—she'd passed on hiring her in the first place a year earlier, but was forced to take her on after the Georgetown dustup.

"We caught the bitch," Jayna said.

"I'm going to fire her in the morning," Rachel said.

Six minutes after leaving the store, Brittany made a call of her own, telling coworker Eila Rab that she'd left her wallet in the store and needed Jayna's number so she could come back and unlock the door for her. Eila suggested Brittany call their store manager, Rachel Oertli, who lived across the street from the store and also had a key.

"Well, Jayna was just here," Brittany said. "Can I just get her number?"

"I can give it to you now," Eila said.

"No, just text it to me," Brittany said.

A moment later the text arrived, and Brittany called Jayna, leaving her a voice mail. As Brittany waited, she dashed off a quick text to the coworker: "Thank you!" She tried calling Jayna again, couldn't get through, and followed that with a text: "Hey Jayna it's Britt I think I forgot my wallet in the store."

Jayna called back, spoke with Brittany briefly and said she could come back to the store. "I noticed I didn't have my laptop anyway, so that's fine." Ten minutes later, Jayna pulled her silver, two-door Pontiac G5 up near the front of the store. Brittany was waiting for her at the teak bench. It was 10:05 P.M. They opened the door and walked inside.

ZEROING IN

CHAPTER NINETEEN

Monday Night: Piling On

By the evening of Monday, March 14, 2011, detectives had spent three days piecing together what happened after Brittany Norwood and Jayna Murray returned to the lululemon athletica store. At first, they'd been alarmed at the idea that two men could have been so bold as to slip into a popular nightlife area and unleash mayhem. Then they became wary, as parts of Brittany's story didn't add up, but backed off, swayed by the parking-lot video that seemed to back up her story, and the discovery of a bloodied homeless man, Keith Lockett, who seemed to know about the case.

But the prospect of Keith being the killer had fizzled. And even if he was, the statements he'd given in the wee hours of the morning had been so incoherent as to be useless. The only way to tie Keith to the crime would be through DNA analysis, and those results were at least several days away. Detective Jim Drewry, one of the two lead detectives on the case, wasn't even sure whether to ask the crime lab to analyze Keith's blood yet. He knew they'd be bombarding the lab with such requests in the case, and wanted to maintain goodwill. Citizens had continued to call in with tips, which other detectives checked out, but none were leading anywhere.

Drewry and Detective Dimitry Ruvin, the other lead detective, didn't know much about the two victims, and had yet to meet Brittany personally. There'd been no immediate need to hit their stunned friends and family members with questions about them, and what information about the women that was available online and in law enforcement databases offered only broad overviews. Still, they'd been able to form some initial impressions. Jayna Murray was obviously a go-getter. Her LinkedIn profile showed that she was getting two master's degrees at Johns Hopkins University, and before that listed her as having held an international marketing position at Halliburton. She had no criminal history. Brittany Norwood was less visible on the Internet, though she, too, had a clean criminal history. She'd clearly been a star soccer player in high school, good enough to earn a college scholarship. A Google search of her home address indicated that she lived in an apartment unit of a large renovated town house owned by her sister and her sister's fiancé.

"What do we have? Do we have any credible tips?" Ruvin asked Drewry, before answering his own question: "No. We have nothing."

They knew Brittany was out of the hospital now, resting at home. Maybe they should go introduce themselves, see if she was relaxed enough to offer more details and better descriptions of the suspects. Drewry had her sister Marissa's cell-phone number and called her. Marissa said it would be fine to stop by that evening.

Drewry and Ruvin climbed into Drewry's Dodge Intrepid and headed south. The detectives enjoyed each other's company, despite their differences: Ruvin the gadget freak; Drewry the man twice his age with no Facebook account. As Ruvin liked to tell him: "You're the only guy around here who can say you were a cop before I was born and not be lying about it."

Drewry parked near the town house, and the detectives walked up the single flight of stairs to the door of Marissa's immaculately renovated, century-old home, where they were greeted warmly. Many of Brittany's family were there, including those who'd flown in from the West Coast to rally around her. The whole scene—big home, successful African American family, everyone sticking together—seemed to Drewry like something right out of *The Cosby Show*. As he and Ruvin introduced themselves, a diminutive young woman walked in from another room. "Hi, I'm Brittany." She spoke softly and said she lived downstairs. "That will probably be the best place to talk."

The detectives walked down the outside flight of stairs, entering a tidy apartment and taking seats around a dining table. Ruvin got out a legal pad to take notes. Brittany's roommate, Lisa, made a brief appearance before ducking back out of sight. Brittany told the detectives her family wanted her to move back to Seattle. "They're very concerned for me."

But Brittany said she wasn't going to let the attackers scare her into leaving. "Before this all happened, I was talking to Equinox gym. I was looking for a job. They reached out to me since it happened and said the job is mine when I'm better. I can come work there anytime."

Ruvin knew the gym was just two blocks from the yoga

store, and thought she was brave to consider going back
to the area in such a visible job. His partner tried to put
Brittany at ease. "We just want to go over the story one
more time," Drewry said. "A lot of times, a couple of days
later, people remember a small detail that may be important to us."

Brittany told them the same thing she'd earlier told
Detective Deana Mackie in the hospital, adding in more
details. Friday evening had been fairly slow in the store.
She and Jayna closed at 9:00 P.M., cleaned up and left,
heading in opposite directions. Brittany realized she'd left
her wallet behind and called Jayna to ask if she could come
back to let her in. "I noticed I didn't have my laptop anyway, so that's fine," Brittany recalled Jayna saying. "So I'll
just meet you at the store and we'll walk in together."

Brittany said there weren't many people left on Bethesda
Avenue when she'd waited for Jayna. The fancy bakery,
Georgetown Cupcake, was closed, as was the Apple Store.
When Jayna arrived, the two went inside but couldn't find
Brittany's wallet. Jayna offered Brittany her plastic subway
fare card so she could board the subway. "Why don't you
just take mine, and we'll look for it in the morning?" Brit-
tany recalled Jayna saying.

Drewry pulled out his digital recorder. She told him
how she and Jayna were walking out when the two men
suddenly appeared, with one of them striking Jayna. Drewry asked Brittany where the man was who attacked her.

"Behind one of our clothing racks."

"Okay," Drewry said. "And what did he do?"

"When I noticed him is when he jumped up. When I
tried to turn around, he yanked me back by my hair and

was telling me to shut up. At this point, Jayna and I are both yelling for help."

Brittany spoke clearly. She said both men wore dark clothes, gloves, ski masks with narrow slits cut around the eyes, and hoodies over the masks. "My suspect was taller than me by a couple of inches, maybe five five," she said, adding that "Jayna's suspect" was taller. He dragged Jayna by her hair. The two men laughed, almost as if they were acting out a violent video game, Brittany said, the name of which she couldn't place.

"*Grand Theft Auto*?" Ruvin asked.

"Yeah, that's it," Brittany said. Her hands started to shake, tears sprang to her eyes. She told the detectives that her attacker forced her to the cash registers to get money, whacked her across the head, pushed her to the back of the store, then shoved her onto Jayna's bloody, dead body.

Ruvin was stunned at the horrific scene Brittany described, and his own emotion took over. He stopped writing. *We will find these assholes*, he told himself. *I don't care how long it's going to take*.

Brittany suddenly paused, looked down, then back up at the detectives. She said there was something she hadn't told the female detective back at the hospital. "They know where I live."

"Well, how would they know?" Drewry asked.

"I don't know. They probably looked in my purse and maybe found my bills. I had Comcast bills and a gas bill."

Drewry tried to get more detailed descriptions of the attackers.

"Okay. And describe the guy that assaulted you."

Brittany was vague, saying he was covered from head to toe.

"Okay. And from his voice, how old do you think he was?"

"I guess, I'd say midtwenties."

"And from his voice, can you give me a race or an ethnicity?"

"I would say he was Caucasian."

She said Jayna's attacker was taller, about six feet. "As far as the color of his skin, I have no idea," Brittany said.

"Do you think he was white, black, Asian from the way that he spoke?"

"The same: Caucasian."

As Brittany continued to speak to Drewry, the detective started getting an uncomfortable feeling. Something was bothering him about Brittany's crying. It didn't feel . . . real. Maybe the effects of the trauma, he told himself.

At the same time, however, Detective Ruvin was also feeling his earlier rush of emotion—the comment to himself: *We will find these assholes*—start to recede. It was Brittany's detail about the bills that had started it for him. How would that have worked? Brittany just indicated her assailant left during the attack to go through her purse. Couldn't she have made a break for it?

And the more he thought about how the guy pushed Brittany onto Jayna, the more it didn't sit right. It was *too* evil. Brittany continued talking to Drewry, saying how her suspect called her a "nigger" as he raped her.

Drewry didn't want to push with the questions. He moved to wrap up the interview, and asked Brittany if she'd told her family that the assailants knew where she lived.

"No, I haven't told them. Should I?"

"We can't tell you, but I think you should, because they have the right to know," Drewry said.

The three made their way back upstairs to Marissa and her fiancé's place. Family members gathered around. "I think Brittany has got something to tell you guys," Drewry said.

"They know where I live," Brittany told her family. "These guys know where I live. I think they found my bills. They were in my purse. They knew my name and my address."

Brittany's father, Earl, spoke up. "I guess the obvious question is what do we do?"

Drewry tried to put them at ease. In 99.99 percent of cases, he said, the suspects don't return. But he added: "If you see anything suspicious, even if it's something little or if you think it's irrelevant, but if it's suspicious, you need to call the police and express that."

Drewry sought to assure them that the case would get solved. "We're working every lead we can. We're getting all kinds of tips. Our whole shift is working on it nonstop."

As the detectives prepared to leave, Ruvin thought about the sneakers that his sergeant had found in the store the day before, in particular the pair of size-14 Reeboks that matched the bloody tracks. "Hey Brittany, can I ask you something real quick?" Ruvin asked.

"OK," Brittany said, walking over to him.

"Do you guys sell shoes?" Ruvin asked.

"No," Brittany said.

"Were there any shoes in the store?"

"Yeah, there were two pairs, men's and women's. The men's are really big. And we use them for alterations."

Alterations. The thought hadn't crossed their minds. Who knew yoga pants had to fit so well? It sent their theory that one of the killers had brought the shoes inside the store out the window. But why would the killer put *those* shoes on? How would he know where they were in the first place? Ruvin's head was starting to spin when Brittany's brother Chris approached.

"Can I come down with you guys?" he asked.

"Of course," Ruvin said.

The three walked down and stood on the sidewalk. "You know, I'm happy that my sister is alive. I'm thankful my sister is alive," Chris said. He was cordial, then bluntly starting talking about the case. "But I just can't get over the fact that like, why would they spare her? This girl was killed, and my sister only has a few injuries."

The three stood in silence. It was certainly something the detectives had considered. But they'd worked off of the theory that only one of the masked men was totally deranged, or they'd been scared away by something before killing Brittany.

"Do you think your sister had something to do with it?" Ruvin asked, realizing after he'd done so that the question was too strong.

"No, no, I don't think that," Chris said.

Ruvin tried another angle. "What kind of person is your sister?"

Chris seemed to be both trying to help and worried about what he was saying.

"My sister is a very secretive person," Chris said.

Then he told the detectives a story. When Brittany was six or seven years old, their dad once ran out of gas while taking her to a soccer game. He told Brittany to stay in the car while he went to a gas station, yet when he returned, she was gone—she had hitchhiked home. He didn't add much more to the story, nor explain why he was telling it. Chris politely said good-bye and went back inside.

But that word—*secretive*—stuck in Ruvin's head as he and Drewry walked back to the car. So did the strange information about the shoes, and the utility bills. There was only one good explanation: Brittany knew the killers. She had let them into the store for some reason, a robbery, perhaps, and things had gone terribly wrong. Whatever relationship she had with them caused them to spare her life. And most everything Brittany had done since was an attempt to cover up her involvement.

The two detectives climbed in the car. Drewry started driving to their station in silence, but the quiet didn't last long, as Ruvin couldn't ignore how quickly his mind had changed.

"Jimmy, something's not right," he said to Drewry. "You know, we have a store in the middle of Bethesda Avenue. It's still busy. These guys go in there. They got no weapons. They rape and kill one girl. And now they're like, sticking around? They threw Brittany on Jayna's body, like to mess with her. You can find probably one guy that's like this Hannibal Lecter. But to find two guys like that?"

He couldn't bring himself to say out loud that he suspected Brittany. Instead, he kept repeating what bothered him, that two guys would choose to rob a store in Bethesda on a Friday night, when people are still around. They don't have weapons, and they stick around—*to shove Brittany onto Jayna's murdered body*? "They were so cool, calm, and collected that they stayed in the store to mentally torture Brittany?" Ruvin asked Drewry.

Something else didn't square with Ruvin: Brittany's assertion that the attackers had called her a nigger. Ruvin had come to the United States in 1995, enrolling in an integrated public high school. At thirty-one, he had plenty of white friends who adopted urban, hip-hop language— the very terms and phrases used in the video game *Grand Theft Auto*. "A twenty-year-old *Grand Theft Auto* guy, he's not going to use that word," Ruvin said. "He's going to call her a fucking bitch."

On this much, however, Drewry disagreed. He'd grown up in an America where white people used the term all the time to keep black people "in their place." When he'd gone to visit relatives in southern Ohio, he'd seen the "Whites Only" drinking fountains. That was only one generation ago. And the term lingered on. After he became a cop, in 1979, people he arrested uncorked it, as did other cops. And although the term was fading in its use, the idea that two white guys of any age would call Brittany a nigger, particularly the kind of guys who would rape and kill, was hardly a stretch.

"I can see that happening," Drewry said.

But the young detective still struggled to believe it. "I think the story is very exaggerated, and two guys are made out to be villains. They're villains."

As they drove, Drewry had a nagging feeling about where this case might be going—a place he didn't want to follow, but one all too familiar for a detective in his shoes. He did not want to believe that this polite young African American girl—a presumed *rape* victim—was lying. In the United States, African Americans represented just 13 percent of the population but committed half the murders, a rate made to seem higher by decades of media portrayals. Every time there was a high-profile, unsolved murder case—and this one certainly qualified—African Americans held their collective breath. Drewry couldn't help but do so as well, even if in his job he never made the distinction. Murder was murder was murder.

Drewry had barely slept six hours over the previous two days. He didn't know if Brittany knew the killers or had anything to do with Jayna's murder, and he wanted to continue giving her the benefit of the doubt. He wanted to believe that the odd parts of her actions and explanations could be some kind of trauma-induced confusion. Hell, the case was only three days old. He didn't want to doubt the *Cosby* kid.

"Jimmy, something's not right with this girl," Ruvin continued.

Drewry's anger and worry and exhaustion came to the surface. He decided to give himself this much: a suspension of the discussion for the next fifteen minutes, the time they had left before arriving at their station. Drewry held up his right hand. "Don't go there," he said. "I don't want to hear that shit right now."

The detectives rolled into their headquarters shortly after 9:30 P.M. They walked into the homicide unit and went to their cubicles. Another half-dozen detectives were there. Among them were Sergeant Craig Wittenberger and Detective Randy Kucsan, who'd both had early doubts about Brittany's story; Detective Mike Carin, who'd talked to the Apple manager and seen her cry; and Detective Deana Mackie, who'd interviewed Brittany at the hospital and found her so believable. Just that afternoon, she'd fielded a question from a detective not involved in the case, who pondered if Brittany could have killed Jayna. "Absolutely not. No," Mackie had replied.

Without support from Drewry, Ruvin feared he wouldn't be taken seriously. The young detective sat down and quietly started typing notes into his computer, but the other detectives could sense something was up.

Drewry stood up and walked to Ruvin's cubicle. Others needed to hear what Ruvin had to say.

"Just tell them. Tell them what you think," he said.

Ruvin stood up. His head was spinning, not just from what he'd heard at Brittany's apartment, but where his thoughts had gone since. Again, he hemmed and hawed—asking questions rather than making statements. He wondered aloud why Brittany's attacker looked through her purse instead of making a quick escape. "Who does that?" Ruvin asked the others. "Who's so calm, in the middle of Bethesda, 'Let me go back and get her bills?'" Ruvin finally circled around to what he really wanted to say. It had come to him on the car ride from Brittany's.

It wasn't that Brittany was involved and knew the killers. It was that she did it all by herself.

It was the size-14 shoes that had convinced him—specifically, the fact the shoes were kept in the store. Why would one of the men have put them on? And even if he had, why then try to clean them up and put them back? No, it was Brittany who had stepped into those shoes, who'd walked in Jayna's blood and then around the store to create the illusion of a big male attacker. "The shoe prints never left the store," Ruvin said. "The killer never left the store."

Mackie sat only a few feet away. "What do you mean? What are you trying to say?"

"I think Brittany killed Jayna," he said.

Silence followed the assertion. The detectives looked at each other.

Wittenberger liked Ruvin's bold accusation, even if it went beyond his own, earlier supposition that Brittany merely *knew* the killers. As the sergeant realized, trying to explain the abnormalities in Brittany's story by saying she knew the killers hadn't made them go away. But if *Brittany* was the killer—if she was the kind of person who could inflict hundreds of nonstop blows with whatever tools she could find—that rendered her subsequent actions positively tame: of course she could stage two rapes, of course she could cut herself and lie all night in the dark next to a mutilated corpse, of course she could patiently wait for the cops to come so she could tell an endless stream of lies. She could do all that, Wittenberger thought, if she was truly evil.

And with that, it was open season on Brittany. The detectives threw everything they had at her, some realizing for the first time that they hadn't reviewed key evidence. Ruvin pulled out the report completed by the nurse who examined Brittany for rape injuries. "Patient vaginal examination revealed no tears or tenderness. Cervix had several white lesions." That seemed kind of light for a wooden coat hanger. He read the account of what Brittany told the rape-exam nurse. "Patient says that was her last memory until this morning being in the ambulance." Of course: Brittany's bottom line excuse for all the holes was memory loss.

Wittenberger wanted to look at the photographs of Brittany's injuries taken at the hospital. The sergeant called them up on his computer screen, clicking until he came to a photo depicting two long, superficial cuts across the small of Brittany's back.

"Can she get to her back like that?" Ruvin asked. Wittenberger stood up and demonstrated so with his hand—showing the natural direction the blade would travel, the same angle shown in the picture.

The detectives pored over the photos of Brittany's face when she came into the hospital. Yes, it was caked in dried blood from the cut to her forehead. But the blood flow was down and straight—covering the nose and lips and chin—indicating she'd been standing when she bled. That matched Brittany's story of how she'd been struck, but was at odds with the idea that she'd then spent the night on the bathroom floor, on her back. "The blood flow would have shifted. It would have flowed to the sides, too," Wittenberger said.

He and the others discussed where the wound came from in the first place—maybe a backswing as Brittany was pummeling Jayna with one of the weapons. They talked about the missing cash from the store—about $900. Brittany would have had plenty of time to ditch that to stage a robbery.

Kucsan, the tall detective who'd found the zip-ties, believed Ruvin's theory but still struggled to picture it. *This little girl turned into the fucking Tasmanian Devil*, he thought.

Drewry worried they were moving too fast, blowing past the possibility that others might still be involved. No one had any forensic evidence attaching Brittany to the crime, let alone putting a weapon in her hand. Still, when Drewry finally went home that night around midnight, he couldn't sleep. The more he played it through, the more he could come up with only one explanation for the holes in her story.

Ruvin stayed at the station longer, going over the evidence with Wittenberger, and didn't get home until 1:30 A.M. He walked in to find his wife, Yasra, asleep on the living-room sofa, having tried to wait up for her husband after putting their six-month-old son to bed. Ruvin sat down next to her. It had been so much easier to believe two masked men attacked both women, so much easier to want to protect Brittany and her family than to believe she was a savage killer.

He still felt like he needed validation. He woke Yasra, and made her promise not to tell anyone what he was about to say.

Yeah, yeah, of course, Mr. Dramatic, she thought.

"I think I know who killed Jayna," said Ruvin.

Yasra had already been following the case more closely than any other her husband had worked. She was the same age as the murder victim, and she, too, was into fitness and working out.

"You can't tell *anybody*," her husband said again. "I think it's this girl Brittany."

Yasra sat up on the sofa. Goose bumps shot up on her arms.

CHAPTER TWENTY

Tuesday:
"Let Me Throw This at You"

The few hours of sleep recalibrated Jim Drewry's thoughts. At 8:00 A.M. on Tuesday, March 15, the detective walked up to Dimitry Ruvin's cubicle. "I think this girl did it," Drewry said.

"I think so, too," Ruvin agreed.

Drewry turned his attention to keeping a lid on their suspicions.

"This cannot leak," Drewry said, "because if we're right, we're right; but if we're wrong, then it's like the worst-case scenario."

The theory fit the evidence, but neither detective was *certain* that Brittany Norwood was Jayna Murray's killer. They wanted to continue collecting evidence, waiting for the analysis, and keep Brittany talking. She had to believe they still believed her.

Drewry also recognized the potential racial politics at play—in both directions. At first, he'd been frustrated by the way the media had again given so much attention to a white victim. Now, he worried that word would get out that he and the other detectives had turned on a black rape victim who'd told them two white madmen were on the loose. He invoked a notorious case out of New York from the 1980s. "We don't want this to be another Tawana Brawley," he said. "You don't want Al Sharpton down here."

Drewry's point was how explosive race and crime could be. In the Brawley case, an African American teenage girl had accused several white men, including one wearing a badge, of raping her in the woods and smearing her with excrement. It was an awful story, and Al Sharpton had taken up her cause, holding a series of press conferences alleging that detectives weren't taking the girl seriously because she was black. It was a huge media storm—and it turned out that she had made the whole story up. The problem here was that if they ended up wrong about Brittany, their situation could end up even worse: it would be Tawana Brawley if Tawana had been telling the truth.

Ruvin didn't know who Tawana Brawley was. At the time of that case, he'd been seven years old and living in the Soviet Union. But he certainly understood the broader point. On a personal level, he knew that if they did file charges against Brittany and they turned out to be wrong, he'd be humiliated and would resign from the homicide unit.

The detectives strategized with their sergeant, Craig Wittenberger, about how to go full speed at Brittany in the quietest way possible. Drewry thought briefly about simply not telling anyone else. But that was impossible: the crime-scene investigators had to be looped in, to say nothing of his entire chain of command. The sergeant turned his attention to how they might exploit Brittany's personality. Assuming she was indeed the killer, she hadn't fled or panicked after committing the murder. No, she'd slunk around in a dark, bloody store, staging a gruesome cover-up because she thought she could outwit the cops.

You sometimes got that kind of thing in Montgomery County. Spouses who hired assassins. Fathers who suffocated their infants for insurance money. Coworkers who struck inside contained workplaces. Such had been the case for Wittenberger and Ruvin ten weeks earlier, when they found themselves standing over the body of Roosevelt Brockington Jr., stabbed seventy-four times by someone who'd left the twelve-inch knife lodged in his neck.

"Who even knows this place exists?" Ruvin had asked. The room Brockington had been found in was an office inside a locked boiler room in the basement of a hospital. Talk about a contained murder scene. The detectives started going through the backgrounds of boiler-room staff like they were playing a game of Clue. One staffer jumped right out: Keith Little, who had been charged with killing a coworker years earlier but who'd been acquitted at trial. Little clearly knew the detectives would zero in on him. What he didn't know was that they'd also be able to figure out that in a different part of the boiler room, he'd used a spigot of chemically treated water to clean a pair of gloves and a ski mask. Ruvin and Detective Deana Mackie eventually charged Little with first-degree murder. The motive: Little killed his boss because he'd changed his hours and given him a bad performance review.

The case to be made against Brittany had obvious similarities. But despite his last name, Keith Little stood six feet one, weighed 225 pounds, was built like a linebacker, and acted like a complete badass. "You ain't got shit on me," he'd snarled to the detectives while riding an elevator up from the boiler room, handcuffs around his wrists.

Wittenberger wondered about the hundreds of wounds inflicted on Jayna. Maybe Brittany had known Jayna was dead or dying, and kept going as part of the cover-up. *She wants us to look for the crazy guys forever*, the sergeant said to himself.

When high-pressure cases push down on police departments, there is a tendency for all those involved to *do* something—like return a tipster's phone call, go back to the scene to look for more clues, reach out to informants. Important observations get relayed verbally, sometimes turning into a version of the parlor game Telephone, where one player whispers a story to another player who whispers to another player and down the line, until the whole thing is peppered with errors and omissions.

It was in that context that the department's shoe-print expert, David McGill, had learned about the parking-lot surveillance video, the one showing the two men walking outside the rear entrance of the yoga store the night of the killing. By the time the video was described to McGill, it showed two men walking *out* the back door of the yoga store. And that amounted to solid confirmation of the survivor's account. It had certainly governed McGill's thinking the day prior—on Monday—when he'd examined and analyzed the bloody shoe prints inside the store. He figured he'd find tracks linked to Brittany's shoes, and to the size 14s found in the store. And McGill quickly found both. But that was it. That he couldn't find any tracks for Jayna made sense, since she had apparently suffered the brunt of her attack where she fell. But what about the second guy from the video? Surely, McGill thought, he should be able to find at least one partial shoe print from him out of all the tracks and bloodstains in the store. He looked over and over, but couldn't find a third type of shoe. To enhance the shoe-print stains, he sprayed them with Leuco Crystal Violet, a chemical agent that turns bright purple in the presence of blood. Still, no third pair of shoes. *What the hell am I doing wrong?* McGill kept asking himself.

Now, on Tuesday morning, he decided to find a copy of the video and watch it himself. There were the two men, dressed in black, walking from the direction of the yoga store's back door. But they weren't coming out of an open door to the yoga store. It was impossible to know exactly where they'd come from. How different reality—human foibles, bureaucratic breakdowns—was from the smash TV franchise *CSI*. McGill, forty-four, and his colleagues had watched the inaugural episode eleven years earlier, ordering pizzas, to see what it was all about. They'd laughed over the sexy and all-powerful crime-scene investigators who fed evidence into impossibly fast computers, inter-rogated bad guys themselves, and sewed up cases inside of an hour. McGill had only watched it once since.

McGill decided to go see the detectives himself, walk-ing down a flight of stairs to Wittenberger's office and finding the sergeant inside with Detective Ruvin. He joined them, taking a seat, and could sense something was up.

"Hey, Dave, let me throw this at you," Ruvin said. "Let's say the two guys don't exist and Brittany is the killer. What would you think?"

McGill thought about how far Jayna's car had been found from the store, and the likelihood that Brittany would have moved it after the attack. He thought about how she could have zip-tied her wrists by herself. "We'd find blood in Jayna's car and we might find teeth marks on the flex-tie."

The detectives said they'd check the car as soon as they could. McGill said he'd get to work on the flex-tie, also known as a zip-tie. McGill had actually worked a previous murder case involving zip-ties. And he knew what he needed: the zip-tie that had been wrapped around Brittany's wrist, plus dozens, perhaps hundreds, of extra zip-ties to act as comparisons, and a microscope. He went off to get them.

At his desk, Ruvin fielded a call from Marybeth Ayres, a prosecutor assigned to the case. She was at her courthouse office three miles away and wanted to know about Keith Lockett, the homeless guy who'd been released from jail the day prior. "Do you have him under surveillance?" she asked.

Ruvin didn't know what to say. All around him were veteran colleagues who feared leaks—feared them to a degree Ruvin thought bordered on paranoia. "I'll call you back," he said.

Ruvin got up, walked down the hall, and ducked into a large room that housed the police department's computer-networking equipment. He knew Ayres and trusted her. And he knew he would be working on the case with her for months, possibly years. He had to be honest with her. He also hoped he could keep her from asking too many questions.

"Let Lockett be," Ruvin said.

"What are you saying?" Ayres asked.

She was relatively new to the county, but had prosecuted murders in Baltimore in her previous job. And she now had the detective under a form of cross-examination. Ruvin hesitated, then tried to use some of Drewry's language to describe Lockett.

"We're just not feeling him."

"Do you have any other suspects?"

Screw it, Ruvin thought. He told Ayres they were looking at Brittany as the killer. "Marybeth, why do you think the footprints never left the store?" Still, Ruvin told Ayres, they weren't *sure* Brittany did it and not to fear—they knew better than to arrest her too quickly. "If we charge her and we get it wrong, we're fucked."

Twenty miles south, in Washington, D.C., Brittany Norwood's family members were deeply worried about her. Brittany wasn't sleeping. They wondered if she should get out of the house. It wasn't like her family members were going to let anyone hurt her again. They convinced Brittany to go out with them to a grocery store and to Bed Bath & Beyond. It was something, at least.

Brittany didn't have her iPhone with her, having left it at the crime scene when her bag fell to the floor. Friends were still trying to reach her, leaving voice mails and text messages.

"Hey Brittany. I'm thinking, praying, and sending you all the love I can muster up," one former coworker from the Georgetown store wrote.

"I can't stop thinking about you," wrote another. "Let me know if I can help with anything at all."

And the bank kept calling, leaving automated messages. "Please call Citi, regarding your Citi account . . ."

The recording tracked with a deposit slip Brittany had recently tucked inside her wallet, one showing her balance had dropped to $7.25.

For Jayna Murray's parents, each day brought ever-more unimaginable horrors. The calls on Saturday from Drewry, the news that Jayna might have also been raped, the sudden need to buy her a gravesite, a flight to Washington, D.C., to claim their daughter's body. Amid all that, they also had to inform Jayna's brother Hugh what had happened. They did so by getting news to Hugh's supervisor in Baghdad, who tracked Hugh down in the northern part of Iraq.

"Is there anybody there with you?" the colonel asked.

"No," Hugh said. He was sitting alone inside the windowless plywood hut that served as his office. Hugh figured they were about to discuss classified information.

"Is there anyone you can get to sit with you?" the colonel asked instead.

"Not really," Hugh said. His office mate had just gone on leave.

"Hugh, there's been a family emergency."

"What is it, what kind of emergency is there?"

"Your sister's dead."

"No, there's no way. She's healthy."

"No, Hugh, she was murdered."

It took Hugh fifty hours and a series of flights to get to Washington. He didn't sleep, staring straight ahead at the seat in front of him. He couldn't help but think about what he'd been doing the moment Jayna was murdered. It had been early in the morning in Mosul. Protected by a group of Army infantrymen and traveling in mine-resistant trucks, Hugh had left his base to meet with an Iraqi judge. As they headed out, everyone was aware of a recent intelligence report that said insurgents were trying to target Americans meeting with judges—and they were the only Americans meeting with judges. The caravan rolled up to the courthouse. There was no judge. No local police. No protection. The infantrymen climbed out and took up positions. Finally the judge arrived, Hugh met with him briefly, and the trucks headed back to the base. Who could have guessed that a luxury retailer in a wealthy suburb would be the deadlier place?

The Murrays met Hugh at Dulles International Airport outside D.C. and drove him to their hotel for a quick rest. And now—on Tuesday afternoon—Hugh said he wanted to go see the memorial outside the store: the flowers, cards, and notes to Jayna. His parents and brother, Dirk, wondered about all the reporters camped outside. "I want to see the notes," Hugh insisted.

The Murrays struck a compromise, deciding to first drive by the store and see how many reporters were parked outside. Once they arrived, and slowly drove by the memorial and the reporters, Hugh made a quick left into Bethesda Row's hidden parking garage, pulled into a spot, and turned off the car. For about fifteen minutes the Murrays discussed what to do, what to say if a reporter approached. Finally, they got out and walked across the street.

As they approached the lululemon store and the memorial, they also saw the yellow police tape and brown paper taped over the windows. Whatever was behind those windows wasn't a store anymore, but a crime scene. Until that moment, Phyllis Murray had tried to convince herself that her daughter wasn't really dead. That was now impossible. "You can't hurt any more than you hurt" is how she would later describe it. Next to the flowers someone had left an empty can of Diet Dr Pepper, Jayna's favorite drink. Another person had left an accounting textbook, a subject Jayna had struggled with at Johns Hopkins. The Murrays slowly started reading the cards and notes. Journalists mumbled to each other: "Is that the family?" A television reporter approached David and asked if he knew Jayna. When it was clear David did, he asked a follow-up: "How does this make you feel?"

Four days of devastating grief hadn't just robbed David of sleep; it had weakened his ability to keep anger under his surface. Rage burst forward, transporting him back to combat mode. He walked toward the newsman, but was halted by Captain Paul Starks, the police spokesman, who put his hand on David's chest. "Mr. Murray, I'll take care of this," he said.

Hugh grabbed the back of his dad's coat and helped get him away. Starks got the reporter to retreat.

As quickly as the rage had surfaced in David, it was replaced by a sense of shame—that he had embarrassed his family, embarrassed Jayna. Starks approached again, saying they could keep reading the cards. The captain also asked, whenever they were done, would they be willing to go to a nearby police facility and meet with the detectives? The Murrays agreed.

Thirty minutes later, the Murray family sat around a table with Detectives Drewry and Ruvin. David and Phyllis asked about Jayna's coworker who'd been in the store.

"How is she doing? Is she okay?" The detectives said she was recovering well. They chose their words carefully. "We've still got a lot of stuff to do. We're finishing things up at the store," Ruvin said.

He and Drewry guided the conversation to Jayna. They wanted to cross all their t's in case the case against Brittany fell apart. Her family walked them through Jayna's life: she traveled a lot growing up, attended several different high schools, studied overseas, worked in Houston, and moved to Washington to get her MBA. Drewry asked about boyfriends, learning about Fraser Bocell, the PhD candidate on the other side of the country. "Came here to visit New Years and was supposed to come this coming Thursday," Drewry wrote. The detective was interested in any past problems. Jayna's parents described a former boyfriend. "Very controlling," the detective wrote.

The Murrays wanted to know how Jayna died. In nearly twenty-five years working homicides, Drewry had come to expect the question from grieving families. Of course they wanted to know. The fundamental emotion of empathy—the ability to put yourself in someone else's shoes—wasn't something they could cut off. They wanted to know about her final moments, holding out hope that she didn't suffer. "Was it fast?" Dirk asked.

Drewry knew the whole story would be hard, but lies would be just as devastating to them down the road. He tried to tell them the truth but say as little as possible, in this case telling Dirk that no, it wasn't fast.

The Murrays asked about a weapon. "Multiple instruments" was all Drewry would say.

Dirk pushed, asking why the killers had left a witness alive. One of the assailants may have simply been more violent than the other, Drewry offered. "We're still trying to figure that out," he said.

David Murray, Jayna's father, sat across the long table from Drewry, who looked him straight in the eye and said, "Believe half of what you see and none of what you hear."

Inside the county prosecutors' office, State's Attorney John McCarthy had kept tabs on the yoga store murder since the case's opening hours—both as a skilled lawyer and an astute politician. For the past three days, he, too, had thought the murder was the work of two masked, crazy men. Now he was learning otherwise. He called the police department's homicide unit to say he needed to come over for an update.

Around 7:00 P.M., he and an assistant state's attorney, Marybeth Ayres, entered the homicide unit. McCarthy walked through the cubicle area, and stood three feet outside Wittenberger's office, greeting the sergeant he'd known for more than twenty years through an opened door. There was a small table to McCarthy's right. He looked down and saw a startling autopsy photograph: an unrecognizable human face, mangled with slashings and blood. McCarthy picked up the photograph and similar ones stacked below it, leafing through one image after another.

"Holy mother of God, what's this?" McCarthy asked.

"That's your case," Wittenberger said.

Everyone gathered for a meeting. McCarthy had always been of the opinion that every prosecutor, detective, judge, and defense attorney came across three or four cases in their careers that—if handled the wrong way—would end those careers. This one felt like it could be one of those, particularly in a left-leaning place like Montgomery County. Brittany had no criminal record, came from a good family, and was a college-educated African American woman in a nation that historically had been too quick to arrest black suspects. McCarthy urged the detectives to wait for DNA results, invoking a case from 2005 when the twenty-three-year-old son of Iranian immigrants was charged with beating and strangling his mother to death inside her Potomac home. Then the DNA results came in, showing another, unknown man had left either saliva or sweat on the victim's neck. "The Makki case," McCarthy said. "We've been down this road before."

The detectives assured him they were in no hurry to arrest Brittany before they had more physical evidence and more conversations with her. But the prosecutor knew the pressure they were under—given the effect the case was having on downtown Bethesda.

"You've got to get this right," McCarthy said. "This is a hell of an allegation to make against somebody the community has embraced as a victim."

Jayna's car was the logical next step. The detectives had put off examining the car's contents while they focused on the store and, later, Keith Lockett. With Brittany as the suspect, however, and given the story she had told, the car now took on added value. The detectives wanted proof that Brittany had later moved the car, hopefully by finding blood in it.

Just before 9:00 P.M., Ruvin, Drewry, and Wittenberger drove to an evidence garage in a nondescript industrial park five minutes away. Together with three crime-scene investigators, they walked up to Jayna's silver, two-door Pontiac with Texas plates, its hood casting sharp reflections from bright florescent lights overhead. Inside was a stick shift—good news for crime-scene investigators, because a driver had to constantly touch it—and on the front passenger floorboard was a bright-pink workout jacket, and a black, baseball-styled cap was on the rear seat floorboard. A crime-scene investigator named Jennifer Greer slowly started working through the car. She swabbed surfaces, placing each swab in a small box so it could be tested in the lab for any DNA left by someone's skin cells. She found a tiny smudge of what looked like blood on the driver's floor mat and, about twelve inches from that, a dark-red drop the size of a pinhead against the driver's side door. Greer found a possible bloodstain in the jacket, and a red smudge the size of a fingertip on the front, inside band of the cap—one subtly branded with the lululemon logo and a saying stitched in small letters from the company manifesto: "Sweat Once a Day."

The clue on the hat was particularly intriguing. The band was stained in the same location as the center of the wearer's forehead—right where Brittany had been cut. Greer brought the cap out of the car. A colleague conducted a field blood test by swabbing the red mark, pulling the swab away, and dropping three solutions onto it. The swab turned bright pink.

"Oh yeah, we got blood. We got blood," Ruvin said, high-fiving anyone he could.

All anyone knew at the moment was that it was blood. The samples would be submitted for DNA analysis, but results probably wouldn't be ready for at least four or five days. At 10:45 P.M., the five finally left the garage.

Their secret suspicions were still safe. On the *Washington Post* website, the latest story was based on the statements made by the police department the day before: "The masked assailants who slipped into a Bethesda yoga store raped two workers, beat one of them to death and beat and bound the other, Montgomery County police said Monday. It was the first time that police have said how Jayna T. Murray was killed."

National outlets were starting to pay attention. That night, two hours before the crime-scene investigators had started combing through Jayna's car, CNN's HLN network launched into a segment about the case.

"Tonight, a devastating blow in the war on women," host Jane Velez-Mitchell said. "Two young women savagely attacked inside a trendy yoga clothing store in an upscale neighborhood. Two masked men brutally sexually assault them, murdering one and leaving the other tied up. Police desperately searching for any clues tonight. Who are these cold-blooded demons? And I'll tell you why this case has sparked global outrage among women."

The two suspects were described as about six feet tall and about five feet three inches tall. Velez-Mitchell then introduced a guest commentator, Linda Kenney Baden, a defense attorney who earlier had represented Florida's Casey Anthony.

"It is terrible," Baden said. "I mean, this is an upscale neighborhood. It looks like a crime of opportunity. And I would beg people out there who know somebody who pals around with a five-foot, three-inch person and a six-foot person to call them in, because no one is safe, not even their own family, with the kind of violence that these two have engaged in."

CHAPTER TWENTY-ONE

Wednesday:
Setting a Trap

If Detectives Jim Drewry and Dimitry Ruvin starred in a network crime drama, they'd spend their Wednesday morning leafing through a complete DNA workup of Jayna's car search and, minutes later, compare that with a DNA analysis of samples taken from Brittany, Jayna, and hundreds of locations in the store—tools, ropes, Buddha statues, bloody walls, sink handles, and more.

In reality, their crime-lab colleagues upstairs moved in real time. They'd barely begun the series of drawn-out steps needed to make DNA comparisons. Working at the molecular level, they had to break open cells, clear out proteins, carbohydrates, and lipids, extract the actual DNA, count it, try to extract more if needed, and start a process to make millions of something akin to genetic-level photocopies. And that only got them about halfway there. Working around the clock, the lab could push through a DNA analysis and comparison in forty-eight hours. But that wasn't really a good idea. The analysts liked to have the same person do every step, avoiding having to later bring a whole team in to testify at trials—a confusing jumble for juries. Cutting any corners now could render the whole workup useless for court. Drewry and Ruvin, aware of this, limited their DNA-analysis requests to those that followed solid leads, which at this point zeroed in on the evidence pulled from Jayna's car the night before. The detectives hoped to get results by early the next week. They expected it to match Brittany's blood.

Drewry and Ruvin settled on their next move: asking Brittany if she'd ever been inside Jayna's car. Chances were she'd say no, which would make the DNA evidence that much stronger because it would also trap Brittany in a lie. There was a second reason to lock Brittany into this position. Down the road, if she ever went on trial, her defense attorney couldn't fuzz up the car evidence by asserting that it simply could be DNA left by Brittany touching parts of the car when she'd earlier borrowed it or taken a ride inside it.

But the detectives couldn't just call Brittany and ask her if she'd ever been in the car. That likely would spook her, particularly if she'd realized by now she'd left the hat behind. And the last thing Drewry or Ruvin wanted was their suspect calling an attorney. What they needed was a ruse, preferably one that would lure Brittany to the station and into one of their interview rooms with the secret recording system. They could then get Brittany to go through her story again. With so many moving parts, she'd likely have trouble keeping them in the right order with each telling. Something would trip her up.

Drewry proposed the time-tested ruse of telling Brittany they needed to get her fingerprints and hair samples to distinguish them from those of the attackers. Drewry hoped to pass off the request as standard procedure from two slightly bungling detectives. He called one of Brittany's siblings, who said the family could bring Brittany by that day. Shortly after 4:30 P.M., on Wednesday, March 16, Brittany, her dad, and several of her siblings walked into the police lobby. Even in an affluent place like Montgomery County, the police-station lobby was hardly a welcoming space: just a twenty-by-twenty-foot room with brown and gray walls; a thick glass window that forced visitors to bend over and speak through tiny, metal slits; two small, square sofas; three plastic chairs with extended writing surfaces—the kind you might sit at while taking a standardized test—and a pay phone. Drewry thanked the Norwoods for coming, and apologized in advance that it might take some time for them to do the elimination fingerprints and hair samples. The Norwoods said they'd get something to eat and come back. As they left, Drewry figured he'd passed the first test; the family still felt comfortable leaving their daughter with him.

He led Brittany down a narrow hallway into a nine-foot-long, seven-foot-wide interview room with gray walls and a black metal table with part of its paint worn to brown. Drewry let Brittany sit in the only comfortable chair of the three available. It leaned back and had wheels. She was dressed in sneakers and lulu garb, a light-pink running jacket and gray leggings. Drewry wore one of his usual sweater vests—green and checkered—along with a button-down shirt, khakis, and loafers. He told Brittany he'd be right back, leaving the door open that faced the detectives' cubicles. Brittany could overhear them talking.

The open door was no accident. Drewry wanted Brittany to know she was free to leave any time she wanted.

That meant that, legally speaking, he didn't have to inform her of her constitutional rights to remain silent and consult a lawyer. Defense attorneys often challenged the open-door technique, but courts had adopted a standard: it didn't matter what the detectives thought—and right now, Drewry and Ruvin thought Brittany was a cold-blooded and possibly psychopathic killer—it mattered what the suspect thought. If Brittany felt she could go, she wasn't entitled to hear her rights.

As it happened, the department's fingerprint machine, on which a suspect merely had to roll his or her finger across a glass scanner, wasn't working. Drewry exploited the development, part of a broader strategy to present himself and his department as bungling. He walked back into the interview room. "Okay, let's do the—I'm trying to think of the best way to do it. We got to do elimination fingerprints. Okay, and it gets really messy and whatnot. I thought that we had this new system still here where it's inkless, okay, but apparently it's . . ."

He paused for effect, emphasizing the next word.

". . . broken."

Ruvin walked up to the doorway. Drewry told him they'd probably have the hair samples taken first. He updated his partner on the broken fingerprint machine. "They ain't going to replace or repair it." To hear Drewry tell it, Brittany was dealing with a department stuck in the Stone Age, though even as Drewry complained, analysts upstairs were working up DNA samples in a lab stocked with more than a million dollars' worth of equipment.

Drewry and Ruvin had developed a rhythm from earlier cases. With his experience, Drewry would lead the

Jayna Murray's smile lit up the room— or, in this case, part of the River Walk in San Antonio, Texas.
(Matt Deschner)

Brittany Norwood was quick with a beaming smile, even when posing for her driver's license.
(Montgomery County State's Attorney's Office)

Both women worked inside the high-end lululemon athletica store in Bethesda, Maryland. No one could have guessed it would become a vicious crime scene. *(Montgomery County Circuit Court)*

Behind a mannequin and behind the front sales counter, police found signs of a robbery. *(Montgomery County Circuit Court)*

Signs of a struggle were evident in the back dressing room area. *(Montgomery County State's Attorney's Office)*

Jayna Murray was attacked in a tight corner, near a yoga poster. *(Montgomery County State's Attorney's Office)*

What police saw upon arriving at the crime scene

Bloody shoe prints

Opened cash drawer and boxes. Signs of a robbery at checkout counter.

Note: Store merchandise not depicted for clarity.

MAIN

SALES

FLOOR

Brittany's bag and iPhone

Bloody palm print on wall

Brittany Norwood found tied up

APPLE STORE

(beside lululemon)

FITTING ROOM AREA

Jayna Murray's body: A hammer, wrench, rope, toolbox, and Buddha statue were found on or around her.

STOCKROOM

Jayna's BlackBerry

BACK DOOR

Jayna's bag

Brittany's wallet

Employee kitchenette

A diagram showing the crime scene. Brittany Norwood was on the floor of the second bathroom, and Jayna Murray was found in a rear hallway. (*Todd Lindeman*)

Sergeant Craig Wittenberger (LEFT) supervised two lead detectives on the case, Dimitry Ruvin (CENTER) and Jim Drewry (RIGHT). *(Dan Morse)*

When detectives entered the rear hallway, they saw that victim Jayna Murray appeared to have been savagely attacked. Near her body, detectives found a hammer, rope, wrench, toolbox, and box cutter knives. *(Montgomery County State's Attorney's Office)*

Investigators measured blood spatter indicating Jayna Murray had been struck while standing. Later analysis of the lower, more concentrated blood spatter established that she was also struck repeatedly after she fell. *(Montgomery County Circuit Court)*

Brittany Norwood was found bloodied and tied up on a bathroom floor and rushed to a hospital. Investigators marked a bloodstain near a rock. *(Montgomery County State's Attorney's Office)*

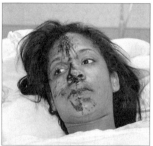

(TOP LEFT)
Nurses didn't wash the blood off of Brittany Norwood until police could take samples for evidence.
(Montgomery County Circuit Court)

(BOTTOM LEFT)
From her hospital bed, Brittany told police that she and Jayna were attacked by two men dressed head to toe in dark clothing. That matched surveillance video that detectives later reviewed, taken behind the yoga store just after the murder.
(Montgomery County State's Attorney's Office)

Even after she got out of the hospital, the strain of the case showed on Brittany's face.
(Montgomery County Police Department)

Jayna Murray's body was taken to the Maryland Medical Examiner's office, where Dr. Mary Ripple counted at least 331 wounds, including at least 152 to her head.
(University of Maryland Medical School)

Autopsy technician Mario Alston, who helped examine Jayna Murray's body, called the case the most horrific murder he'd ever seen.
(Amanda McGinnis)

Possible weapons collected from the store.
(Dan Morse)

This merchandise peg, part of store displays, was likely used to crush Jayna Murray's skull.
(Dan Morse)

Crime-scene investigator David McGill provided key analysis of bloody shoe prints inside the store. *(Dan Morse)*

The rear hallway, after Jayna Murray's body was removed, shows bloody shoe prints. In the foreground, at evidence marker 37, is her BlackBerry. *(Montgomery County State's Attorney's Office)*

(LEFT AND BELOW) McGill tracked bloody shoe prints into the rear stockroom. *(Montgomery County State's Attorney's Office)*

Defense attorney Doug Wood, who'd won a series of acquittals in murder cases prior to the yoga store trial, speaking to reporters.
(*Nikki Kahn,* The Washington Post)

Brittany Norwood's father, Earl, came to the trial from Washington State, hoping for answers.
(*Bill O'Leary,* The Washington Post)

Prosecutors John McCarthy and Marybeth Ayres walking to the first hearing in the case.
(*Ricky Carioti,* The Washington Post)

The case left two families devastated. Behind prosecutor John McCarthy, from left to right, are Jayna Murray's oldest brother, U.S. Army captain Hugh Murray, and her parents, retired U.S. Army captain David Murray and Phyllis Murray.
(*Mark Gail,* The Washington Post)

questions, while Ruvin would sit back and take notes, giving him time to jot down inquiries his partner missed, and interject his own questions at the end. The two hadn't been able to come up with a solid plan for bringing the car up, but in two-dozen years of talking with suspects, Drewry had learned that plans didn't work well for him anyway. He preferred to get people talking about anything, let them lead the conversation, and respond accordingly. "Flying by the seat of my pants," Drewry liked to call it.

When Drewry finally took a seat, he did so atop the metal table, his head turned slightly away from Brittany toward the open door as he waited for the hair-sample technicians to arrive. He hardly wanted to seem eager. Brittany broke the silence, asking if there were any more developments in the case. "Any other good news?"

Drewry seized the opportunity to assert that Brittany's fingerprints were just one of many they needed to get to distinguish innocent store employees from the killers. "We're just still working on it. And that's one of the things, like, what we have to do is, because we got a ton of doggone prints gathered inside of there. And so, we, like, need to get stuff from you, and from, like, everybody else that would have been, you know, working there."

Drewry told her about receiving lots of tips and leads. "I'm trying to follow up on them. But again, like, you know, you're one of our best sources, because you were there."

"The only source," Brittany said, quietly and quickly.

Drewry asked Brittany if she'd had a chance to talk to one of the counselors the county provides to rape victims. Not yet, Brittany said. He asked about lululemon. Brittany said a company executive had come to check on her earlier that day. And she said she enjoyed working at the Bethesda store. "It's like a little family."

Drewry engaged Brittany in more chitchat, asking about her family and where she'd gone to college. Brittany said she graduated from Stony Brook, something she'd been saying for the past seven years, since it had almost happened.

"What was your major?" the detective asked, still sitting on the table, dangling his feet a few inches above the floor.

"Sociology and psychology—originally wanted to be a social worker, and then ended up, when I graduated, I wanted just to hang and actually have fun. I moved to D.C. because I have family here," Brittany said, waving her left hand, the fingertips of which still shone from her manicure five days earlier. "Had no idea what I really wanted to do. I used to say I was going to play soccer all my life. Ended up working with Bank of America for a little bit. It's where I met one of my boyfriends. He was a dentist. I worked for him. Parents hated that."

"They didn't like him?"

"They didn't like me working with him."

"Oh, okay."

Drewry and Ruvin felt confident the DNA results would point their way. But what if they didn't? What if the blood in the car was Jayna's, what if she had cut herself a few weeks earlier? What if the DNA from the store had Brittany's and Jayna's blood in so many places that the chaos was difficult to sort through? Their case would become more and more circumstantial: *Brittany was the only known person in the store, and her explanation of what happened amounted to a series of lies.* Could they even arrest her on those grounds? The more lies they had—and the more provably false they were—the better their chances.

The detectives knew Brittany was smart enough to think through the inquiries they were making. She likely figured they'd delve into what happened at the Georgetown store. Drewry wanted to bring up the topic, if only to shoot down the notion that he cared about it.

"How come you transferred up to the Bethesda store? Is it a larger store, or what?"

"Well, the reason why is a long story behind it."

"Oh, okay. Drama?"

"Yeah. It's kind of a blessing in disguise, you know?" Brittany said, waving the back of her left hand in a gentle, flowing motion. She talked about how it had led to the job offer at the fancy health club. "Just with the way things kind of happened with Equinox and everything."

At 5:05 P.M., Drewry gave way to two women in blue uniforms who walked in. They weren't dressed like cops and weren't: they were there to get the hair samples. The duo—Cheré Balma and Amanda Kraemer—had worked with Jennifer Greer on Jayna's car the night before. They knew the detectives' suspicions, but acted their parts, deferring to Brittany as a traumatized victim. Snapping on a pair of rubber gloves and holding a pair of tweezers, Balma began to go to work. Brittany politely helped, offering to pull her hair to this side or that, to remove her bobby pins. At one point, Balma warned that a certain pull could be painful.

"Oh my gosh," Brittany said. "Is it going to hurt a lot?"

It took twenty minutes to pull the hair samples. Drewry walked back into the interview room and took Brittany out to get her a bottle of water. When they returned, the detective casually stepped in front to naturally guide Brittany to the straight-back chair in the corner, the one nearer the hidden microphone and facing the hidden camera.

"Do you want me to sit here?" Brittany asked.

"I got a bad back," Drewry said, pointing at the rocking seat. "If you don't mind, if I can sit here."

"Sure."

"Okay thanks," Drewry said. Next to Brittany's knee, welded to a metal table leg and clearly visible, was a ring familiar to anyone who'd watched crime drama on TV. That's where they cuffed the bad guys in place.

It was another part of what the detectives hated about their cramped, outdated police station. With only two interview rooms—often in use at the same time—they had to equip both with restraint rings. Ideally, they'd have other, less threatening rooms with the recording equipment. But they had to make do to try to keep things casual.

Ruvin tried to do his part by making himself out to be little more than a stenographer. He walked into the room, took a seat across the table from Brittany, and held up a folder that held his legal pad. "I usually do the writing," he said. "I guess I'm a faster writer."

Ruvin imitated a typing action and said he was thinking about buying an iPad.

"Well, for this, it'd probably be really good," Brittany said with a smile and a soft voice on the border of flirtatious. "My brothers just bought me one."

"Yeah? The new, new one?"

"Yeah, I don't want it . . I haven't even opened it."

Brittany gently lifted her bottle of water. Her right hand still had the cut. "Can I maybe ask, could you possibly open this?" she said.

As Ruvin did so, Drewry casually shut the door that led to the squad room. Brittany was now inside a room with two locked doors, which could only be opened with a swipe card. Drewry felt a judge would not view locked doors literally—that all Brittany had to do is ask to leave and she'd be allowed to do so. But it became that much more important for him and Ruvin to not come across as dominating or threatening. He gently suggested they speak for a bit before the fingerprint people arrived, asking Brittany about Jayna and any boyfriends she might have. She told him about Jayna's boyfriend, Fraser. "He's at the University of Washington. She was planning on moving in May, and so that's how we kind of bonded right away is, because like, 'Oh, you know, I'm from Seattle.'"

Brittany sat with her legs crossed, calmly answering questions. She spoke about the last night she and Jayna worked. As far as Brittany knew, she told the detectives, Jayna headed home. To Drewry, it seemed liked an opening to ask the car question, even if it had presented itself early.

"And she lives in Arlington?"

"Uh-huh," Brittany said by way of affirmation.

"And she drives?"

Brittany nodded her head.

"Do you know what kind of car she has?"

"I don't. I saw it once," Brittany said. "But I don't know the make and model."

Drewry and Ruvin realized Brittany had answered the question in a way that left wiggle room down the road. *Sure, Jayna gave me a ride once, but I wasn't paying attention to whether the car was a Toyota or a Honda or a whatever.* Drewry decided to let the car questions go for a while.

He got Brittany going again with her recollections of the night of the attack: closing down the store, leaving behind the wallet, going back inside with Jayna, being followed in by two masked men. If it was all lies, the detectives thought, Brittany was painting the broad outlines of how she killed Jayna. Brittany needed masked men to match the evidence; and the best way to do so, wherever possible, was to substitute what she did to Jayna with what they did to her. But Drewry had trouble picturing the attack Brittany was describing. He turned to Ruvin. "Give me your diagram," he quietly asked.

Ruvin reached into his folder, pulled out a floor plan of the store, and gave it to his partner. Drewry placed it on the table between himself and Brittany. He wheeled his chair closer to her. "I should have done this before, I'm sorry," he said, holding a pen over the diagram and readying himself to follow her lead. "Okay, here's the front of the store, then, and this is where the alarm pad would be?"

"Uh-huh," Brittany said, and spent the next twenty-five minutes helping Drewry draw a map of the attack.

He'd need it. In Brittany's telling, the assault covered all four sections of the store: starting in the fitting area, where the bathrooms were, and moving back and forth among the three other sections—the rear stockroom, the main front portion, and the back exit hallway. As Brittany helped Drewry fill out his diagram, she had one of the masked men pushing and pulling her in eight directions. For the most part, Brittany spoke calmly, using her right hand to point to the diagram and using her left hand to wave and open and close for emphasis. Her facial expression didn't change, but at one point her right foot under the table fluttered nineteen times in four seconds.

Brittany sometimes spoke in the present tense, like when she described Jayna getting pushed into the rear hallway, behind the purple door, where her screams started to fade. "She's a lot more faint. And, like I, you, can't make out what she's saying," Brittany said. She described breaking free of her attacker, squeezing into the rear hallway to try to help Jayna, seeing her, and getting dragged back. Brittany helped the detective draw a figure of Jayna's body, where it was lying, what direction it was facing. Brittany's voice began to quiver at the memory: "I remember seeing a lot of blood and stepping in it."

As Ruvin took notes, he could hear when Brittany was trying to cover holes in her story. This was one of those points: she knew she had tracked Jayna's blood in the store on the bottom of her sneakers. And so Brittany had just offered an explanation. In Ruvin's mind, however, Brittany had a deeper hole to fill: coming up with reasons why the detectives would find Jayna's blood on Brittany's clothes and her hands, and why the detectives would find Brittany's blood on Jayna's body. She'd started her explanation Monday night in her apartment with the notion the two masked men shoved her onto Jayna's bloody body. Now, Brittany was taking it one step further—explaining how she had bled onto Jayna. She pointed to the diagram and asserted what came next.

Her attacker dragged her back into the fitting-room area, she said, where he struck her in the forehead with something heavy. Then he forced her onto a bathroom floor and cut her hands and her stomach. Suddenly, both men wanted to know how to get out the back door. So Brittany's attacker dragged her into the rear hallway to tell them how to disconnect the fire alarm.

Brittany was starting to whimper.

"I know it's rough," Drewry said, "but you're almost through it." The detective stood up, reached into a back pocket, pulled out a stack of tissues and put it on the table next to Brittany. Then he reached over, pulled a tissue off the pile, and put it next to her as well, so that Brittany had tissues next to both hands if she wanted them.

Brittany continued, offering an explanation for the biggest hole of all: why Jayna had been brutally massacred yet she herself was sitting there in relatively fine health. It was told to her by her attacker after he dragged her into the bathroom for the second time.

"Back out here," she told Drewry, pointing at the diagram. "Back into the bathroom, he tells me that I'm like more fun to fuck with or something: 'You're lucky like,' I don't know, something like I'm more fun to fuck with, 'You're lucky you're cute, you're more fun to fuck with.'"

Deep down, Drewry was growing more convinced Brittany was a coldhearted killer. But he didn't show it, having long ago learned to suspend his emotions in the interview room. Best to just try to treat a suspect like he or she was a regular person. "I try not to judge people" is how he described the technique.

Drewry pushed back from the diagram, gave Brittany a bit of space, and asked her quietly about the rape.

"He has a hanger," Brittany said. "He says he's not going to stop until I came."

"How long do you think this went on?"

"Forever, it seems like," Brittany said, her voice cracking.

"I'm sure," Drewry said.

He moved on, getting to how they bound her in the

zip-ties. Drewry decided to push a little bit, hoping to trap Brittany. "Okay. Where did he get the zip-ties from?"

"I don't know."

"Because it sounds like he was probably with you the entire time?"

"Yeah, he was. I don't know. He had them with him."

"When they came into the store, they had them with them?"

"I don't know where he gets them, I don't know."

Drewry stepped off the gas, inferring that he didn't understand the whole zip-tie thing either. "Because there is a box of ties in, in the back, in the storage room. And I don't know if those are the same ones or not."

He could tell Brittany was now itching to get out of the interview room. "I really don't want to talk anymore," Brittany said, following that a few moments later with, "Can I just get my fingerprints and then go? I'm sorry."

Drewry had to make a split decision. Both doors to the room were closed. Brittany was asking to leave. It was getting to the point where if he wanted to ask more, he would have to inform her of her rights. He wasn't about to do that, not this early in the case. But he didn't want her to go, figuring he might never have a chance to ask her about Jayna's car. Drewry forged ahead, resetting the table with a couple of questions about the rape, all structured as if he absolutely believed it had happened. Brittany still was asking if she could quit talking. There was no time left for a subtle approach.

"Has she ever given you a ride home or anything?" Drewry asked out of left field.

"No," Brittany said.

The detective had gotten the response he was after, but

at a price. Who knew if Brittany would ever come back and talk to them now?

Drewry tried to cover up the randomness of the question, asking Brittany how she got back and forth to work, hoping to convince Brittany that he was pursuing the notion that the masked men had somehow been following her to work. Drewry had one more card to play, one he hoped would make him appear so lost he was looking everywhere. The detective showed Brittany a picture of a lululemon coworker—another apparent outlier—who'd been involved in a bizarre criminal case. She'd been charged with arson for allegedly trying to set her estranged husband's house on fire. One of the tips the detectives had actually received was that the estranged husband had hired a hit man to go after her in the store, and in a case of mistaken identity, the hit man took out Jayna. Drewry figured it would do him good to play the string out in front of Brittany. He pointed to the photo. "What's she up to? Is she cool?"

"Always fun to work with," Brittany said. "Always energetic. I don't know anything else, I mean, nothing personal with her."

Drewry said he'd go get the fingerprint technicians and see about getting her home. "Let me go out and see if your family is here."

In front of Brittany were the two tissues. She'd never used them.

It had been two hours since Brittany's family dropped her off. Drewry wondered what Brittany might tell them on the way home. *The detective kept making me go over the story. He asked me questions about Jayna's car.* Drewry wanted Brittany's dad and siblings to counter Brittany by saying the detectives were just doing their jobs. He tracked one of the family members down on a cell phone. "Sorry it has taken so long. Where are you folks?" Turned out they were waiting up front, in the dumpy lobby. "Oh, okay," Drewry said. "You guys want to come in and just talk for a minute?"

Drewry brought them all back to the homicide unit, walking the Norwoods past the open door of the interview room, where the technicians were deferentially fingerprinting Brittany. "They're just finishing up, doing some elimination prints," Drewry said.

He sat them down at a long table with Ruvin. The detectives tried to keep things light, and largely succeeded. One of Brittany's brothers, a semiconductor-design engineer, joked at being directionally challenged by the area around the police department, a common ailment for newcomers navigating the looping roads that wound through the office parks. Conversation veered to how one of Brittany's other brothers studied criminal justice, and whether the detectives liked their jobs. Drewry talked about his earlier career as a letter carrier: "It was either become a cop or go postal at the post office, literally."

The Norwoods also wanted to know about the case. "You guys know anything new?" one asked.

"We still got a lot of tips," said Ruvin, unsure what to add.

Earl Norwood asked about the murder three months earlier in the basement of Suburban Hospital, less than two miles from the yoga store. The detectives didn't know how Earl knew about that case—maybe from one of his other daughters who lived in the area—but it seemed like he was grasping for a connection to what had happened in the yoga store.

"Can you be more specific as to what that one was?" Earl asked them.

"An arrest was made," Drewry said. "So the guy is locked up."

Brittany could hear the conversation, could hear her family's concern and worries. She calmly cooperated with the fingerprint technicians, apologizing when she failed to lay down a clear print, even as the procedure stretched past thirty minutes.

Out around the table, conversation fell back to casual subjects. Earl spoke about living near Puget Sound. Drewry said he'd traveled to the area once. Earl said he hoped Drewry would return. "Look me up, and we can go fishing," he said.

The detectives felt for the family. Every word the Norwoods had said since they'd met them had been gracious, cooperative, and even, where appropriate, humorous. If the detectives' theory about Brittany was correct, the Norwood family had perhaps a week, maybe even less, left to their lives as they knew it. For now, of course, the detectives' charade that Brittany was a victim continued. Ruvin could hear the technicians finishing up. He walked back into the interview room to get Brittany.

"Do you want to hang out with your family?" he asked her.

"Sure."

As she stood up, Ruvin could see she'd taken off her running jacket for the fingerprinting, and was wearing a tight, athletic T-shirt. She was small, but only around the waist. Brittany's torso extended upward in an inverted triangle to broad, muscular shoulders. Her arms were equally defined.

Brittany joined her family, but only for a few minutes. The technician reviewing the fingerprints announced they were all in order. Drewry walked the Norwoods out of the station. He returned and spoke to Ruvin, talking about Brittany's family, repeating the offer that Ruvin had also heard. There was sadness in the detective's voice: "He invited me out to Seattle to go fishing."

CHAPTER TWENTY-TWO

Thursday:
Tracking and Trailing

Detectives Jim Drewry and Dimitry Ruvin returned to the office Thursday, March 17, worried they'd spoken with Brittany Norwood for the last time but convinced more than ever she was the lone killer. It wasn't just the holes in her story. No one was stepping forward who had seen men enter the store, heard men's voices inside it, or seen men leave. The tipsters who were now calling increasingly lacked specificity and, in some cases, a connection to reality.

A local musician said she'd gone for a walk down Bethesda Avenue the night before the murder and saw a tall, muscular black man with a "criminal face" pass in front of her while wearing a dark polyester hoodie—possibly casing the store. "Didn't fit in," a detective wrote, taking notes of the call. "Hardened face, looked angry, walking in middle of street, criminal face." An anonymous tipster suggested detectives look into a group seen one or two days before the murder, gathering a block from the yoga store in front of Barnes & Noble. "Caller stated the group was having a meeting before being sent out to go door-to-door to solicit magazine sales. Caller stated in their experience the people involved in those door-to-door sales are from outside the area."

A performer from a well-known strip club in Washington, D.C., submitted a tip on one of the police department's online-reporting forms. She offered the name, e-mail address, and employer of one of her more rabid fans, and recalled a recent conversation with him: "He said a lot of his women friends died, that he wanted to join the Army to kill people for the last war and he was serious." The stripper said she practiced yoga in Bethesda. Her implication, seemingly, was that the fan went looking for her at the store and slipped into a rage. "I get a creepy feeling from him," she wrote. If the police wanted to talk to the man directly, they could find him at the strip club. "He will most likely show up on Saturday morning right when we open."

A psychic reported a vision that one of the yoga store victims suffered internal bleeding because she'd been raped with a knife. Another tipster said he had *spoken* to a psychic who saw the killer as a heavyset man, possibly named Raphile, who could be identified by his tattoo of a non-English word surrounded by a circle. And there was the person who called with simply a gut feeling: "The suspect might have a disease on the foot or bad odor on one foot."

Drewry and Ruvin didn't personally have to field many of the calls or sift through the tips, but their colleagues kept them up to speed on the more outlandish ones as a form of comic relief. A more serious pursuit, the detectives knew, was under way inside the store, where evidence was adding up in support of their theory that Brittany had killed Jayna while wearing her pink, size-7½ New Balance running shoes, then took them off, stepped into the store's size-14 Reebok running shoes, and walked through the blood to create another set of tracks.

The pursuit was being led by David McGill, one of the crime-scene investigators, who was an expert in shoe prints. His wife constantly teased him during beach vacations for allowing his eyes to wander off at the sight of tracks left by shoe-clad tourists. He was an expert in the discipline, and had studied shoe prints in more than 500 cases.

Until now, McGill's time in the yoga store had been limited to locating each shoe print. What he wanted to figure out now was the movements of the shoes. It wasn't going to be easy; in many places, the shoe prints and partial prints crossed over each other in different directions. McGill's plan was to lay down pieces of bright tape next to each shoe print, along with an arrow when he could establish a clear direction. He'd use yellow for Brittany's sneakers, and red for the ones found in the store.

McGill wanted to study all four parts of the shop: main sales floor, fitting area, rear stockroom, and rear hallway exit. He wanted cleared-away, open spaces to lay down his tape and get clear photographs of any established trails. By now, almost all of the scattered clues and evidence first encountered had been photographed, cataloged, and taken away to the crime lab. So he was free to roam, except on the main sales floor, which was filled in the middle with its normal assortment of merchandise tables and racks. So McGill and two colleagues pushed the displays into corners easily enough, since the displays were meant to be cleared out for community yoga classes. What a difference that scene must have been—a roomful of people on their mats, legs crossed, soft sitar music playing—versus a middle-aged crime-scene guy with a slight paunch, staring at blood-stains.

As McGill laid down his red and yellow tape and arrows, he encountered a challenge. In a small patch in the middle of the sales floor, there was a different type of bloodstain: drops that were not near any of the shoe prints. McGill didn't know what it meant, but he wanted to encircle the drops with a different colored tape. Problem was, he didn't have any other color of tape.

"Hey, Paula, I'm going to cut up one of these yoga mats," McGill said, calling out to Detective Paula Hamill, a homicide investigator who was there to guard the place and help him while he worked. "Go ahead," Hamill said. McGill had several colors to choose from, and quickly selected purple for its contrast to the floor and his tape markings. He marked off the drops using three-inch strips. As McGill completed his layout—the tape, arrows, purple strips—the store began to take on the look of some kind of inverted, macabre game of Twister.

When he was done, one thing was clear: how often the New Balance prints and Reebok prints crossed paths. It made things confusing but offered valuable data in the form of smudges and smears, which McGill examined closely. As far as he could tell, Brittany's New Balance tracks were always made first.

The New Balance tracks were abundant in the rear hall-way, where Jayna's body was found, and the fitting area near where Brittany herself was found. In both locations, there was too much back and forth for clear direction. But coming from the fitting area, a track of yellow arrows pointed toward the front door of the store. They stopped just before an interior deadbolt lock, turned around, and headed back to the fitting area.

By studying how the tracks grew fainter, McGill surmised that at some point, the person in the New Balance shoes—most certainly Brittany—had returned to the rear hallway and got more blood on the soles. What she was doing back there wasn't clear. But when she came out, according to the shoe prints, the soles were soaked. McGill's yellow arrows led into the stockroom and toward a sink in the rear corner. It was in this area, he knew, that Windex, Formula 409, and a scrub brush had been found on the floor, and a drop of diluted blood had been found on the hot water handle. What McGill *couldn't* locate was equally compelling—there was no evidence of the shoes walking away from the sink. Brittany, it seemed, had removed her shoes here and cleaned them.

McGill was thinking on two levels. On the first, he was documenting the clinical observations he needed to put together reports and testify to in court. On the other, McGill was drawing a mental picture of what Brittany might have done, one he would share with the detectives to give them ideas of how to question Brittany. And here at the sink, after she cleaned her sneakers, Brittany either slipped them back on or walked about in her socks—in either case walking around the existing bloody prints and making her way to the back fitting room, where she knew the Reeboks were kept.

McGill studied the red-tape patterns, representing the trail Brittany presumably made after putting on the Reeboks to create the illusion of a large male killer. One of the first things made clear by the tape was, again, where the tracks *weren't*: no Reebok tracks in the front of the store. Just New Balance tracks. That meant that for Brittany's masked men story to be true, she would have had to either walk up to the door by herself, which raised the question of why she didn't open it and flee, or she had to have walked up to the front door in the company of a masked man who didn't have blood on his shoes, which seemed unlikely given how much blood was on the floors in the back of the store.

As for the back portions of the store, the Reebok tracks appeared to go in and out of the rear hallway at least twice. McGill imagined that Brittany, having already killed Jayna, may have used the pool of blood around Jayna's head as a sort of giant inkwell from which to soak the Reeboks to be able to make more tracks. In any case, McGill surmised, Brittany eventually walked into the rear stockroom and into the small manager's office. Inside the office, McGill noted, the Reebok prints suddenly went backward and sideways, as if Brittany had literally walked herself into a corner. It wasn't surprising, really, given all that Brittany must have had on her mind inside the darkened store: Could someone have heard the commotion? Were the police coming? How do I imitate the steps of a tall man? How do I do so in huge, unlaced shoes without them falling off? In any event, McGill would later write, the Reebok tracks in the office represented movements "inconsistent with normal biomechanical movement," which was more evidence the tracks had been created as part of a cover-up.

Immediately outside the office, the Reebok trail

appeared to halt in front of an orange chair. It was here, McGill thought, that Brittany took off the Reeboks, cleaned them in the nearby sink, and gingerly walked around even more bloodstains to return the sneakers to the table.

As 2:00 P.M. approached, Drewry and Ruvin still weren't sure how to proceed with Brittany. She'd grown weary of their questions the night before, maybe even wary of their suspicions. The detectives didn't want to start digging into her past—calling friends, coworkers, past employers—for fear that news of the inquiries would get back to Brittany and spook her. With the DNA test results still days, if not weeks, away, they found themselves in a stressful holding pattern.

Drewry's cell phone beeped. It was Chris Norwood, Brittany's brother. He told them that Brittany had withheld an important piece of information about the attack because she'd been so rattled by the whole thing: the men actually made his sister move Jayna's car the night of the murder. And Brittany wanted to talk to the detectives about it, to give them the whole story.

Drewry reacted as calmly as he could to this new twist in Brittany's story, as if the development was perfectly understandable. They made plans for Brittany to come back to the station either later that day or Friday. He and Chris chitchatted a little longer about Brittany possibly moving back to Seattle. Then Drewry hung up, walked over to Ruvin's cubicle, and gave him a report. "This is going to be a good story," Drewry promised.

It was clear to the detectives what had happened.

Brittany had figured out why Drewry had asked her about being in Jayna's car. She'd realized that she must have left blood there. The detectives updated Sergeant Craig Wittenberger. "What's she going to say?" Ruvin asked, laughing. " 'The two masked men walked me out to the car on Bethesda Avenue.' Maybe she'll say they took their masks off, but told her not to look at them."

Drewry realized that his car questions the day before had spooked Brittany. She must have felt she could still lie her way out of this bind. Drewry told Ruvin to be ready for anything, that there was no way to know what she'd come up with: "You'll go nuts trying to speculate."

Back at the store, McGill was finishing up his shoe-print and tracking work. But one thing remained a mystery: a series of what looked like worm-shaped bloodstains in the stockroom and the fitting area. The worms had ridges, like the side view of a scallop shell, such that McGill dubbed them "scallops." He had first noticed the faint stains earlier in the week. Now he'd seen the scallops throughout the day. Some of them were next to shoe prints. Others were off on their own. The isolated ones had originally been faint, but became more noticeable after he sprayed the Leuco Crystal Violet agent. McGill made sure he had pictures of all the scallops before heading to his office at police headquarters.

Thirty minutes later, he was sitting in his second-floor cubicle. Like those in the rest of the building, his space was cramped—roughly five feet by five feet. If he moved too far to the left, he hit a wall. If he wheeled back more than a foot, he rammed into the refrigerator he and his colleagues used, a three-footer he'd bought in college. McGill pulled the scallop photos up on his computer. He and a colleague—Cheré Balma, who'd searched Jayna's car and taken Brittany's hair samples—took a look.

"Maybe they're shoelaces," she said.

Certainly some of the marks were positioned next to shoe prints. But what about the scallops off on their own, with no corresponding shoe prints? As McGill and Balma talked about it, he mentioned how Brittany had likely washed her own shoes—probably so that she wouldn't make tracks outside to Jayna's car when she moved it. What if Brittany had cleaned her shoes and soles well, but left diluted blood on the laces? McGill looked at evidence photos of Brittany's shoes. Two things jumped out: the laces weren't tied, and the laces had a stylish twist to them, so they effectively formed up-and-down ridges. *Scallops,* McGill thought.

This was getting complicated, but McGill was able to advance a theory: first, Brittany walked around in her New Balances, which had blood on the soles and the laces. That created the scallop images on either side of her shoe prints. Then she washed her New Balances, unwittingly leaving diluted blood on the laces. She put the New Balances back on, walking with clean-soled shoes but whose laces left faint scallop marks as she went to get the Reeboks. Put another way, this was the possible order of things: wear New Balances, kill Jayna, get blood on them, make tracks, remove them, clean them, put them back on, walk to Reeboks, put Reeboks on, walk through Jayna's blood, make tracks, get trapped in office, take off Reeboks, clean Reeboks, return Reeboks to table. It was an amazing sequence, one made by someone who likely was either scared or calculating, or both.

McGill knew he'd have to conduct an experiment the next morning to support his shoelace-markings theory. He planned out how he'd do it. First, he'd bring in an old pair of sneakers, like the ones he wore when he was doing yard-work or taking his six-year-old daughter fishing on the Potomac River. Using sheep's blood kept in the crime lab for experiments, he'd be able to get the laces bloody. He could line the floor of a long hallway outside the lab with white paper. Then he'd step into his old sneakers, keep the laces untied, walk down the paper, and see what happened.

Downstairs, news of McGill's findings was tempered by the fact they had gotten no word from Brittany's family about the pending interview. People were getting nervous, wondering if Brittany had gotten an attorney or if she was going to rush off to Washington State. At 7:45 P.M., Drewry called her sister Marissa, trying not to sound eager. She told him that Brittany was simply too tired to talk, but they would bring her to the station the next morning at 10:00 A.M.

So far, Brittany's family members had seemed straightforward and accommodating, even warm, to the detectives. Drewry believed that still to be the case. And he told his colleagues not to worry if Brittany bolted for the West Coast because they would inevitably track her down. "Flight is great," he said. "It's an indication of guilt."

CHAPTER TWENTY-THREE

Friday:
Offering an Out

Friday morning, March 18, 2011, opened with a heated debate inside the office of the Montgomery County Police Department's major crimes commander, David Gillespie, over how far to push Brittany Norwood. One camp—essentially, all of the top commanders—contended it was time to confront Brittany with the evidence they had against her. Their feeling was that Brittany had grown wise to the detectives' suspicions, this was likely their last shot with her, and she might even flee.

"We need to find out what her story is, and then we need to grill her from there," Gillespie said.

Detective Jim Drewry pushed back. He worried about the strength of the case. Yes, they could go into the interview room, blow holes in Brittany's story, and prove straight to her face that she was a liar. But what did they really have to convince Brittany they could prove she was the *killer*? Not DNA. Not eyewitnesses. Drewry certainly wasn't above deceiving suspects that they had the goods, but he didn't think that would work with Brittany. He favored letting her tell as many lies as she wanted to tell, into the next week if Brittany was willing. "Let's give her as much rope as possible."

One of the meeting's attendees, Marybeth Ayres, was in a tricky spot: Not only she relatively new to the county, she looked so much younger than her thirty-nine years that she'd been mistaken by some outside the murder scene for one of the lululemon workers, and this was her first high-profile case in Montgomery County. But Ayres had held similar positions in Baltimore and Queens, New York. She stepped up and told the half dozen cops and commanders in the room that she'd watch the interview on the closed-circuit monitor in Gillespie's office, keep her boss informed—State's Attorney John McCarthy was on his way to New Jersey for a family funeral—and advise them as the interview unfolded. Ayres stayed silent on whether to confront Brittany, but told the detectives that if they did so, they had to first advise her of her rights to remain silent and consult a lawyer.

The meeting broke up by 9:45 A.M. Drewry knew what his bosses wanted him to do, but he wasn't sure he was going to do it.

Brittany did not strike him as someone with a natural urge to tell the truth, a force that was somewhere deep inside a surprising number of killers. Drewry had spoken with David McGill, the shoe-print expert, and knew how Brittany appeared to have deliberately and repeatedly dipped both pairs of shoes into a pool of Jayna's blood. Who does that? Someone who made the decision a week ago not to flee, but to doctor the scene, tie herself up, wait for the cops, and tell one lie after another. The biggest problem Drewry had with confronting her was that it disarmed him of two of his favorite tactics. Suspects like Brittany mixed their lies with the truth, and the longer Drewry could speak with her in a conversational tone, the closer he could get to some version of the truth. It was akin to peeling back at least the outer layer of the onion. Drewry also viewed back-and-forth conversation as the best way to fully back a suspect into a corner, which often was the only route to a confession. The veteran detective approached Ruvin.

"Let's take a walk and talk," Drewry said, leading the young detective outside to the parking lot.

"How are you doing?" Drewry asked.

"All right," Ruvin said.

"Whatever happens, we've just got to do what's best. Don't worry about what everyone else is saying. Don't worry about all the pressure. Don't worry about that stuff. We'll just play it by ear, and we'll see where it gets us."

Ruvin had been leaning toward the bosses' view on confrontation—largely because he agreed that this was their last chance with the suspect. But he remained silent. He knew how he and Drewry had succeeded in past cases by letting Drewry take the lead on the questions in the interview room, while Ruvin quietly took his notes, biding his time until Drewry gave him a natural opening to come in with an inquiry. By 10:00 A.M., the detectives were back in their squad room, waiting for Brittany.

Upstairs, shoe-print expert McGill finished the rounds of his sheep-blood experiment. He'd soaked the laces of his old sneakers and walked down a hallway covered with a roll of wide, white paper. The results were just as he and his colleague Cheré Balma had predicted: the lapping laces generated stains similar to what he'd seen in the yoga store. And by keeping the soles free of blood, he could see how these stains seemed to be dancing off on their own, independent of actual shoe prints. McGill walked downstairs to share these results with the detectives, arming them with even more information ahead of Brittany's arrival.

Just before 11:00 A.M., Drewry got word that Brittany was out front with her brother Chris and sister Marissa. "They're here, Dimitry," he called out, loud enough that other colleagues overheard. They knew how much pressure Drewry and Ruvin were under, and tried to keep them loose.

"Jim, keep your phone with you because I may have some suggestions," one called out.

"Thank you, I will," Drewry said. "As a matter of fact, I'll crank the volume all the way up."

Drewry, wearing a cream-colored sweater vest, walked to the lobby to greet Brittany and her siblings. He tried to make Chris and Marissa feel as comfortable as he could in the dumpy lobby, and brought Brittany back into the homicide unit, placing her in the same room she'd been in two days earlier. Again, he subtly eased her toward the chair in the corner, near the hidden microphone and facing the hidden camera. She wore gray lululemon workout pants and a gray zippered lululemon jacket.

"Did you want some water or something like that?" Drewry asked, holding his own cup of coffee.

"No."

"You sure?"

"Positive," Brittany said quickly, staking out a pleasant but slightly edged tone that gave a clear message: I am here to amend my story and then I'm leaving.

Ruvin walked in. Brittany greeted him softly. "Hi, Dimitry."

Drewry learned back in his chair and folded his hands behind his head. "Thanks for coming back in. In talking with Chris and Marissa, it sounds like they've finally been able to convince you, like, to go back to Seattle and stay with Chris for a while."

It was part small talk and part establishing the framework of a "noncustodial" interview, which didn't require him to inform Brittany of her rights to remain silent and consult an attorney. Drewry wanted Brittany to feel that as far as he was concerned, she was not only free to leave the interview room; she could head across the country.

"It's definitely an option," Brittany told him, assuring the detectives she didn't want that to become an obstacle to them solving a case. "I told them my only concern was being here throughout this, and if needing anything from me, I didn't want, you know, to be like unreachable. They told me that was the last thing I needed to worry about, and, if need be, I could fly back and forth. They would fly with me. They said not to worry about that."

"Okay, good," Drewry said.

Brittany spoke about how rattled she was—how she hadn't slept, how she was scared even to walk out of her basement apartment and ascend the outside stairs to Marissa's place. Brittany said she'd spoken to her brother Chris about her fears, and how that had led her to talk about what had happened Friday night. It was Chris's idea, Brittany said, for her to come in and share additional details with the detectives.

"So I'm here now," Brittany said, fumbling over a few words before coming out with it. "Prior to him sexually assaulting me and zip-tying me, they made me move her car."

"Okay," Drewry said, rolling his chair slightly back, displaying little reaction, and reaching to shut the door. He didn't want any noises interfering with the recording on this one. Drewry nodded to Brittany, hunched his shoulders, leaned forward an inch. It was an acceptance of what she just said, an invitation to keep going. Brittany did.

"They asked, they said, 'Where are her keys?' I said. 'I have no idea.' One of them punched me in my head, and made me look through her coat and her bag for them. When I finally found them, they said if I was to pass any-one and open my mouth, I can consider myself dead, and that one of them would be watching the entire time."

Brittany told them about the lot where she'd moved the car. Drewry offered one word, "Okay," followed by silence. It was one of his favorite techniques, the pregnant pause. Suspects often felt compelled to end it by saying some-thing, as Brittany did. "I remember seeing a cop, and I was just too scared to even flag him down."

Seeing a cop and not running to him for help? Maybe what really happened was that Brittany had seen Officer Justin Tierney ease his cruiser past her when she was parked in Jayna's car—and she was trying to get in front of that story, too.

Drewry asked a few more questions about Brittany moving the car, biding his time to segue into a broader discussion about the case. His tone was apologetic. "Okay, well, let's, go, ah, through it step-by-step then as far as your returning to the store then, because you might remember some other things, too." Brittany stuck to her earlier story. To help explain Jayna's movements, she took her left hand out of the front pocket of her gray lulu jacket, extended her index finger and moving it across the metal table. Nine minutes after Brittany arrived, though, her tone had shifted to exasperation. "Do I have to go through it?"

"Yeah," Drewry said, "because you left out some things, okay? So let's, like, see if you remember some other stuff."

"Left out what?"

"Well, as far as like the car thing is concerned."

"I know," Brittany said, raising the pitch of her voice, leaning back, and looking at the ceiling. "And that's the only thing."

The best detectives are also skilled con men. Judges have ruled again and again that detectives can deceive and lie during interrogations. It gave them permission to use an arsenal of tricks, ones Drewry and Ruvin had employed together in the past. They planned to use some with Brittany.

Drewry wanted to come across like he was in Brittany's corner, but that he needed some more explanations to get his superiors off his back. Ruvin wanted to eventually toss Brittany an "out," a term detectives used to tempt suspects to lie their way out of trouble, only to get into more trouble. The "out" here would be that it was somehow not really Brittany's fault for trouble that erupted inside the store; it was Jayna—she'd started a fight.

For forty minutes, the detectives kept coming back to questions about the weakest links in Brittany's story, in particular, this most recent notion that the men had sent her out, alone, to move Jayna's car, and she came back to the store anyway, even knowing that one of the men had just viciously attacked Jayna. But Brittany edged forward, trying to add a detail to fill in another hole: the black cap she must've by now realized she'd accidentally left in the back of Jayna's car. Before going out to move the car, she told the detectives, the men made her put the hat on.

"Okay," Drewry said.

"I had a hat on. It's a black hat."

"Okay. Why did they make you put the hat on?"

"I don't know."

"Well, what did they say?"

"I don't remember. I don't remember," Brittany said, raising the pitch of her voice. "Do you know how many times they hit me in my head?"

Drewry shook his head no and turned the question around. "How many times did they hit you?"

"I don't know."

Drewry leaned his chin atop his clasped hands, creating gaps of silence stretching past ten seconds. He returned to his questions about Brittany leaving the store to get Jayna's car, acting out the role of just a cog in the wheel. "Okay, people would probably ask, 'Well, why didn't you just keep on going and not go back,' you know?"

"Because I was scared for my life."

Drewry asked Brittany why she didn't flag down the cop she saw. "You know, people would probably ask stuff like that. And I guess I have to try to be able to answer that. So what's the answer to that one?"

"I was scared for my life. I mean I was scared for my life. That's all I can tell you."

Drewry got Brittany to again confirm that she had

blood on her face when she moved the car. Edging up the heat of the flame below her, Drewry asked Brittany about her three-block walk *back* to the store among late-night pedestrians. "Did they kind of look at you funny or anything like, you know, 'Whoa, what's she doing all bloody?'"

"I don't know if they saw, like I would have been more in front of them," Brittany said.

Ruvin smiled inside over Brittany's contortions. It must have been a gut-wrenching moment for Brittany, he thought, when she realized that she left behind such a telling, bloodstained clue in Jayna's car, the hat. And Drewry was returning to that subject, asking Brittany where the attackers got the hat. "I don't know," Brittany said, "maybe on like one of our mid-racks."

Drewry kept pushing on what happened inside the store. Brittany said she didn't want to go over the horrifying details yet again, even as Drewry continued to go back over them.

"And how did you fall onto Jayna, I mean, were you on your hands and your knees? Or straight down, facedown?"

"On my knees."

"Okay. Were you straddling her, or were you actually physically, like, pancaked on top of her or what?"

"He pushed me on her," Brittany said, pausing for several seconds, and turning her voice into a soft, whispering cry. "I touched her head."

Drewry's only concern about Brittany's soft cries was that they weren't being picked up by the recording equipment. In a gambit he repeated several times, Drewry pointed to his right ear and spoke of his own pretend limitations. "I understand that you're emotional, and that you're crying, okay. But with my, my hearing, and you know, and your crying, I can't hear you."

"One of my hands," Brittany said, "fell on her head before like sliding to the ground in the blood." From the detectives' point of view, Brittany played up her whimpers about having to relive what she'd seen, about how she had just wanted to come into the room that morning, give them her car-moving addendum, and leave.

"I wanted to feel better after coming here," she said.

"Well, hopefully you will, okay?" Drewry said.

"I don't," Brittany snapped.

By 11:44 A.M., nearly an hour after the interview had started, Brittany had indicated she didn't want to talk with them anymore. The detectives knew they were getting to decision time—either let her go or inform her of her rights to remain silent and get a lawyer. Drewry put his hands on the table and stood up. "Let's take a break, okay. Do you want to use the bathroom, or some water, or something like that?"

"Can I go?"

"Probably in a couple of minutes. I just need to take a break, okay."

The detectives opened the door, leaving it that way so Brittany could see into the cubicles. They took a sharp left and walked forty feet down a hall to their captain's office to strategize.

It was the same crowd as the morning. At issue was if and when to confront Brittany. Drewry still didn't want to. He advocated going back into the room and getting Brittany to agree in front of the camera that she didn't mind staying; then, ask a few more questions and see what happened.

But it meant that they should be willing to let her walk out, to see if they could go after her next week with more evidence. His commanders returned to their same point in the morning: if she leaves, she's not coming back. Go in there and confront her, they told Drewry. Ayres, the prosecutor, chipped in too, reminding the detectives they needed to advise Brittany of her rights before confronting her.

Drewry walked back to his cubicle, collecting the evidence he had to blow holes in Brittany's story. He still wasn't sure if and when he would follow his orders. He and Ruvin walked back into the interview room. Brittany sat expressionless, with her left leg looped over a chair arm.

"I just wanted to clarify a couple of things," Drewry began, getting Brittany to talk about how she may have gotten blood on her clothes. The detective saw an opening to try to evoke a feeling of guilt or sympathy.

"When he pushed you on top of Jayna, was she moving at all?"

"She moved when I fell on her, but she didn't say anything."

"Okay, did she moan or anything like that?"

Brittany softly whimpered and nodded her head yes. But like earlier that morning—and two days before—the detectives noticed that she couldn't seem to make tears come out.

"She was moaning?" Drewry asked.

More nods.

"She was probably dying, right?"

Brittany eked out crying, barely audible sentences. "I don't know. I don't know."

Drewry spent a couple more minutes asking Brittany about her clothes. Then he made a decision. Fuck it, he thought, pausing for sixteen seconds and leaning back in his chair, arms crossed.

"Brittany," Drewry began, "there comes a point sometimes when we have to break down and get everything off of our chest, okay. I know this has really been rough for you as far as, like, I'm sure that you have been going absolutely nuts for these past couple of days as far as what the cops have found out, what the cops have figured out, what the cops know."

"No, no one will tell me anything," Brittany said. "I can't even watch the news."

"Oh, I can only imagine, you know. You have got to be going absolutely nuts with worry, with fear, you got to be, got to be. And you got to tell us what really happened."

"I'm telling you."

"Because I know what really happened."

"I told you what really happened."

"No, what you have done is, you've concocted an incredible story that doesn't make any doggone sense."

"No."

Drewry lifted his right index finger. "Listen to me, okay. I've been doing this, I've been a cop for over thirty years, I've been working homicide for damned near twenty-five years, and I've seen a lot of stuff. And I've heard a lot of tales, and I've seen a lot of people—good and bad—and sometimes people get into situations way over their heads, and it's like, 'What the hell am I going to do now?' You know, 'How do I explain this? What the hell am I going to do now?'"

He paused, reaching into the back pages of his legal

pad for three printed photographs from the hospital. "I guess we can start off with the injuries that you have. They're self-inflicted."

He moved his coffee cup out of the way and arranged the photos in front of Brittany. He explained to her how superficial and straight the scratches were.

"I wouldn't do this to myself," Brittany said.

Drewry told her he didn't believe she was knocked out during the attack. Even bound up in those zip-ties, he said, she could have lowered her arms and wiggled to a phone. "Brittany, I know about the thefts. I know that Jayna found clothing in your bag and that you had been suspected of stealing."

"No," Brittany said. "Jayna did not think that I had stolen anything."

"So why did you kill her then?"

"I didn't."

"Yes you did."

"No, I didn't. I would never do that. Jayna was my friend."

Drewry told Brittany how shoe prints in the store had revealed that there were never two men inside—just the tracks made by Brittany's shoes and the store's size 14s: "You put those shoes on."

Brittany shook her head, lifted it back, and spoke in a whimpering whine. "I would never do that. Who do you think I am?"

"I think you need help, okay? And I am very, very concerned for you," Drewry said, seeing an opening. "And I think that you need to, like, really get this off your chest."

As the two went back and forth, Ruvin prepared to throw Brittany her "out." He would tell Brittany that he understood the cover-up and all, but that what he didn't get was what had actually happened.

"May I say something?" Ruvin asked, prompting Drewry to reach for his coffee cup, take a sip, and lean back—a display to Brittany that he now had all day to listen to his partner's questions.

Ruvin continued, trying to do so in the casual language of someone struggling to understand: "We deal with this kind of stuff all the time, right, and, and I can see two things that are kind of wrong with this. The second thing about, like, making up these guys, and that's very, very common, I've done it, Jim has done it . . . I can understand that, and I can appreciate that, because you're not evil enough to just, you know, do all this. But the other part is how it happened. We already know there was a fight between you and her. We just know that all the forensic evidence that we have points that there was a fight between you and her, but we just don't know why. We just don't know."

He talked of his memory of first meeting Brittany and her family. "I was just, like, Brittany is just such a nice person. Her family, I've never seen a family so loving and understanding of her. And I can't understand or believe how this thing transpired. And the only thing, the only way I can explain it, something happened between her and you, some things went down."

Ruvin had no evidence that Jayna started a fight, or any evidence there'd been much of a fight at all. Brittany had only two injuries of note: the cut to her right hand and the cut to her forehead. In all likelihood, the hand cut was accidentally self-inflicted, the result of a knife slipping in her hand. The forehead cut? Who knew? Could have been from Jayna. But Ruvin thought it was more likely a back-swing of one of Brittany's weapons or a cut she gave to herself. None of that really mattered to Ruvin right now. If he could convince Brittany to tell one more lie—that Jayna had started a fight, and Brittany only reacted to it—that would instantly do away with the masked men. Then Ruvin would give her what he termed a "reward." He'd thank her for coming clean, for doing such a hard thing, before adding, "But here's the thing . . ." And then he and Drewry could really go to work: How did the fight start? How come you weren't injured? Why didn't you stop fighting after, say, the fifth blow, the tenth blow, or the two-hundredth?

Ruvin offered his sympathy to Brittany. "It's very hard to come out and say, 'There was a fight between Jayna and me.' It's so hard. I can understand that, and I can appreciate that. But at the end, it's going to come down to, are you a good person and this bad thing happened to you?"

But Brittany wasn't biting. She wasn't even showing any expression. "I am a good person," she said.

Drewry broke in, appealing to Brittany about what her family would think.

"I understand that you're probably thinking, 'God, what are my parents going to do now? What are my parents going to think about me? How are they going to think about me? How are my friends going to think about me? What's going to happen?' You got to do the right thing, you got to get this off your chest, okay, because you're, you're going to go flat-out freaking nuts. You can't carry this weight around with you, you can't. Marissa said that like you guys had to sleep together on the couch, on the sofa, okay? Because this is tearing you up. This is tearing you up inside physically and mentally. It's got to be. For yourself and for your family, you got to tell us what happened, how it started."

Brittany pushed back, saying she wanted to go home. At one point, thinking ahead to a judge reviewing the video recording, Drewry said he couldn't stop her. But he also decided to take another break—walking out with Ruvin and leaving Brittany inside.

The detectives again walked to Gillespie's office. Everyone liked an idea Drewry and Brittany had talked about just before the break, of bringing her brother and sister into the room. The detectives would present the evidence to them. It was a terrible thing to do to them, but could prompt Brittany to offer a meaningful explanation—that there'd been a fight, she lost control of herself, something. Ayres, the prosecutor, worried that Drewry and Ruvin should have read Brittany her rights about forty minutes earlier. She insisted they do so now, adopting the language of the Montgomery County Police Department, which had an Advice of Rights form that was labeled *MCP 50*.

"You've got to MCP 50 her," Ayres said.

The detectives returned to the room, with Drewry advancing the always delicate dance of reading someone her rights—those thunderous-sounding words everyone had heard on television—without making it seem like all that big of a deal. He talked about wanting to make sure they were on the same page, that Brittany wasn't under arrest, but this was something he had to do. He told her she had the right to be silent, to consult a lawyer, that anything she said could be used against her. It was, as always, ominous sounding. But it did give the detectives a break from feeling like they were always on the edge of having to let Brittany leave. Now they could settle in for hours of more questioning. And the detectives knew that they still had cards to play. They could bring in a new detective, maybe a woman, claim to have more evidence of a fight, appeal to Brittany about what Jayna's family was going through, appeal to her about what the world would think of her. Still, unlike even some hardened, longtime cons who'd been in that same chair—men twice her size— Brittany didn't seem like someone who was going to break down and admit what she'd done. "Can I just see my sister and brother?" she asked.

"Sure," Drewry said, "Let me go get them."

Moments later, the three walked back into the room. Marissa smiled at Ruvin and took a seat. Her brother said he could stand.

"Have a seat, Chris," Ruvin said.

"You might be here for a minute," Drewry added.

"Oh, okay," Chris said.

Drewry put his hands in his front pockets and stood in the center of the tiny room. On the left side of the table sat Marissa. On the right sat Brittany and Chris.

"You guys," Drewry said, looking at Marissa and Chris, pausing, hating this, but hating what Brittany had done a whole lot more. "Let's start from the beginning, I guess."

Drewry told them about the holes in Brittany's original story about the masked men, and how she must have realized in recent days that she'd left blood in Jayna's car. So she'd decided to tell the police that the assailants had made her move Jayna's car, then come back. "That's when she came up with this story," Drewry said.

"Came up with a story?" Chris asked.

"Thank you," Brittany said in a haughty tone that effectively conveyed her feeling that at last there was another reasonable person in the room.

"No," Drewry said. "What she's saying, and it is incredible to me, that she and Jayna are inside of the store, and they're attacked by these two guys. And that Jayna is taken into the back room, or hallway, where she's bludgeoned to death, killed, possibly sexually assaulted. And that they then force her to get Jayna's car keys, and give them to her, and tell her, 'Go move Jayna's car, and then come back, and if you don't come back within ten minutes, we're going to kill you.' And that's when she walks out of the store, she sees a police car drive by, but she doesn't do anything. And then she walks down the street to Jayna's car, gets in her car, and drives three blocks away and parks her car, covered in blood by the way, because they had already forced her facedown onto Jayna, who is dead and covered in blood. And so, she gets in the car, and she drives off, parks the car, and then walks back. And this is Friday night in Bethesda, everybody's out all over the place. A black girl in Bethesda covered in blood walks back to the store, and goes back inside, so they can either rape or kill her. Does that make any sense to you?"

"None," Chris said. "Let's cut to the chase."

Drewry told them about the shoe prints. He laid the photos of Brittany's wounds on the table. Marissa was silent, covering her face with both hands. Chris picked up one of the photos. "I've been doing this a long time," Drewry said. "Those are self-inflicted wounds."

"What's your theory?" Chris asked the detective.

"Brittany killed Jayna."

"Uh-uh," Brittany protested.

"That's not possible," said Marissa. "This is not. This isn't . . ."

"Marissa, wait," Chris said. The electrical engineer picked his words carefully. He would later describe his thinking as a whirlwind of emotion, a search for some kind of objective reality. In front of him, one sister sat accused of murder and the other was falling apart. "Let's say that you're right, say Brittany kills Jayna, why does she move her car?"

"That's what we're trying to figure out, too," Drewry admitted, speculating it was part of her cover-up.

"It's not true," Brittany said matter-of-factly, turning toward Marissa, who covered her mouth, a blank look in her eyes.

Seeing Marissa's distress, Chris asked, "Can you guys take her out of here, please?"

"Sure. I'm really sorry," Ruvin said, walking Marissa into the squad room.

Marissa burst into loud sobs, hugging the nearest woman she could find, Detective Paula Hamill. "This is not my sister," Marissa told Hamill. "This is not my baby sister. I don't understand. It's like we're talking about a different person."

Back inside the interview room, Drewry explained how the zip-ties were too hidden for two intruders to find, and how they expected tests would show Brittany's saliva on the zip-tie that had been around her wrists.

Drewry told Chris that Brittany had been suspected of shoplifting.

"Chris, it's not true at all," Brittany told her brother.

Drewry reached into the back of his legal pad, placing

another photograph on the table. It showed a person facedown.

"Can I see that?" Chris asked.

"Yup," said Drewry.

Chris picked it up and stared at it. The person was wedged into a corner. Blood was spattered on the walls next to her and pooled on the floor all around her. "This is Jayna?"

"That's Jayna," Drewry said, turning his head quickly toward Brittany. "Ripped the seat of her pants to make it look like she had been raped."

Chris continued to stare at the photo. He again tried to stay analytical, tried to ask about shoe prints around the body. He wondered if Jayna had been found in a common hallway shared by other stores. No, Drewry said.

Chris sighed quietly. "Oh my . . ." His voice trailed off. He laid the photo back on the table.

Drewry and Ruvin kept it coming: the shoe prints in other parts of the store, the fake moaning for the medics. "The physical evidence knocks down everything that she tells us, everything," Drewry said.

"Chrissy, can we go?" Brittany asked.

"I don't know," Chris said, looking up at Drewry. "Can we go?"

"We're trying to make that decision right now. I don't know. I was kind of hoping that with your help that Brittany might be willing to tell us what happened and why."

"Do you want to say anything?" Chris asked his sister. She said she didn't.

Drewry asked Chris what his gut feeling was, based on what he just told him.

"My gut feeling is there was never a robbery. That never

made sense to me. I told you that," Chris said, recalling his conversation with the detectives five days earlier. "I was concerned that the assailants, there was a connection, right. Like I told you, some of the story didn't make sense. I didn't know how much of the story was things I heard in the media or what. I didn't know. You guys have the facts; I never did. There were things that didn't add up. I never addressed it with Brittany, because I figured when she wanted to talk, she would talk. I mean, something like this happens, you're not just running around, 'Hey, you know: this and this happened.' And she needed, needs to, to slowly accept what's happened, and I figured she would talk to me when she was ready, so I have tried not to assume. I told my brothers, you don't react until you have enough evidence, or enough information to make an intelligent decision. You guys have convinced yourselves that Brittany did it . . ."

"The evidence," Drewry interjected.

"The evidence has convinced you."

"I did not want to believe it at first," Drewry said.

Brittany sat silently in the corner as Chris continued.

"Naturally, I'm Brittany's brother, and I love her, and it's going to take like, either she's going to have to tell me that. She's going to have to look me in the eye and say, 'Chris, I did this, and this is why.' Because I don't, naturally, I don't want to believe it, okay? There's a lot of people that don't want to believe this."

"And that's fair," Ruvin said.

"Yeah, so that's, you can't expect me to just sit here and turn my back on my little sister."

"Absolutely," Drewry said.

"Right now, I'm confused, and I'm, I could get defensive, and I could come up with something like, 'Oh, we're in Montgomery County. This is Bethesda. They need a story, you know. They need to solve this, because people are uneasy.'"

"Yeah, and kick the—throw the—black girl under the bus," Drewry said, trying to pitch in.

"No, this isn't, I'm not saying race. It's not race. I'm thinking as a socioeconomic thing, right? You don't, nobody wants people that are afraid. There's little boutiques, and little ladies in boutiques in Bethesda saying, 'Oh my God, I'm not working at night,' things like that. And as soon as the police can restore order in the area like that, everyone's happy. I'm not saying that."

Chris asked the detectives more about their case, trying to gauge what they had. Drewry tried to turn it around, back to Brittany, saying she was the one who could say what happened. Chris moved to cut him off. He still thought he could get Brittany out of the station before they arrested her. Maybe if they couldn't get Brittany to admit anything, they couldn't charge her. He needed to stop Brittany from coming across as such a liar.

"Can I talk to her for a minute alone?" Chris asked.

"Sure," Drewry told him.

"I'm sorry," Ruvin added on the way out.

The two detectives shut the door and walked as quickly as they could to the closed-circuit monitors. In Sergeant Craig Wittenberger's office, thirty feet away, other detectives crowded inside. Someone wondered aloud what the two would say, and was told to "Shut the fuck up, shut the fuck up" so people could hear. In major crimes commander

Captain David Gillespie's office, another group gathered in front of another monitor: Gillespie, Assistant Police Chief Drew Tracy, and Marybeth Ayres, the prosecutor.

The image on the screens was grainy, but it was in color and clear enough. Chris was visible on the right, closest to the camera, sitting on a chair against the wall and facing into the room. He wore jeans and a long-sleeved T-shirt, which, when he turned a certain way, showed the physique of someone who clearly worked out. Brittany sat behind him, in a corner, facing the camera, slouched in her gray lululemon garb.

Chris turned toward his sister. "Should I ask you? Did you?"

"I don't want to talk about it here. I just want to go, Chrissy."

"Listen, listen. I don't know if they're going to let you go. You need to tell me right now. Did you do it?"

"Chrissy, I just want to go home."

"Brittany, I'm not going to fucking rat you out. But you need to tell me so I know how to talk to these guys. Because if you did it, we have to get you a lawyer to defend you."

"I just don't want to talk about it here. But I will tell you everything."

"Just nod your head if you did. Please tell me. Please," Chris said.

Brittany kept her head still.

"Chrissy, I don't want you to be disappointed in me like everyone else."

Chris was sitting in the one chair with wheels, allowing him to turn and move toward his sister. "What? What did you say?"

"I don't want you to be disappointed in me like everyone else."

"No one is disappointed in you. Brittany, we're your family. No matter what, we're going to be here for you, okay? Because everything he just told me? And I didn't look like I was convinced, but that is really fucking convincing, okay? So you're going to just tell me so that I can at least try to get you out of here. Because this is going to get a hell of a lot fucking worse."

Brittany continued to apologize to her brother.

"I'm going to ruin our whole family," she said.

"You're not going to ruin our family, okay?" Chris said. "I'll take that as a yes. Why?"

"I don't know how it happened."

Over in Gillespie's office, prosecutor Ayres couldn't believe what she was hearing. And she thought Maryland law was on her side as far as for the surreptitious recording of Brittany and her brother. The two were in a police station. How could they expect privacy? And then there was what Brittany had just said after her brother had given her a chance to explain herself. Instead of saying something like, "What are you talking about?" Brittany had said she didn't know how it happened. Ayres walked out of Gillespie's office, and ran into Ruvin, who was coming that way. "We can get a conviction off that," she told him.

Ayres and Ruvin hustled back to the monitors.

Up on the screen, Brittany was worried. "Are you sure they can't hear us, Chris?"

"I looked around for listening devices," her brother said. "There's nothing in this room. And if they did, even if they did record this, there's nothing they could use in court."

Chris asked Brittany if Jayna had accused her of shoplifting, how the fight started, if Brittany had planned out what happened. Brittany gave vague answers, even as Chris cut her off from saying too much. "Okay, stop, listen, listen. No, no, no. What we're going to do is, we're going to have to get you a defense attorney."

"I know."

"Okay, hold on. We have, we're going to have two options. One option is going to be, they could do some temporary insanity or something like that. But the problem with that is that you've talked to too many people. You've talked to counselors and people know that you're not insane, okay? So that's probably not . . ."

Ayres couldn't believe her good fortune. Down the road, if it evolved into an insanity case, she could put Chris on the stand and ask him about his sister's mental health.

"I haven't talked to anyone, Chris," Brittany said.

"No," her brother said. "I know you talked to the counselor on the phone for like forty minutes yesterday."

"No, no, no. Like maybe ten minutes if that."

Chris had already moved on. "You've talked to people," he said, searching for words, his sentences trailing off. "You've been . . . So that's not going to work. So what we're going to have to do is . . . You're going to have to be very honest with us and with an attorney mainly, and we're going to have to try to concoct some sort of plan, like she attacked you. But that doesn't look good, because you tried to cover it all up. Oh, God. Let me see if I can get you out of here, okay?"

Brittany again told her brother she was sorry, that she

hadn't been accused of shoplifting. The prospect of the personal-trainer position flashed into her head—the new job she wanted so badly.

"I damn near had a job," Brittany told her brother. "I don't know if she didn't like me. I don't know, Chris."

"So she attacked? Wait, she came to let you in, right? And then what? What did she say?"

"That she was going to like, I don't know, make sure our manager knew or something."

"Your manager knew what? That you were shoplifting?"

"But I wasn't. I didn't have anything."

"Had you stolen from that store before?"

"Never. Chris, honestly, I wouldn't. I was doing good."

Speaking barely above a whisper, Chris started to instruct Brittany on how to lie. "I'm going to tell you something. You've done it three times. When they ask you a question, you're looking down and you're looking to your left. That means you're lying, okay? If you're going to lie when you talk to them, find something in the room. See that red button? Look at that red button every time. Do not look at anything else."

Chris got up to knock on the door. He would have to move fast to get Brittany out. Ruvin came in, and he and Chris walked into another interview room. The young detective had just listened to Chris advise his sister to lie, yet he couldn't help but feel for the guy. Ruvin had a sister, too. He could see going into that kind of protective mode.

"I'm sorry you're going through this," Ruvin said.

"Hey, listen, you don't, you don't have to apologize," Chris said. "Let me say a couple of things first. You're just doing your job. I know that I told my dad when I first met you guys, that I didn't sense any ill intent. I'm not playing the race card or anything like that. What you guys put in front of me, it's, it's compelling."

Ruvin said he knew it was going to be hard on them. "I don't know what I would do in your shoes as far as believing my sister or not. And you got to do what you got to do to take care of your sister. As far as her going home tonight, the evidence against her is just overwhelming, overwhelming."

"I understand. I understand."

Ruvin said he would get Marissa. "If you can just sit tight, we'll try and bring your sister in."

Less than a minute later, another detective arrived with Marissa. She and Chris were left alone in the room, with the door closed. Ruvin scrambled back over to his sergeant's office to join the crowd watching the monitor. None of them had seen a case unfold like this, where siblings were being led in and out of the rooms, where they talked to the suspect or talked about the suspect.

"She did it," Chris told Marissa. "She told me."

"She did?"

"I never thought this," Chris said, allowing that he'd suspected Brittany was involved, but only in the sense that she knew the killers. "Oh my God, Marissa."

So here they were: alone in a dank interview room, facing the notion not just that their little sister Brittany was mixed up with crazed killers; she *was* the crazed killer. Apparently over something as stupid as shoplifting.

With an arrest seemingly imminent, Chris had a sudden jolt of terror. He realized that reporters might get to the town house—where their parents were staying—before he and Marissa had a chance to tell them what was going on. Chris took out his cell phone, called his dad, and told his parents to head over to another relative's house nearby. "You're not in danger, but right now, you guys need to leave that house, okay? When I can give you more information, I will."

He hung up and continued speaking with Marissa. "The girl accused Brittany of shoplifting and Brittany lost it. She snapped. She said, 'Chris, I don't know what happened.' Then the rest of the night she was trying to cover it up. That's why she can't sleep."

The conversations being recorded continued to amaze prosecutor Marybeth Ayres, who watched some of them while eating tacos from Chipotle that someone had brought in for lunch. She needed to update her boss. McCarthy was still in the car on the way to the family funeral. He'd earlier told his wife that the drive to New Jersey would be a nice chance for them to catch up on things. Instead, he'd spent the whole drive on the phone with Ayres, talking about what Brittany had been saying. He turned his attention to whether the conversation between Brittany and Chris would get past a judge. "Do you think it's coming in?" McCarthy asked her. "You're there. You're watching it. Will we be able to use that?"

Yes, Ayres told him.

The detectives kept shuttling Brittany's brother and sister between the two interview rooms or other waiting areas. At 1:30 P.M., Marissa asked to go see her sister. "Sure," Drewry said, leaving the two alone together. Marissa reached down to hug Brittany, who was still in her corner chair—not under arrest, not in handcuffs. "I just wanted to say I love you, honey."

"Are they going to let me go?"

"I don't think so, baby."

Marissa sat down. She covered her mouth and spoke softly: "What happened to you?"

A minute later, the door opened, Marissa was led out, and Drewry and Ruvin came back in. The older detective cut to the chase.

"Do you want to tell us why the fight started?"

"I just want to see my family, that's all," Brittany responded.

Drewry said she could, in a little bit, and played a new card, saying he had listened to what she told her brother.

"This is recorded. We all heard you when you admitted that you fought with Jayna."

"I didn't."

"Yes, you did."

The detective and suspect were both kind of right—Brittany had never directly said she fought with Jayna, but she'd implied it. Still, right now, she certainly wasn't going any further. Ruvin gave it a shot: "We just don't want you to like go down with the story, like, you're still, like, denying it to the end. And just like Jim said, this room is recorded, and even when your brother said we can't use it against you, we can, because for murders we can tape and listen for anything, okay? And we just don't want you to go down as this evil person that stays like this to the end. We know there was a fight, and now you already told Chris there was a fight, and we knew, like my gut feeling was telling me there was a fight."

Drewry chimed back in, swallowing his own true

opinion of Brittany. He was used to doing that with murder suspects, but Brittany was making it particularly tough.
She'd already ruined one good family, the Murrays, and
was in the process of possibly ruining her own. "Everybody's here to help you," Drewry said. "Nobody's going
to judge you."

He again invoked Brittany's parents: "You can be the
person your parents raised you to be. You can do this."

Brittany didn't respond, the silence passing fifteen seconds. She drew a long, deep breath. Drewry raised his
hopes, having seen the expression before, just before someone caved.

"I can't," Brittany said.

Drewry and Ruvin walked back out and huddled with the
other detectives. One thing worried them: when Chris had
been alone talking with Brittany, he'd had his cell phone
out. Had he been recording the conversation, too? They
didn't need that in the hands of a defense attorney, well
ahead of when the recordings were normally turned over.
Drewry tracked down Chris in the lobby, and got him to
return to an interview room. He told Chris the rooms were
in fact video recorded, and got right to his point.

"We know that you recorded part of the conversation
on your BlackBerry."

"No, I didn't record any of it."

"Okay, well, we're going to seize your BlackBerry and
have it examined, and then we'll give it back to you.

"Right now, okay."

Chris said he hadn't been recording anything, he was
trying to send a text to an attorney. That didn't bother

Drewry as much. He took the opportunity to both extend sympathy to Chris and work a new angle: trying to figure out if Brittany had a traumatic or psychiatric past that would become part of an insanity defense. "It's fucked up," the detective said sympathetically.

"That doesn't begin to explain the situation," Chris said.

"What do you think is in her background?"

"Listen, our whole family dropped everything they were doing to come to her aid. If any of us suspected this, we wouldn't have reacted this way."

"I mean, any kind of, like, emotional problems, before?"

"No."

"Anything?"

"We were a normal, as normal as a family gets, normal. We all make our mistakes, but no." Chris told the detective that just because he wasn't showing it didn't mean he wasn't churning inside. "Don't think that I'm not reeling. I am, okay?"

"Oh I know you are."

Chris spoke about trying to protect his family. "This is going to be a media shitstorm."

"Yeah," Drewry said. He told Chris he'd try to keep Brittany's address off paperwork he would submit as part of his charges against her. Chris appreciated the gesture, but doubted it would be possible. "This is a big case."

"Yeah, well. It sucks. I know."

As for Chris's phone, Drewry offered an alternative to confiscating it. If Chris gave him permission, he'd have someone in the squad room look at it right now to make sure he didn't record anything.

"That's fine," Chris said.

Drewry took the phone and walked out, leaving the door open. Chris could quickly sense the detectives were having trouble figuring out how to work his phone. In a surreal twist, given the circumstances, he found himself calling out technical information, saying any audio recordings in the phone would be stored where the videos are kept. Ruvin walked back in with the phone.

"It's the original Palm Pre," Chris told him. "If you hit the center button in the middle. I'll just talk you through it."

"Thank you," Ruvin said, looking down at the phone.

"Now swipe it away, push it up top, just, and yeah, that's gone, keep going with that, there you go, you can keep going. No. Up, just straight up, there you go. Keep swiping straight up, just go up here. You can just throw the app away, right."

Minutes later, Ruvin confirmed that Chris hadn't recorded anything. He gave Chris his phone back.

"I don't envy you," Drewry told him.

Minutes later, Chris and Marissa were allowed to say their final good-byes and hugs to Brittany. The detectives cleared out, hustling back to the monitor. The chances they'd hear anything useful had faded, now that they were all aware of the recordings. Still, with the volume cranked up, they heard intriguing murmurs.

"I fucked up our whole family," Brittany said.

"Don't ever say that," Marissa said.

"We're never going to judge you, you know that. We all love you," Chris said. "Your family's going to be fine, okay?"

Leaving Brittany alone in the interrogation room, Drewry and Ruvin started putting together their arrest affidavit. Nearly an hour passed. Ruvin heard a sound from the other side of the door, walked over, and opened it.

"You knocking?" he asked Brittany.

"Is anyone allowed to sit in with me?"

Ruvin said he'd see what he could do. "We're actually trying to order some pizza. I don't know if you want some?"

Brittany said she just wanted company. The detectives brought in Detective Paula Hamill, the female detective who had consoled Brittany's sister. Married to another cop and the mother of five kids, she worked a different shift, and beyond helping David McGill do his shoe-print work, she hadn't been directly involved in the case. But she had interviewed homicide suspects for nearly twenty years. The detectives thought maybe Brittany would open up to another woman. Drewry brought in some water and left the two alone.

"I met your brother and sister," Hamill said. "They're very nice. Very nice family."

"I have a wonderful family. I really do."

Hamill slowly went to work on her, talking about her kids, how Brittany, too, had been raised around a lot of brothers and sisters, and no doubt taught to tell the truth. "You've done the easiest thing already by, you know, I say, by lying. But really, it was like a defense mechanism."

Hamill told Brittany how the evidence kept leading them back to her, keying in on how the gynecological exam in the hospital hadn't corroborated her story about the wooden coat hanger: "You just had no injuries that would support that. And you know, as a chick, we, you know that, that you would have some significant type of trauma of some sort. I mean, people get trauma, or bleeding, whatever, just from having sex sometimes."

Like Drewry and Ruvin, Hamill offered Brittany an "out." "Brittany, you know what? If something, if you guys had a whatever, I don't even care, if you had an argument about stealing, money, men, women, whatever, then you know, like tell us . . . If it was something silly, you know, and it was initiated by her, then just reach in, honey."

"I'm trying," Brittany whimpered.

"I know. You know what? I know you're trying. And you know what? You can do it."

Over the course of an hour, Hamill told Brittany she was a good person, that she wasn't judging her, that everything happened for a reason, that Brittany telling right now might be the hardest thing she'd ever done—but that made it so important to do.

Hamill got Brittany to talk about going back into the store with Jayna the night of the murder. "Did you guys do anything while you were there? Smoke dope, anything like that? I mean, you guys didn't have any like sexual relationship or anything?"

Brittany shook her head no. She whimpered, mumbled, curled her legs up on her chair, lowered her head, asked Hamill if she would get hurt in jail. "Thank you for staying with me," Brittany told the detective.

At one point Hamill left, coming back with a slice of pizza. Brittany didn't eat any. Ruvin came in to join them, again trying to get Brittany to say there'd been a fight. She didn't respond. Her sobbing sounds became panting. She told Ruvin and Hamill that she wouldn't answer their questions, but she didn't want to be alone. Ruvin stayed, trying again with the notion Brittany was the only one who could explain what happened.

Drewry watched Ruvin and Hamill's gallant efforts, growing more frustrated. He figured he'd give talking to Brittany one more try, but gone was any patience, any sense that she shouldn't be treated like a killer. He had Ruvin handcuff her right wrist to the ring on the table leg. She slouched, looked at the ground.

"Brittany, we've given you every opportunity in the world to tell us what happened, how this thing started," Drewry said. "It is entirely up to you at this point as far as how people are going to see you. Are they going to see you as a cold-blooded, heartless, goddamned killer, or are they going to see you as a person that got into a situation over her head? That is entirely up to you if you're going to tell us what happened."

Brittany looked up. He told her he was going to have to call Jayna's parents about the arrest, and he would like to give them some kind of explanation of what happened. "The only person that can tell us why their daughter is dead is you. Is it because Brittany is psycho, and cold-blooded?"

"No," she sobbed.

"Or is it because they got into a fight?"

"I'm not psycho. I'm not cold-blooded."

"What are you? What happened? Who started the fight? Let's get it out. Who started the fight? Either you started it, or Jayna started it, because they're going to have to be told of the amount of injuries that Jayna had. Multiple, multiple injuries. And somebody's going to have to explain how she got those injuries. I'm trying to be nice to you, kid. Told your brother and your sister that I would do everything I could to help you. You got to help yourself. Who started it?"

Ten seconds passed.

"I didn't start it," Brittany said, looking down.

"You didn't start it?" Drewry asked. "Jayna started it?"

"Uh-huh," Brittany seemed to mumble.

"I can't hear you, baby," Drewry said, crouching down next to her. "Talk to me, put your head up and talk to me."

At one point, Brittany seemed to whimper that Jayna had started the fight. Drewry thought they might be on the verge of hearing something valuable. He reached out with his left hand to hold Brittany's right hand, still cuffed to the table leg, and stroked her hair with his right. The detective had a running joke with his colleagues about how at this point in interviews they were willing to try anything, though Drewry liked to say he stopped short of a stunt others pulled—breaking out a Bible—because it conflicted with his agnostic beliefs.

"I can't hear you, okay?" he told Brittany. "You're crying."

But all Drewry could make out were hysterical mumbles, which sounded like Brittany lamenting going off to jail. She bent further forward, her face on her knees. "Come on, baby. Lift your head up for me," Drewry said.

Brittany did, her head lobbing to her right and knocking a cup of water across the table. Ruvin pulled tissues out of a box to begin wiping it up. Drewry continued holding Brittany's cuffed right hand and right knee, begging for answers as he grew more frustrated.

"I'm sorry," Brittany said. "I can't. I just can't talk. I'm sorry. I don't want people to think I'm horrible but I can't talk anymore."

Drewry again invoked Jayna's parents, Brittany's own parents. He waited nearly ten seconds. No response. At 6:01 P.M., a little more than seven hours after Brittany had arrived at the station, it was over.

"Okay," Drewry said with a shrug. He stood up and walked out to get paper towels to help Ruvin soak up the rest of the water. Then they left together, shutting the door behind them.

The police press office sent out word that there would be a 7:00 P.M. news conference about the lululemon case. Montgomery Police Chief Tom Manger walked into the homicide unit from upstairs, congratulating the detectives and trying to figure out what he was going to say. He looked over Ruvin's shoulder as the detective typed up his affidavit to support first-degree, premeditated murder charges against Brittany.

Drewry went to a quiet area to call the Murrays, who had returned to Texas after claiming Jayna's body. Their week had been one soul-numbing task after another. One of the worst had been having to buy Jayna's gravesite. Her dad, David, never thought she would die before him, and had planned to be buried in a military cemetary in Texas with his wife, Phyllis. But at the funeral home the day after finding out his daughter was dead, David switched his plans. "The military plot can go to someone else who needs it," he told the woman selling them the gravesite, saying he needed at least six more for the rest of the family. "I'm going to be buried next to my daughter."

It was about 5:30 P.M. Texas time on Friday, March 18, 2011. David and Phyllis, their sons, and their sons' families were getting ready to leave for a visitation set for Jayna at a nearby funeral home. David's phone beeped. He answered and Drewry greeted him. "We just made an arrest," the detective said.

"That's good," David said.

"There's more to it," Drewry said, going on to say how the case had taken a turn, how they had charged the purported survivor with murder.

David exhaled a long sigh. His hand started to shake. He thanked Drewry, hung up, and told the others. No one knew what to say. Jayna's brother Hugh called one of Jayna's friends, and word quickly spread, reaching those already on their way to the funeral home—including Chasity Wilson, Jayna's friend from Halliburton, whom Jayna had been so helpful to during her divorce, and who she'd encouraged to return to college. In the years since, Chasity had earned a degree in business and moved into a new house with her kids. During the previous week, even as Chasity had been rocked by Jayna's murder, she'd been worried about the purported survivor. "That poor girl was laying there all night," she had told her coworkers. "How is she going to go on?"

Now in her car, hearing news of the arrest, Chasity burst into tears. She pulled off the freeway, onto a road with less traffic where she could stop her car. That the police in Maryland were saying the killer knew Jayna and tried to cover it up made it all the worse, if that was possible. Chasity sat behind the wheel, shaking as she wept, eventually composing herself to start driving again to the visitation.

The Murrays arrived at the funeral home. Hugh asked the director if he had a computer on which they could watch the news conference, which he figured might be streamed live on Washington, D.C., television stations. In short order, the Murrays and a few friends were inside a small room, watching the news conference begin.

"Tonight we have arrested Brittany Norwood," Montgomery's police chief said, "for the murder of Jayna Murray." His statement was brief, and gave the vague possible motive as "a dispute between the two women."

Reporters asked follow-up questions, but the chief didn't want to go into many details of the case. David and Phyllis Murray knew that hundreds of their friends and family members were outside in the main room, including David's best friend, who had come all the way from a drilling site in China. The Murrays left the small room to greet them, even as the press conference continued. The couple stood next to Jayna's closed casket, receiving words of comfort from those lined up. By then, word had spread among the crowd about the coworker's arrest.

After a week of horror, the Murrays were paralyzed by a new question: why?

WHY?

CHAPTER TWENTY-FOUR

Neuropsychiatry

With Brittany Norwood's arrest for the murder of Jayna Murray, the fears that had gripped Bethesda vanished, replaced by heightened fascination over the case. Residents devoured news accounts describing Brittany's respected, successful family; her lack of a criminal record; and the possibility that the whole thing started over stolen clothes.

At Parker's restaurant, a few doors down from the lululemon athletica store, customers were more interested in Brittany than they'd been with the infamous "Beltway Snipers," who'd killed ten people in the region nine years earlier. "This isn't two clowns from out of town," the group of regulars was telling owner and bartender Matt Touhey. "It's the girl down the street."

Three days after the arrest, Jayna's parents appeared on *Good Morning America*, sitting on an interview sofa in the show's New York studio. For much of the three-and-one-half-minute segment, David and Phyllis Murray smiled, recalling their daughter's outgoing, spirited nature. David even summoned up some humor, saying he was being "as objective as a father can get." But when he and Phyllis were asked about Brittany Norwood's relationship with Jayna, their faces went blank.

"Jayna never mentioned her," Phyllis said. "There were always people that she would have dinner with and go to movies with, but Brittany's name was never mentioned."

The arrest tore through Brittany's family as well. News accounts presented a devastating case against her. Her siblings—Chris and Marissa—had been in that interrogation room, had heard the detectives lay out evidence against their sister. The Norwoods couldn't help asking themselves: Could this really have happened? And if so, was there something we missed? Reporters called, rang doorbells, stuffed business cards into doorjambs next to the cards of their colleagues. The Norwoods stuck together, publicly saying nothing but privately researching and calling several of the best defense attorneys in Maryland. As Chris had promised Brittany just before she was taken to jail: "No matter what, we're going to be here for you."

One of the lawyers they reached, Doug Wood, enjoyed a particularly aggressive reputation in the courtroom. "I think the system works best when it's adversarial," he had once told the *Washington Post* in a profile posted on his website. The story told of Wood cutting his teeth in the rough-and-tumble world of Washington, D.C., courts in the 1980s before going on to nearby Prince George's County, in Maryland, where he won five murder acquittals over a two-year streak.

"When I was younger, I tended to trust that police got the right guy and used the right process in finding him," Wood said in the profile. "The more you see and hear, the more you learn you just can't trust what they say. You have to look at every case with skepticism; that's the only way to do it." And Wood tried not to get chummy with his opponents. "I don't have a cordial relationship with the police, and I like that," he said.

Outside of court, the slim, six feet one, fifty-nine-year-old Bethesda resident, who wore his wave of silver hair about an inch longer than most lawyers, was friendly, and quick with a joke. He had an equally skilled law partner in Chris Griffiths, who in 2007 had won acquittal for a murder suspect in Montgomery County—the first time in more than a decade that Montgomery prosecutors had outright lost a first-degree murder case. The Norwoods hired them.

As is typical early in cases, Wood and Griffiths didn't know exactly what the police had. But they could see three apparent pathways ahead, none of them easy.

For one, they could embrace Brittany's story about the masked men and assert that their client had nothing to do with Jayna's death. The problem here, at least according to early media reports, was that Brittany had left evidence tying her to the crime and the cover-up. And to hear the prosecutors tell it, Brittany had lied to detectives hundreds of times during video-recorded interviews. Still, there often were ways around such challenges.

For instance, what if the cops hadn't properly handled all those tools, clothes, and other clues they'd collected? Wood and Griffiths could raise issues about mishandled evidence, and the possibility of blood transfer. Besides, could the prosecutors really use bloodstains to re-create Brittany's movements in the store? Might not all that evidence be explained by Brittany's fending off a furious, chaotic attack? As for the lies she'd allegedly told the detectives, they knew how detectives were forever playing games to get around reading suspects their rights to remain silent and contact a lawyer. Brittany's words would mean nothing if Wood and Griffiths could get the interrogations ruled unconstitutional and excluded from evidence.

The second path was based on the dramatic differences in sentencing for different categories of murder. Under this strategy, Wood and Griffiths would concede that Brittany killed Jayna, but assert that she hadn't done so in a "willful, deliberate and premeditated" fashion, the elements of first-degree murder. The number of injuries to Jayna, if initial news accounts were accurate, would make this tough going—but what if Jayna had attacked Brittany first, causing Brittany to flash into an uncontrolled rage? And what if they could show that Jayna received at least some of her injuries by striking Brittany? The goal here would not be exoneration, but a conviction for second-degree murder and Brittany's release from prison within fifteen years—when she'd be forty-three, still young enough to make a life. First-degree murder likely meant a life behind bars.

The final option was an insanity defense, known in Maryland as "not criminally responsible." In taking this route, the defense lawyers would likely concede that Brittany had killed Jayna, but would contend that she had an underlying mental disorder that made her unable to tell right from wrong. The challenge here was twofold. First, if evidence showed that Brittany had tried to cover up the murder, it was likely she knew it was wrong. Second, she apparently had never undergone mental-health treatment. But Brittany had said she'd suffered two concussions while playing soccer in college. Wood and Griffiths knew just whom to call: Dr. David Williamson.

Williamson graduated with academic awards from the University of Edinburgh, then went on to Johns Hopkins Hospital, in Baltimore, and launched a dazzling career exploring how traumatic brain injuries could induce "neurobehavioral" complications. He ran a private practice specializing in the role of brain illness in criminal and legal matters. For six years, he served as an attending psychiatrist at Maryland's maximum-security hospital for the criminally insane. Killers who were sent there received treatment and, in some circumstances, were released back into society.

Williamson had gained international acclaim in his position as medical director at the traumatic brain injury unit at Bethesda's National Naval Medical Center, a temple of American medicine where U.S. presidents went for checkups and treatment. Williamson and his colleagues used advanced brain imaging, behavioral therapy, and combinations of medications to treat soldiers injured in Afghanistan and Iraq. He had briefed Congress and the president on the effects of traumatic brain injury, known as TBI.

Of course, colliding with an opposing soccer player or "heading" the ball too many times didn't bear comparison to being blown up by a roadside bomb. But the idea that sports injuries could induce behavioral changes was at least plausible. As it turned out, soccer players were suffering concussions in large numbers. In a 2007 paper published in the *Journal of Athletic Training*, researchers estimated that high-school girls who played soccer sustained 29,167 concussions a year, often from head-to-head collisions, and college soccer players, on average, were apt to sustain one concussion in every 556 games they played. That was in the same ballpark as college football players, who were apt to sustain one concussion in every 331 games they played, according to the paper.

"I am writing to request that Dr. David Williamson be permitted to have a contact visit with my client, Brittany Norwood," Wood wrote seven days after Brittany's arrest. The next day, on Saturday, March 26, 2011, one of the world's leading experts on brain trauma and behavioral changes pulled up to the county jail in the sleepy Clarksburg community, twenty-two miles north of the yoga store.

CHAPTER TWENTY-FIVE

Murders in Montgomery

Charging someone with murder is one thing. Proving it is another. Leading that effort, from the time that Brittany Norwood was charged, was Montgomery County State's Attorney John McCarthy. Fifty-nine years old, he'd grown up in a neighborhood in New Jersey near Philadelphia, and had come to the Washington area by virtue of a baseball scholarship to Catholic University, where he learned firsthand the career ceiling of five-foot-eight catchers. McCarthy graduated college, got a job teaching social studies at a local high school, then put himself through law school at night and joined the State's Attorney's Office as a line prosecutor in 1982. He took on tough cases, bided his time, and in 2006 ran as a Democrat for the elected position that headed up the office. McCarthy won by a landslide, and four years later was unopposed in his reelection.

His morning newspaper-reading routine reflected his passion for sports and his skills as a politician. International news? Reports from the White House? Local news?

In a pinch, they could all be passed over as he read deep into the sports section for the box scores of local high school football, basketball, and baseball games. He scanned for Montgomery County results, arming himself with details to deploy in the halls of the nine-story Montgomery County Circuit Courthouse. "Before we get to that case you were asking me about," McCarthy might say, "let's talk about what's really important. I saw your daughter had fourteen points the other night."

McCarthy worked from a corner office on the fifth floor of the courthouse, though his office felt less of a legal sanctuary than a reflection of his affection for family, sports, and his Irish Catholic heritage. There were photographs of his wife, Jeanette, their four children, and their first grandchild. There were trophies from recreational softball leagues, a row of baseball caps from the area's top Catholic high schools, a Philadelphia Eagles helmet. There were two unopened bottles of Jameson Irish Whiskey, a black-and-white photo of John Kennedy, and a color shot of himself standing arm in arm with Maryland Democratic Governor Martin O'Malley and President Bill Clinton.

Prosecuting high-profile murder cases was nothing new to McCarthy, who'd done so many he'd long considered writing a book titled *Murders in Montgomery*. The cases McCarthy was talking about descended to depths of depravity that amazed him. One chapter might recount the story of onetime Motown recording engineer Lawrence Horn, who stood to inherit $1.7 million dollars upon the deaths of his ex-wife and eight-year-old son, who had been awarded a civil judgment after a hospital mishap left him a quadriplegic. So Horn hired a man named James Edward Perry, who purchased a pair of how-to books titled

Hit Man and *How to Make Disposable Silencers* and read them carefully, then slipped into the former Mrs. Horn's house in Silver Spring, quietly and fatally shot her and the boy's overnight nurse in their heads several times with a .22-caliber rifle—including one round each into one of their eye sockets, like one of the books said—and then smothered the boy by using one hand to cover his mouth and nose and the other hand to cover the tracheotomy opening in his throat. Another chapter could cover Bruman Alvarez, a handyman who tied up and raped a fifteen-year-old girl inside a Potomac home where he was working. A short time later, when his boss arrived, Alvarez took him out with a hammer and a knife. Then the girl's father and two sisters came home. Alvarez killed them all before returning to the bound girl and stabbing her to death. And what about Samuel Sheinbein? The seventeen-year-old killed another teenager; went to Home Depot to buy a Makita circular power saw, propane tanks, and trash bags; returned to the garage; sawed off the corpse's arms and legs; and torched the remaining part of the body. A more recent entry would be Renee Bowman, who'd adopted two children through a government program that paid her to raise them. She then suffocated the girls and stuffed them into a chest-style freezer under ice cubes and packaged meats, where they remained for two years while she continued to collect her checks. "By killing the children, keeping them literally on ice," McCarthy had said in his closing arguments, "the money continued to flow."

In recent years, he'd become more of an administrator, but he still prosecuted one or two murder cases a year. He'd assigned himself the yoga store case in the opening hours, when it looked like a search for two masked men, but it had quickly taken shape as among the most violent, bizarre, and closely followed that he'd ever seen.

In the days after Brittany Norwood's arrest, McCarthy learned that defense attorneys Doug Wood and Chris Griffiths were representing Brittany. McCarthy didn't know either well personally, because they practiced primarily in neighboring Prince George's County. But he certainly knew about Griffiths's 2007 murder acquittal in Montgomery. "Came in here and fucking walked a guy," McCarthy told a colleague. To learn more about Wood, McCarthy spoke to prosecutors who'd squared off against him, hearing again and again to get ready for anything. "Watch out for the other shoe," said McCarthy's deputy, John Maloney, who used to work in Prince George's, "because it's going to drop."

McCarthy knew the three options open to Wood and Griffiths: stick with Brittany's masked-men story, go for second-degree murder and the shorter prison term, or claim criminal insanity. To attack any of those defenses, McCarthy needed to learn exactly what happened inside that store.

He knew the blood drops and spatter could help recreate the fight—or the attack. There was a science to bloodstain-pattern analysis, complete with conferences and research papers. By measuring the width and length of the drops and applying principles of physics and trigonometry, forensic scientists could track the blood backward, determining where the blood came from and how it got there. On the witness stand, those guys could be great, as captivating to jurors as if they'd climbed into an episode of *CSI–Montgomery County*. McCarthy had a favorite blood-spatter expert, William Vosburgh, a top forensics official for the D.C. police department. McCarthy reached for his phone.

It was 6:30 P.M. on a Tuesday night when Vosburgh made his way to the back of the yoga store, still locked and under the control of the Montgomery Police Department. He was met by four of the key players in the investigation—Detectives Dimitry Ruvin and Jim Drewry and Sergeant Craig Wittenberger—and shoe-print expert David McGill. They all wanted to slip in through the back because they knew reporters were still making regular rounds in the front of the store to try to catch people going in and out. Vosburgh knew the outlines of the case, but asked the others not to tell him too much as they walked him through the four sections of the store: the narrow rear hallway, the back stockroom, the fitting area, and the main sales floor up front. In these opening minutes, Vosburgh wanted to form his own impressions.

Vosburgh hadn't always wanted to be a forensic scientist. After studying chemistry in college, he went to dental school and started a practice in 1981. But he soon grew to hate the monotony, the screaming kids—feeling so beat down by 1987 that he went to see his physician, who diagnosed him with acute stress and prescribed two weeks off. Vosburgh took them and felt so much better that he took two more, then two more. Then he simply walked away from the profession for good. In need of a job, he got one as a chemist evaluating drugs seized by police in a county just south of Baltimore. That led to other forensic assignments, promotions, and eventually his current post in the D.C. forensics lab.

Inside the yoga store, what struck Vosburgh about the main sales floor, fitting area, and stockroom—particularly compared to the chaotic mess in the rear hallway—was the decided lack of blood spatter. Yes, he saw lots of bloody shoe prints, a bloody floor in one of the bathrooms, and blood droplets scattered about. None of that told him much about the assault. But one clue caught Vosburgh's attention—the partial, bloody palm print on the wall near where a television had fallen. He studied it closely, and learned that tests were pending that could confirm that it was made by Brittany or Jayna. "That's really important," he said.

Vosburgh and the others returned to the rear hallway and shut the purple door behind them. The hard, gray floor was stained red with blood, and all along a three-sided corner defined by the closed door, the back wall, and the metal shelving unit, Vosburgh saw dense, saturated blood spatter just above the floor. Higher, and near his head to the right, he saw several tiny drops of blood. Upon close inspection, they looked like ovals with tiny tails, and they formed an arc. It was the classic sign of "cast-off," droplets that fly from a blood-covered weapon as an assailant draws it back. "Kind of what I was looking for," Vosburgh noted.

Bending over, he studied more concentrated spatter about four feet from the floor, noting additional "cast-off" arcs. He also noted "impact" droplets, which result when an assailant pounds a weapon onto a hard, bloody surface, such as a skull. The pattern was clear: the lower Vosburgh went, the more spatter—the beating was turning into a massacre. These drops were perfect circles, meaning the blood hit the wall at a 90-degree angle at the same height as Jayna's skull.

Vosburgh looked to his left, at the shelving unit. The lowest shelf was only twenty-two inches off the ground. Vosburgh wondered if they'd find impact spatter on the bottom of that shelf. "I need to look at the underside of this," he said to the others, bending down to get a better look. What he saw there, in his mind, confirmed it: the beating had continued after Jayna was flat on the ground.

The next day Vosburgh was on the phone with McCarthy, reporting what he had seen. He had to couch his conclusions—more analysis of the spatter photographs was needed, he wanted to compare his findings with McGill's shoe-print work, DNA results were pending, and he wasn't sure where the altercation had started. But some things seemed clear to him. At some point, Jayna tried to make a run for it out the rear, emergency door and got close enough to leave blood on the handle. But Brittany pulled her back, trapping her in that corner. She started beating Jayna while they were standing, then continued as Jayna fell to the ground—causing blood to bounce upward from her skull onto the underside of the low shelf. "There's significant blood spatter from the ground level, going up," Vosburgh told the prosecutor.

McCarthy was optimistic about how this would look to a jury asked to convict Brittany of first-degree murder. Yes, maybe Brittany's attorneys could argue that the first few strikes had been leveled without much thought, but the longer she'd gone on, the more Maryland's definition of premeditation played against her. It was something the prosecutor could cite by memory. "Premeditated means that the defendant thought about the killing and that there was enough time before the killing, though it may only have been brief, for the defendant to consider the decision whether or not to kill and enough time to weigh the reasons for and against the choice."

And there was more, Vosburgh told McCarthy.

It had to do with additional "cast-off" blood-spatter patterns he'd spotted in the back hallway—about four feet off the ground, to the left and right of where Jayna's body had been. They suggested that at some point, Brittany had changed from an up-and-down pounding to a back-and-forth slashing—almost as if she was trying to disfigure Jayna. McCarthy thought about Jayna's autopsy photos— wondering how many he'd be allowed to show the jury—as Vosburgh told him how evidence on the bathroom floor eroded Brittany's claim of masked assailants. The bloodstains looked smeared. Vosburgh said that after the murder, Brittany probably had taken a shirt or a towel, dipped it in Jayna's blood, carried it to the bathroom and created the bloodstain. It even looked diluted, as if she used water to increase it.

"The story of the outside intruders, it just doesn't add up," Vosburgh told the prosecutor.

Vosburgh's findings lessened the chances Brittany's attorneys would use a defense that stuck to her original story. So did continued work over at the police department. There was David McGill's shoe-print analysis. And there was follow-up work Ruvin had done behind the yoga store. He'd been able to uncover two men who matched the description of the two men dressed in black seen on the surveillance videotape from outside the back of the Apple store, just after the time of the murder. The detective had set up in the parking lot in his unmarked car at 10:00 P.M. on a Friday night, and sure enough, a little past 11:00 P.M., two men, dressed in black, walked right by the back door of the yoga store. Ruvin went to question the men, showing them photographs from the surveillance camera. The men were nervous, and spoke only broken English, but said they were kitchen workers at a restaurant several doors away. Ruvin returned to their restaurant the next day, with his laptop, and showed the surveillance video to one of the kitchen workers. Yes, that is me and my coworker, the guy told Ruvin, adding that they were walking away from the restaurant after their shifts had ended, and that one of them was carrying a backpack. To Ruvin and McCarthy, that loop was closed—there was an explanation for the video if it came up at trial.

The thought of Brittany's lawyers advancing a second-degree murder defense still worried McCarthy, however. All he had to do was look back at three Montgomery murders in which Vosburgh had testified. In the case of Robert Lucas, who was accused of breaking into a church rectory and repeatedly stabbing Monsignor Thomas Wells, Vosburgh told jurors that blood spatter on a wall had started at standing height and continued downward as the priest fell to his death. Two years after that, Vosburgh had been brought in for the murder trial of Dr. Zakaria Oweiss, a popular obstetrician whose wife, Marianne, had been found in their basement, bludgeoned to death with the hard rubber mallet the couple used to tamp down the tarp over their swimming pool. Citing blood spatter on the shin of one pants leg and the front thigh of the other,

Vosburgh testified that Oweiss had kept swinging the weapon as he dropped to one knee while his wife fell to the floor. In a 2008 case, detectives were able to show that an ex-U.S. Army soldier, Gary Smith—who had served as an elite Ranger in Iraq—pulled up to his apartment building, loaded a revolver, and climbed a set of stairs to his apartment, where his roommate, fellow ex-Ranger Michael McQueen, sat watching television. Vosburgh testified that blood spatter from a single shot to McQueen's head indicated Smith had been right next to him when the fatal shot was fired. Yet in all three of those cases, jurors found no premeditation and returned verdicts of second-degree murder. And the verdict in Smith's case was later overturned because of a witness-testimony issue. Smith was given a new trial and convicted of involuntary manslaughter and use of a handgun in the commission of a felony. McCarthy didn't want to accept such a verdict in the yoga store case. He was thinking not only of Jayna's family, whom he was getting to know, and all the people who had worked on the case and were counting on him. There was also his political future.

In late 2010—months before the murder occurred—McCarthy had begun weighing a 2014 run for attorney general of Maryland, the top law enforcement official in the state. The post could set him up to run for governor in 2017 or 2021. Yes, the ever-increasing media attention on this case could be very good publicity, but that same media attention had also already cemented the image among voters that Brittany was guilty of the worst kind of premeditated murder. A verdict that freed her in fifteen years would hardly play well on the campaign trail.

Although McCarthy wasn't the youngest person to

consider an extended run in the upper echelon of Maryland politics, he also cheated age every day, following the exercise regime of a twenty-five-year-old. Lunch hours meant a quick drive to the county's police-academy training gym. Some days it was a forty-minute run on the treadmill while speaking to other lawyers on his phone. Two days a week, it was five-on-five basketball with cops. Every Sunday morning, in a park behind his house, he played quarterback in a standing game of touch football with his buddies, a routine that one morning left him with two cracked ribs, courtesy of a blitzing prison guard. And he still taught, giving criminal-justice lectures at a local college two nights a week. McCarthy turned his attention to the bloody palm print. Tests confirmed that it matched Jayna's left palm, supporting one of Vosburgh's theories: Brittany had first struck Jayna in the rear stockroom or the fitting area, causing blood to soak into Jayna's hair but not fall to the floor; Jayna instinctively reached up to her head as she pitched forward, catching herself by slamming her palm into the wall. The early DNA results also looked encouraging. McCarthy read a report about the bloodstains found inside Jayna's car and on the brim of the hat in the back of the car. The prosecutor took notes, using the Greek delta as shorthand for the word *defendant*: "Black hat, interior driver side handle, gear shift—All Δ." McCarthy also noted that although some of Jayna's DNA was also found in the car, Brittany herself had said she had gotten Jayna's blood on her. "Some Jayna in her car too. Okay," McCarthy wrote.

As much as he'd wanted quick DNA results before the arrest—to make sure the detectives had the right person—the prosecutor now wanted to slow the process down. He was sure Brittany was the killer. But of the hundreds of pieces of evidence, the county's crime lab could only test a limited number of additional spots, due to requests from other cases. For two days, McCarthy, Ayres, and the detectives met with a DNA analyst to decide what to test. They also recognized how certain results could work against them, such as the palm print that had been confirmed as Jayna's on the wall. McCarthy already seemed to have enough evidence to tell jurors that Brittany had struck Jayna on her head, causing Jayna to grab the wound with her hand as she stumbled into the wall, leaving the print. So why test that print for DNA? If the results came back as Brittany's blood, that could just confuse matters. In the end, the group decided to concentrate tests on sections of the hammer, rope, and wrench found near Jayna's head; sections of the inside of the shoes Brittany appeared to have worn as part of her cover-up; and various parts of a serrated bread knife found in the kitchenette area.

McCarthy knew that the more weapons he put in Brittany's hands, the more likely he could prove premeditation. Suppose she started with a hammer, switched to a wrench, then a rope. Each time she rearmed herself, she would have had to pause, giving herself time to think about what she was doing. Meanwhile, at the forensics-autopsy lab in Baltimore, Dr. Mary Ripple was having trouble matching all the photographs of Jayna's injuries with photographs of the possible weapons found at the crime scene. She called Ruvin and said she wanted to drive down to look at the tools in person. Ruvin called McCarthy and invited him and the assistant prosecutor on the case, Marybeth Ayres, to come to police headquarters.

In nearly thirty years of homicide prosecutions, McCarthy had never heard such an offer from a medical examiner—and he was happy to accept. He and Ayres joined detectives Ruvin, Drewry, and Wittenberger, and two forensic pathologists, Ripple and Kristin Johnson, around a table at the homicide unit, where Ripple went over some of her preliminary findings. Her final report, which would total almost thirty pages, said that Jayna had no signs of drugs or alcohol in her system. She had suffered at least 331 pummeling, cutting, and stabbing injuries, including at least 152 to her head. She had 105 injuries to her hands and arms, a clear indication she had been trying to block the attack. Simple multiplication revealed an astounding ordeal: if the assailant had struck once every second, the attack would have lasted about five and one-half minutes. A more likely scenario, particularly if the attacker had to pause for a break or to switch weapons, was one strike every three seconds. Nearly seventeen minutes.

Tests on Jayna's brain showed deep bruises, the kind typical of car-crash whiplash victims, which suggested the killer wielded an instrument that was heavy but could be swung with great velocity.

Ripple and Johnson pulled out their autopsy photos, along with rulers and calipers. Drewry and Ruvin cut open evidence boxes and bags and spread their carefully sealed contents neatly on the table—hammer, wrench, screwdriver, Buddha statue, rope, and several small box cutters. Looking at the autopsy photographs, Ripple quickly matched a series of tiny, circular pounding wounds to the side of the adjustable wrench, just as she'd hypothesized at her lab in Baltimore. She also matched rounded, crushing injuries to Jayna's skull to the hammer. The slashing injuries to Jayna's face seemed to match the box cutters.

What Ripple couldn't find was the weapon that had inflicted a catastrophic series of straight-lined gouges in Jayna's skull and forehead. "I need something with some weight behind it," she said. "What about that Buddha?"

The detectives handed over the two-pound statue, with its square seven-inch-by-four-inch base. But the edges didn't jibe with the wounds. There were other still-mysterious wounds as well, shaped like Ls, as if delivered with a club with some kind of right-angle attachment on the end. The doctors drove back to Baltimore.

Despite their not having matched all the wounds to weapons, for McCarthy, it had been a fruitful session. He knew how to present murder weapons dramatically at trial to jurors. But he still didn't have a complete accounting of exactly how Jayna was killed, and he could imagine a skilled attorney like Wood cross-examining Ripple: "So you really don't know what caused all these injuries, do you, Dr. Ripple?"

McCarthy was certain that Brittany's lawyers were exploring their third option, an insanity defense. "Let's see who they're bringing into the jail to see her," he told Ayres.

He got his answer simply by asking the jail to provide Brittany's visitation requests and logs. McCarthy scanned them for doctors he knew from previous cases. He didn't see any familiar names, but he caught an unfamiliar one: Dr. David Williamson. McCarthy looked him up, and saw articles detailing world-renowned work on behavior problems caused by brain trauma. *Uh-oh*, McCarthy thought.

Next up—and on this score it didn't matter what defense Brittany's lawyers chose—the prosecutor needed to learn more about both Brittany and Jayna, their relationship, and their interactions on the night of the murder. The lead detectives, Drewry and Ruvin, already had interviewed three of the women's coworkers, so McCarthy and his assistants popped the interview DVDs into their computers. The images were incongruous—attractive, ambitious young women in designer fitness clothes seated in the dank interrogation rooms, at worn metal tables with little rings for attaching handcuffs.

One of the lululemon coworkers, Eila Rab, told detectives that she and Jayna had bonded over academics—how she had completed her MBA and Jayna was about to. Eila also knew Brittany well enough to hang out with her after work. "This whole thing is just unreal to me," she told the detectives. "When I first found out that she had been charged, I just couldn't piece it together. Because as much as I want to believe I know Brittany, I don't."

Eila said she had never considered Brittany violent or even aggressive. "She never raised her voice. When she laughed, it was a lighthearted laugh."

Another coworker said the same. "She was so normal," Chioma Nwakibu told Drewry. "She was really friendly. She just carried herself in such a way that you'd never think that she would be stealing or anything like that."

The lululemon staffers said Brittany and Jayna weren't close, largely because Brittany had only worked at the store for six weeks. None of the staffers had picked up any hints of trouble between them.

McCarthy and Ayres also started to interview those who knew both women. People talked about Jayna's knack for imparting confidence and ambition to others. "She changed my life," Courtney Kelly told the prosecutors. Rachel Oertli, the store manager, ticked off a series of characteristics that, to McCarthy, encapsulated what a half-dozen other people had told him about Jayna. "Intelligent," the prosecutor wrote in his notes. "Sassy attitude. Highly motivated. Disciplined. Never late. Honest, always."

The picture of Brittany was more complicated. McCarthy read detectives' paperwork and notes about her years at Stony Brook University. "Known to steal from other athletes . . . Stole from friends . . . Pathological liar," Captain David Gillespie wrote after he'd fielded a call from a classmate. A report from the Stony Brook campus police described a fellow student telling officers that her ATM card, bank statement, and account funds had come up missing just days after Brittany had been in her room. It was unclear from the report how the campus police had followed up, or whether they had had enough information to open a formal investigation. McCarthy learned that soccer teammates accused Brittany of stealing money and clothing, and at one point, Brittany admitted to stealing $20.

Over at the homicide unit, Ruvin had started to find traces of Brittany on the Internet. A high-end hairstylist in Washington—the same one Brittany had given last-minute excuses for cancellations—posted a comment on a blog called *Miss A* regarding a photo of Brittany. The stylist noted that the photo had been taken just after she'd done Brittany's hair, with imported hair and a full weave, but that when the time came to pay, Brittany "claimed that someone in the salon had stolen her money out of her wallet." Despite assurances from Brittany that she would return later to pay, she never did. "After doing Brittany's hair for about four or five years and developing a close relationship with her, I never expected this. She seemed to be a very nice and determined young lady with a huge future," the stylist wrote.

McCarthy also looked into Brittany's life as she moved to Washington, D.C., reviewing the restraining order that her ex-boyfriend, dentist Maury Branch, had filed against her. He called Maury, who wanted to help. The dentist said the two dated for more than a year, but he'd had trouble getting to know her. First Brittany told him she'd graduated from college. Then she said she didn't, because of tuition debts. Then she said it had been because of problems with the soccer coach. Maury also told McCarthy that while he and Brittany were together, $1,000 in cash had gone missing from his house, something he'd initially blamed on a cleaning woman.

"Did she ever say anything about concussions?" McCarthy asked.

"Yes."

"Migraines?" McCarthy followed up, anticipating the kinds of evidence the defense lawyers might be looking for. Chronic migraines were one of the symptoms of athletes who'd suffered bad concussions.

"No," the dentist answered.

The prosecutor tracked Brittany's employment record and tried to get to the bottom of what happened at the lululemon athletica store in Georgetown, where Brittany was fired and rehired. It was murky, with each side still claiming to be right. In McCarthy's mind, supervisors suspected Brittany of stealing but used Brittany's end-of-the-year abuse of "Shop Night" as the technical reason to fire her. And a pattern in Brittany's past was taking shape: dustups rarely stuck to Brittany, and when they did, she could almost always talk her way out of trouble.

Also emerging was the extent of Brittany's dual life. One of the starkest examples to McCarthy was the text messages and Internet browsing histories he was shown that had been lifted off the iPhone Brittany left in the store. Brittany visited "Sugar Daddy" websites. The text messages showed Brittany discussing what to McCarthy were clearly prostitution services: "Just a younger woman with goals/dreams and could use financial assistance," Brittany had written, describing herself to a man in Virginia she met on Craigslist.

Another example came when McCarthy's office researched the lineage of two plastic subway fare cards also found in the store. McCarthy knew that most users added money to the cards via credit card. He subpoenaed the Washington-area subway system for records connected to the numbers on the bottom of the cards. The first fare card, found in a pocket of Brittany's jacket, was traced back to Jayna. That actually matched part of Brittany's account of what happened the night of the murder; Brittany said that after she and Jayna looked in vain for Brittany's wallet, Jayna gave Brittany her fare card to get home. The second card, which had been found on the floor of the stockroom where Brittany's wallet was found, traced back to a group called HIPS, or Helping Individual Prostitutes Survive. An intern in McCarthy's office called HIPS, where an official said they distributed the fare cards as part of an outreach program so prostitutes could get to doctors' offices or treatment programs. The official said HIPS didn't keep records of who received the cards, ending that trail.

To McCarthy, the card was more evidence Brittany had gotten into prostitution. Although he doubted a judge would allow him to present either the texts or the HIPS card to the jury, McCarthy wondered whether Brittany's secret life was a reflection of her character—or something that shaped it. He and Ayres talked about it. Did Brittany get a thrill out of keeping secrets? Did they wear her down? Was it a combination of the two?

The prosecutors watched recorded interviews of Brittany talking to Drewry and Ruvin, looking for more people they might want to question. One individual stood out: Brittany's brother Chris Norwood, who had been at the station the day Brittany was arrested, and who detectives had allowed to speak alone with Brittany so they could eavesdrop on the conversation. Several times, according to the video recording, Chris asked Brittany if she did it. Brittany never really said yes—and never really said no.

"Chrissy, I just want to go home," she'd told him, later adding: "I just don't want to talk about it here."

A short time later, as seen on the video, the detectives arranged for Chris and his sister Marissa to be alone in the room. "She did it," Chris told Marissa. "She told me."

However dramatic that exchange sounded, McCarthy knew it would have limited value at trial. It could even play into the defense's hand. What exactly was the "it"? Without a broader context, it didn't give McCarthy much. And he wanted to ask Chris about other things he had said in the interview room, such as about Brittany going on trips to south Florida, or her never having been treated for mental illness. McCarthy decided to bring Chris in and put the squeeze on him.

Back in suburban Seattle, at the end of a cul-de-sac in the community of Maple Valley, the electrical engineer had been trying to return to some kind of regular life. He commuted seventeen miles a day to an office park in Federal Way, where he worked for a Fortune 500 semiconductor company. But, suddenly, he was served with court papers from Maryland, compelling him to fly across the country and testify in a pretrial process. Chris retained an attorney, who helped hatch out a deal with McCarthy: Chris would come in but would speak in a less formal atmosphere.

On an afternoon in May, Chris sat at a long conference table in the prosecutor's office. In front of him was a video camera, flanked by McCarthy and Ayres on one side and detectives Drewry and Ruvin on the other. If he turned toward a bookshelf to his right, he could see the framed photo of McCarthy arm in arm with former president Clinton.

The prosecutor asked a few general questions before moving on to the events of March 18, 2011, when the detectives had recorded Chris and Marissa's conversation. "Let's play that," McCarthy said.

There in front of Chris was a grainy image of him speaking with Marissa in the interview room. In a soft, clear voice, he was seen telling her that he had been worried Brittany might have been involved, but only in the sense that he'd suspected she knew the killers.

"Marissa, this is the fucking worst scenario," Chris said

on the video. "I never thought this. I thought that she was involved. I thought maybe it was drug-related. I thought a lot of things. I thought about all of her Miami trips: it was like them sending her a warning message."

McCarthy now fired his questions at Chris. How many Miami trips? Who were "them"? Did Chris think his sister was involved in the drug trade? Either way, McCarthy knew Chris's answers would be helpful. If Chris gave him some reason to believe Brittany might be moving drugs, that was just more dirt on her; if he downplayed it, it was just another blow to the idea that masked men, maybe a pair of drug traffickers, had struck inside the store.

"No idea," Chris said, parrying the questions. "I speculated a lot of things. That's exactly what it was. It was speculation."

Chris told McCarthy that anything he said on March 18 should be put in the context of when and where he had said it: a police station, one sister accused of a horrendous killing, another falling apart in front of him.

"I was out of my mind trying to come up—trying to make sense of the whole thing, all right?" he said. "What would you do? I mean we're trying to make sense of this situation. Our little sister just got charged with murder." Pushed by McCarthy, Chris said that on that afternoon, with his head spinning, he fell back to familiar, if illogical, territory. "This is me watching too much Court TV is essentially what it is," he said.

The prosecutor zeroed in on Chris's conversation with Brittany, also captured on videotape. "This was the conversation when Brittany admitted to you that she committed the murder," McCarthy said.

Chris wouldn't bite, looking at McCarthy silently for

several seconds before opening his hands: "Let's play the tape."

McCarthy cued an assistant to play the video, pausing it occasionally after what he considered key exchanges.

BRITTANY: "Chris, I'm sorry."
CHRIS: "Don't, don't apologize. Just tell me."
BRITTANY: "I'm going to ruin our whole family."
CHRIS: "You're not going to ruin our family, okay? I'll take that as a yes. Why?"
BRITTANY: "I don't know how it happened."

McCarthy tried to be as direct as he could. "She's admitting to you that she did it," he said to Chris.

"She's not admitting to anything." The protective older brother was intent on not giving McCarthy anything against his sister.

The prosecutor tried to flesh out other exchanges. Chris responded with what the prosecutor thought were maddeningly simplistic answers.

"You are a college graduate, correct?" McCarthy asked.
"Look, I think you're a very smart, intelligent guy."

"No one's questioning anyone's intelligence here," Chris shot back.

McCarthy fished around about Brittany's Internet activity, asking Chris if he was familiar with Craigslist.

"Yeah, I buy car parts on Craigslist."

"Are you familiar with a website called sugar-daddy dot-com?"

Chris smiled slightly, a hint that he found the site's very name ridiculous. "No, I am not."

At one point, tensions eased when McCarthy asked

Chris if he'd read a recent article about his sister in the local newspaper. Chris smiled and said his hotel hadn't provided newspapers. McCarthy looked around the table. "I think that's a shot at the hotel we put him at."

Before letting Chris go, McCarthy had something else on his agenda. "Are you aware of any point in her life, growing up or as an adult, that she has received psychiatric or any kind of counseling from a professional?"

"No," Chris said, unscrewing the cap on a plastic water bottle and taking a drink.

"Has that been discussed with you by any member of the family?"

"No, it hasn't."

"Do you believe, based on your observation of her, she ever needed that type of assistance or help?"

"No, I don't," Chris said, screwing the cap back on the bottle, and quickly correcting himself to account for the present tense. "Or I didn't."

Forensic evidence continued to mount against Brittany. At the police crime lab, McGill, the shoe-print expert, finally completed his work on the plastic zip-tie that had been found binding Brittany's wrists—he'd held off doing so until the arrival of a new microscope that allowed him to take digital photographs of images he was viewing. McGill had figured Brittany had likely used her teeth to tighten the zip-ties around her ankles and her wrists. This would not be the first time he'd analyzed zip-ties in a case, and McGill knew that he had to account for the way zip-ties were manufactured, with liquid plastic poured into molds. Each mold produces its own set of microscopic imperfections—ridges and scratches—that could look like teeth marks.

McGill spotted a "K2D" stamp on Brittany's zip-tie, which he knew identified a certain mold. The next step would be finding unused zip-ties made from that same mold. Fortunately for McGill, he had a full box of zip-ties found in the store. He found a handful made with the same K2D mold—"exemplars" he called them. With these zip-ties as comparisons, now McGill could look at them under his new microscope to establish the locations of that mold's imperfections—showing up at the same location on each zip-tie. He placed the Brittany zip-tie under the microscope. He could see all the imperfections from the mold, and he saw something unique to Brittany's zip-tie: indentations that likely were left by her teeth.

Still, McCarthy and Ayres had to decide how much science to throw at the jury. They knew McGill's shoe-print work was crucial, but it would be complicated: the overlapping tracks, the difference in blood density, the wormlike shoelace patterns. Maybe adding an explanation of zip-tie manufacturing processes would be too much.

As the summer progressed, McCarthy spent weekends at his summer house on the Jersey shore. As his younger siblings' kids ran around the sand and splashed in the surf, the grown-ups took spots on beach chairs with something good to read. McCarthy pulled out a legal pad and pen to outline questions he'd ask Brittany if she took the witness stand. "Cross," he wrote in cursive across the top of the pad, underlining it twice, and quickly getting lost to all the activity around him.

Six initial questions poured right out, all based on whether Jayna had checked Brittany's bag the night of the murder. "Tag on item," McCarthy wrote, using as few words as possible. "You had no receipt," he added.

He also wanted to ask Brittany about the job interview scheduled for three days after Jayna's murder, the one at the upscale health club where she wanted to be a personal trainer, the one where she couldn't afford a bad reference from lululemon. "New job lose—Equinox," McCarthy wrote.

His next section centered on a bit of courtroom theater. He planned to start by playing recordings of Brittany's interviews with detectives, then direct Brittany to call out every time she heard something that wasn't true. "Play tape. Tell me when lie," McCarthy wrote.

He continued for four single-spaced pages, including what he'd ask after showing Brittany photos from Jayna's autopsy. "What cause crack to skull . . . What crush skull with . . . Knife used, where put it."

During another beach session, McCarthy prepped for an insanity defense. McCarthy had tried a handful of such murder cases, and he certainly believed that some killers, no matter what they'd done, needed to be in secure psychiatric hospitals rather than prison. For instance, in 2002, he was given a case in which a twenty-three-year-old man who had shot his parents had also lined up bottles of urine in his bedroom to ward off evil spirits. After McCarthy learned more about the killer's mental state, he agreed that the man should be sent to the psychiatric hospital without a trial. But in other such cases, the prosecutor had taken aggressive stances. In 1997, he tried to convince a judge that although a forty-nine-year-old man off of his meds may have been legally crazy when he killed his parents, he'd known the risks of not taking his medication and should be held accountable—in prison—for doing so. McCarthy had lost that case, though his novel strategy became the basis for an episode of *Law & Order*.

Sitting in his beach chair, McCarthy knew that he'd get wide latitude to question Brittany's doctors if she pleaded insanity—particularly if he asked the questions in the context of how the doctors had formed their opinions. McCarthy quickly starting writing. The opener: "Which weapon 1st?"

His strategy would be to stay away from medical questions, knowing that any doctor hired—particularly someone such as head-trauma expert Williamson—would be way out in front of him. He'd stick with the specifics of how Jayna was killed, even if it was just to detail for the jury all that Brittany had done, such as running around the store picking up weapon after weapon as Jayna was dying. Again, the prosecutor figured, he would ask the doctors what questions they'd asked Brittany. "Where knife/hammer/wrench/rope/Buddha," McCarthy wrote.

By late summer, McCarthy still didn't know the murder weapon that had inflicted the linear gashes in Jayna's skull, including the ones that turned at a sudden, 90-degree angle. He asked Vosburgh, the blood-spatter expert who had examined the store, to come to his office and review reports and more than 1,000 crime-scene photographs. Vosburgh arrived late on a Thursday afternoon and took a seat at McCarthy's conference table, sitting in front of boxes of document and photographs.

"Take your time, Bill; I've got a million things to do," McCarthy said from behind his desk.

The two were alone in the office, working in silence. Vosburgh came across a photograph of the red toolbox that had been found resting on Jayna's shoulder. As he could see from the progression of photos, the crime-scene technicians working the scene had used the toolbox as a container for other bloody items found near Jayna's head, taking the collection back to the police station. There, they unloaded the contents, took photographs of the items, put them back in the toolbox, and stored the toolbox as a single piece of evidence, labeling it "CS-35."

A lot of the items stored in the toolbox were random and harmless. Paintbrushes, a bike reflector, part of a paper bag. But in the middle of the collection was a black metal bar, about a foot long and an inch wide. At one end was a thin plate, perpendicular to the bar. This plate was two inches by three inches, and one edge of it turned in a 90-degree angle. Vosburgh looked at the bloodstained middle portions of the bar. Much of the stains were meaningless blotches. But outside the blotches were small oval-shaped droplets. To Vosburgh's eyes, those were impact spatter. He pulled out the autopsy pictures, finding close-ups of the devastating linear and L-shaped wounds on Jayna's skull.

Vosburgh called McCarthy over, showing him the photographs of the toolbox and the black bar with impact blood on it. Vosburgh showed him autopsy photographs. "You can literally place this weapon into the wound path on her head," he told the prosecutor. "This is what did it."

CHAPTER TWENTY-SIX

Skirmishes

The Brittany Norwood trial was shaping up to be as big of a media spectacle as the Montgomery County Circuit Courthouse had ever seen. Bigger than the trial of Samuel Sheinbein, the seventeen-year-old with the circular power saw. Bigger than the trial of Zakaria Oweiss, the obstetrician with the rubber mallet. And at least as big as the Beltway Snipers, whose fates had been sealed by juries in Virginia before they were tried in Maryland.

Yet the presiding judge in the case, Robert Greenberg, fifty-nine, had been on the bench only five years and had spent much of the time presiding over civil suits, never over a murder trial. It just so happened that this case came to him because of the standard rotation process among Montgomery's twenty-one Circuit Court judges. An angular, six feet two inches tall, Greenberg had a soft-spoken manner that belied a brisk legal mind often one step ahead of the attorneys in front of his bench.

The longtime Montgomery County resident had started his legal career as a prosecutor, working misdemeanor and traffic cases. His biggest claim to fame was securing a drunk-driving conviction against U.S. Representative Louis Stokes, of Ohio, who, like many other members of Congress, kept quarters in Montgomery County. In 1984, Greenberg switched to defense work, opening a private practice and at one point representing boxing legend Mike Tyson in a road-rage incident involving two other motorists. After Tyson, Greenberg took on more and more complicated cases, and was appointed to the bench in 2006.

Few in the courthouse knew of his pursuits outside of the office. As an amateur baseball historian, Greenberg had published a biography of Swish Nicholson, baseball's best slugger during World War II. As an aging baseball player himself, he still competed in what he termed a local "old-men's league." Once a month, he served food at a soup kitchen. And when he really wanted to take his mind off things—about three nights a week—he descended to the basement of the home where he and his wife had raised three kids; sat in front of his drum set; donned a pair of headphones; cranked up the Marvelettes, Otis Redding, Bruce Springsteen, or the Smithereens; and thumped right along. Back in his office, the judge worked among law books neatly lined up next to baseball figurines and a drumstick autographed by Springsteen's drummer, Max Weinberg.

By late summer, the case against Brittany was heading toward an October 24 start date. Her attorneys filed legal papers asking Greenberg to vacate all five of Brittany's interviews with detectives, arguing that she had been in distress or not free to leave. The attorneys also asked Greenberg to postpone the trial to give them more time to explore a psychiatric defense—known in Maryland as "not criminally responsible," or NCR. "Counsel believe that an NCR defense is warranted," her attorneys wrote, "and an NCR plea is likely." Greenberg took up the postponement question first, calling an August 30 hearing for the matter. Brittany, wearing a tan prison jumpsuit, was driven over from the jail and led into the courtroom through a side door.

"Good morning, ma'am," Greenberg told her.

If she responded, no one heard. In the gallery were members of Jayna Murray's family, seeing Brittany for the first time. Also present were members of Brittany's family, there to support her and to see whether her attorneys could explain what happened. Brittany's lead attorney, Doug Wood, spoke first, indicating that an insanity defense in the case was complicated by the fact Brittany had never been diagnosed with psychiatric problems. "Because someone doesn't have treatment early on in their life doesn't mean they don't need treatment later on in their life," Wood said. "Your honor, the nature of this offense, I think, cries out for a very thorough investigation of the mental health issues."

Harry Trainor, a new member of the defense team and an expert on psychiatric defenses, told the judge that Brittany likely "has a history of concussions." But, like Wood, Trainor was vague on specifics. Greenberg pushed the attorneys, asking why they hadn't demonstrated at least some psychiatric issues in the five months since her arrest.

Over at the prosecutor's table, John McCarthy and Marybeth Ayres certainly wanted the trial to start on schedule; the less time Wood had, the better for them. But the prosecutors had figured Greenberg would likely grant the postponement, given the trial's visibility and forensic intensity. Still, McCarthy hoped he could at least use the hearing to take advantage of Dr. David Williamson's well-earned reputation, which McCarthy figured was important to him. McCarthy wanted to publicly link the doctor to a defense strategy that to the lay public wouldn't make sense—soccer injuries leading to murder. "He's a reputable guy," McCarthy had told Ayres. "Once his name gets mentioned, his family, his neighbors, his colleagues are going to go: 'What, are you kidding me?' I think there's going to be this subtle pressure on the guy to back away from this case."

Before the hearing, McCarthy already had made a point to identify Williamson in court filings. Now, as McCarthy listened to Greenberg bore in on the defense attorneys, he sensed opportunity—both to go to trial on time, and to put more pressure on Williamson. When he spoke, the prosecutor described how calm Brittany was after her arrest. Mental illness, he noted, doesn't just turn off and on like a light switch.

"I know who their doctor is. We've been doing research on this guy. I'm looking into his background," McCarthy said, as a row full of reporters took notes. "What are we going to say? Soccer injuries? Because she did too many headers that now she has a psychiatric condition, because of soccer injuries?"

Judge Greenberg denied Brittany's attorneys' request for a postponement, giving them two weeks to come up with a specific reason for a psychiatric defense. Wood balked, arguing that the whole process was moving too quickly. "I've done a lot of homicide cases and to try a homicide case of this magnitude within five months of an indictment is quite a rush."

He asked the judge to reconsider.

"Mr. Wood, with all due respect, I've ruled, and I'm not going to change my mind," replied Greenberg.

Three days later, the attorneys returned to Greenberg's courtroom to debate the defense attorneys' request to disqualify all of Brittany's statements to detectives.

In documents filed before the hearing, Doug Wood and Chris Griffiths detailed the detectives' five interviews with Brittany: two from her hospital bed, one in her apartment, and two at police headquarters. At the hospital, Wood and Griffiths wrote, Brittany was in distress and hadn't wanted to speak with Detective Deana Mackie. Two days later, according to the attorneys, Detectives Jim Drewry and Dimitry Ruvin already considered Brittany their prime suspect when they called on her at home. Both there and when she later came to the police station, they questioned her in a way that made her feel she wasn't free to leave, the attorneys wrote, meaning she should have been informed of her rights to remain silent and call a lawyer.

State's Attorney McCarthy brought in all three detectives to testify at the hearing. Wood gamely went after them on his cross-examinations, making a U-turn in his case by arguing that Brittany's cover-up story was so ridiculous, she must've been the detectives' only suspect from the beginning. But the detectives wouldn't bend, telling Wood that information in the opening days was being delivered in bits and pieces by various people, not all of them communicating in real time.

Wood's questioning of Drewry lasted over half an hour, evolving into a sharp duel between two gray-haired veterans who'd worked homicide cases for three decades. "Essentially," Wood charged at one point, "you're trying to elicit more facts to get more contradictions with what you knew the forensic evidence would show, right?"

"There's a saying, okay?" Drewry replied, going back to his mantra. "'Lie to me. Please lie to me.' Sometimes a provable lie is as good as the truth."

"So you need a conversation," Wood added. "You don't need a confession."

"Yes."

"That's another saying?"

"Yes."

Wood questioned whether Drewry really had poor hearing and a bad back, both of which the detective had mentioned repeatedly during his interviews with Brittany. Wood suggested that Drewry invented the maladies so she'd speak loudly enough for the hidden microphone to pick up her words, and so that he could sit in the more comfortable chair farther from the microphone. Quietly taking all this in from the bench was Greenberg, the judge, who already had watched hours of interrogation video in the case.

"Are you hard of hearing?" Wood asked the detective.

"No," Drewry said.

"Okay," Wood said, chuckling at the candor. "So during the interview when you tell her you're hard of hearing, that's just to get her to speak up into the microphone, so to speak?"

"Yes."

"And you don't have a bad back, right?"

"Yeah," Drewry said, pausing. "I do have a bad back."

"Okay, so that part was true."

"That much is true."

Greenberg interjected. "You had me convinced you were hard of hearing."

"Oh, he's good, your honor. No question about it," said Wood.

Greenberg listened to the attorneys' final arguments, took a brief break, then came back to issue his ruling. He opened with remarks that he acknowledged went beyond the legal issues at hand: "Let me begin by saying that there's been a suggestion here that the police conduct in this case indicated that very early on, they should have known, or did know, that their suspect was in fact Ms. Norwood."

The judge went on to list the immediate pressures the detectives had been facing.

"We had a community, a rather affluent part of our county, which was in an uproar. This appeared to be the work of some unknown assailants on a night when people typically are out at restaurants or shopping. It was shocking in its nature and immediate police action was required. Now, police action in a case such as this, by its very necessity, takes a while to unfold. We sit here today and look back in hindsight at what investigative techniques were used and what leads were pursued and so forth. But hindsight is twenty-twenty. And what we learned here today was that not every police officer investigating this case knew everything that was going on. Indeed, there were forensic tests that were being conducted, the results of which didn't become immediately available. And it strikes me as taking a somewhat cynical approach in the society in which we live, where we are trying to be more sympathetic to victims than perhaps we've been in the past, that immediately we ought to suspect a young woman who appeared to have been, by all accounts, the victim of a heinous crime."

From there, things only got worse for Wood.

Greenberg said that when it came to detectives' interviews of his client, it didn't matter that at some point the detectives considered her a suspect. What mattered was what the suspect thought. And in this case, Greenberg said, the suspect thought she was in control.

"What really struck me in all of these interviews was the expansiveness of the defendant," Greenberg said. "This woman is a woman of frankly striking intelligence and lucidity. And at appropriate times, as was also pointed out by the state, she could tug on your heartstrings."

The judge ruled that the interviews could be played almost in their entirety to jurors. He tossed out part of the final interview, agreeing that Drewry had kept asking questions without informing Brittany of her rights even as she insisted she wanted to go home. But prosecutors would be allowed to use key statements Brittany made earlier that day, including her dubious explanation of how the masked men had forced her to move Jayna's car and return to the store.

But Greenberg's larger message seemed to be that Brittany thought she had the detectives duped until the end.

"It just came across as very calculated," he said.

CHAPTER TWENTY-SEVEN

Without Conscience

The two hearings had an immediate impact on both Brittany Norwood's and Jayna Murray's extended families.

To the Norwoods, Judge Robert Greenberg had forcefully declared that Brittany was in full command of her faculties, and had not been in some kind of psychotic daze after spending all night in the middle of a bloody crime scene that made her incapable of being herself. Nor had any evidence been presented supporting Brittany's claims about masked attackers. In fact, her own attorneys had argued that the story was such nonsense that detectives should have seen through it immediately.

But her family's support, steadfast since the arrest, didn't waver. They visited Brittany at the jail and talked with her on the phone. As was their legal right, prosecutors and detectives listened to recordings of the calls, hoping she'd say something incriminating, but instead heard only encouragement from her parents and siblings. One of Brittany's sisters, who was engaged to be married, told Brittany she wouldn't have bridesmaids because Brittany couldn't be her maid of honor.

"No, have bridesmaids," Brittany said. "I don't want to take anything from you."

She called her dad in suburban Seattle at least once a week, often reaching him at his upholstery shop. On one call, a ringing bell could be heard in the background, as if a customer had come through the door.

"Do you need to go?" Brittany asked.

"No, it's okay," her father said, telling Brittany he'd been waiting for her call. He always ended conversations by telling her they loved her, missed her, and were praying for her.

Inside his shop, Earl Norwood received visitors who wished him well, even if they didn't quite know how to say it. Tim Longmead, who worked across the street at a woodworking shop, was one of them. "I'm doing fine," Earl told him, but his voice seemed about to crack with every word. The initial hearing hadn't gone well for his daughter.

The import of the judge's rulings and comments were even clearer to the attorneys in the case. In early September 2011, State's Attorney John McCarthy was pulling into a conference-center parking lot to attend a political gathering when his phone beeped. One of Brittany's attorneys, Doug Wood, said he wanted to come in and talk about a plea deal—one that would give Brittany a chance at parole.

"Doug, I don't know," McCarthy said. "I've got to ask the family."

McCarthy wanted a trial, but felt compelled to talk to Jayna Murray's family about the proposed deal first. As it turned out, David and Phyllis Murray, their sons, Hugh and Dirk, and their daughters-in-laws, Kate and April, were all coming into town the following week for a road race to raise money for a foundation to be established in Jayna's honor. McCarthy invited them all to his office.

The outlines of the proposed deal meant that Brittany would plead guilty, but her sentence would be capped, making her eligible for parole in as soon as fifteen years. The prosecutor told the Murrays he had a strong case, but warned that anything could happen during a trial. He cited the much-publicized acquittal of Casey Anthony in Florida, whom a jury had recently found not guilty of murder, aggravated manslaughter of a child, or aggravated child abuse—even after the skeletal remains of her daughter, Caylee, were found near her home.

"Why don't we leave you all alone to talk about it?" McCarthy said as he and Marybeth Ayres got up to leave. It had been 191 days since Jayna's murder, each one horrifying for the Murrays in its own way.

Few were as bad as the morning the family entered Jayna's apartment in Northern Virginia just outside D.C. and tried to decide what to do with her possessions, tried to select the clothes Jayna would wear in her closed casket. Phyllis could tell that her daughter had dashed to work quickly on her last day of life. Jayna's Murphy bed was still folded down. An empty Diet Dr Pepper can sat on her desk. For some reason—perhaps because she could so clearly envision Jayna drinking from it, maybe because she'd seen it at the store memorial—Phyllis couldn't throw the can away. She packed it up. Other things she didn't feel the need to keep, such as Jayna's sheets and towels, but she found herself folding them before throwing them away. It was like that, the grief, prompting behavior that didn't always make sense. Phyllis couldn't take walks anymore, even with other people, because they made her feel even more alone. She could go to the grocery store, but avoided the aisle where powdered drink mixes were kept because she had liked to buy them for Jayna. And every day, she dreaded the hour between 3:00 and 4:00 P.M., which was when Jayna would have called. She had learned to turn her ringer off for that hour. "Some days you're so down you just ache" was how she later described it.

After his daughter's murder, David's thoughts still ran to his combat days, but only in vague terms. The vivid images and bad dreams were instantly replaced by thoughts of his daughter's final minutes. He forced himself back to work, knowing he had to occupy his mind. Alone in his office, tears would often overcome him. But David found that if he put in twelve hours at work and two hours at the gym, then fell into bed, he might get to sleep within a few minutes. If not, he'd be up all night, thinking about how Jayna died.

Jayna's brother Dirk had agonized over how much to tell his young boys, something he'd faced since the opening hours of the tragedy, when he attended his son's scheduled birthday party knowing Jayna was missing, trying to pretend nothing was wrong. Since then, he struggled with how much to tell the kids, well aware of how fast kids grow up when they're surrounded by hundreds of TV channels, computers, video games. In the days after the murder, when masked men were supposedly on the loose, Dirk's six-year-old son told him the police needed to review store surveillance video. "They can go look at the tapes," he'd told his dad.

Hugh, Jayna's other brother, who after the murder had flown to Washington from Iraq, had had to return there several weeks later. When he did, he found a package awaiting him from Jayna, which she had mailed just before her death. Hugh took it to his private quarters, hesitating before he opened it, knowing he was about to read Jayna's last words to him. Inside was a running cap, along with a card that listed things that didn't work when they were apart: *Chips without Dip . . . Macaroni without Cheese . . . Me without You*. She thanked him for his e-mails. "It'll be even better once you're back telling the stories and showing pictures in person. Take care and be safe! Love you and miss you, Jayna."

Now he was in McCarthy's office, listening to the prosecutor ask how he and his remaining family felt about taking a plea deal in Jayna's murder. The family didn't have much to discuss. Hugh and his wife, Kate, as lawyers, had spent countless hours studying Maryland law, studying which homicide statutes applied, and what prison sentences they carried. The family already had asked McCarthy whether Maryland law allowed an inmate's wages from prison jobs to be garnisheed, and whether the state had a "Son of Sam" law preventing inmates from profiting from books or movies about their crimes. They'd created a flow chart of possible plea deals and their effects on sentences. Every one of them was convinced that Brittany had committed first-degree, premeditated murder, and over something as senseless as a pair of yoga pants. Kate got up to find McCarthy, who hadn't even made it to his administrative assistant's office, twenty feet away. "We made our decision," she said. They would go to trial.

So the conversation resumed, this time veering toward Brittany. The Murrays had always been inquisitive people—led by David as an engineer and Phyllis as a trained family therapist—and they couldn't stop themselves now. What would drive someone like Brittany to kill?

Ayres, the prosecutor who had tried killers in Baltimore and rapists in Queens, had wrestled with that question as never before. She told the Murrays about a book she was reading, *The Sociopath Next Door*, which suggested that one in twenty-five people possess little or no conscience. Some of these people were successful businessmen. Others were senseless killers.

"What fuels them is this deep-seated insecurity," Ayres told the Murrays.

The Murrays soon found themselves all reading the book. The first paragraph seemed particularly revealing.

Imagine—if you can—not having a conscience, none at all, no feelings of guilt or remorse no matter what you do, no limiting sense of concern for the well-being of strangers, friends, or even family members. Imagine no struggles with shame, not a single one in your whole life, no matter what kind of selfish, lazy, harmful, or immoral action you had taken. And pretend that the concept of responsibility is unknown to you, except as a burden others seem to accept without question, like gullible fools. Now add to this strange fantasy the ability to conceal from other people that your psychological makeup is radically different from theirs. Since everyone simply assumes that conscience is universal among human beings, hiding the fact that you are conscience-free is nearly effortless. You are not held back from any of your desires by guilt or shame, and you are never confronted by others for your cold-bloodedness. The ice water in your veins is so bizarre, so completely outside of their personal experience, that they seldom even guess at your condition.

The author, Martha Stout, wrote that the condition went by a more familiar term, *psychopathy*, and cited one of the most well-known authorities in the field, Robert D. Hare.

Jayna's brother Hugh also bought Hare's book, *Without Conscience*, a more clinical take on the subject. Hare had interviewed murderers in prisons for twenty-five years. The term *psychopath* was too loosely used, he wrote, conjuring up images of crazed killers depicted in horror movies. Instead, Hare asserted, "Their acts result not from a deranged mind but from a cold, calculating rationality combined with a chilling inability to treat others as thinking, feeling human beings."

Hare acknowledged that compared with widely studied conditions such as schizophrenia and manic-depressive illness, the contours of psychopathy were only starting to take shape. He estimated that there were more than two million psychopaths in North America, existing on a sliding scale of severity. Some had been shaped by their environment. Others were simply wired wrong.

On the outside, psychopaths could charm anyone, making it difficult to know if that carried over to genuine affection. At their worst, Hare wrote, psychopaths weren't governed by an emotion that drives so many daily decisions—the ability or desire to see the world from someone else's perspective. "In short, a complete lack of empathy, the prerequisite for love," Hare wrote.

Hugh read the book while at Fort Bragg, North Carolina, where he'd been sent after his Iraq deployment had been cut short so he could be closer to the court proceedings in Maryland. He couldn't help but think of that country and his final assignment there, as the legal chief of detention operations—and all the prisoners he'd met face-to-face. Among them were insurgents willing to blow themselves up or blow up others. They believed in a greater cause, and in that sense, at least their actions carried logic. Not so for the woman who killed his sister, Hugh thought. "They selfishly take what they want and do as they please, violating social norms and expectations without the slightest sense of guilt or regret," Hare wrote. "Their bewildered victims desperately ask, 'Who are these people?'"

CHAPTER TWENTY-EIGHT

"I Think We Can Live with This Guy"

In the case of Brittany Norwood, her attorneys, Doug Wood and Chris Griffiths, could not make a compelling connection between soccer injuries and mental illness—and abandoned the strategy. Dr. David Williamson, the renowned expert from Bethesda's National Naval Medical Center, would not be testifying. Brittany would be tried as legally sane at the time she allegedly committed the murder.

Prosecutors John McCarthy and Marybeth Ayres, meanwhile, were struggling to figure out a way to tell jurors their theory of motive. In a hearing ten days before the trial, Judge Robert Greenberg told them they likely wouldn't be allowed to call witnesses to testify about telephone conversations they had with Jayna Murray less than thirty minutes before she was killed. In those conversations, two coworkers would have said that Jayna told them she had just confronted Brittany over shoplifting before the two of them had left the store. But Greenberg had ruled it to be classic hearsay—the memory of what someone heard but didn't have personal knowledge of.

The prosecutors had another option to try to present their motive. They could play parts of the video recording of Brittany talking to her brother Chris in the interrogation room. The two had been talking about what happened in the store just before Jayna was killed.

"Did she accuse you of shoplifting?" Chris had asked Brittany. "Is that what it's all about?"

Brittany's answer was muddled. She didn't admit to taking anything, but she indicated Jayna suspected her of doing so. "She was going to, like, I don't know, make sure our manager knew or something."

It was compelling dialogue. But to prosecutor Ayres it was also problematic, something she couldn't get out of her head as she took a shower one morning just days ahead of the trial. Before leaving for the office, she sent a text to McCarthy saying they had to talk as soon as she got there.

They did so, in McCarthy's office. "We can't play the tape," Ayres told him.

In the hands of skilled attorneys like Wood and Griffiths, she told her boss, the conversation between Brittany and her brother could swell into indications of deep friction between Brittany and Jayna—and provide an opening to assert that Jayna had started a fight. And there was something else on the tape that the attorneys could use to build an argument that whatever happened, it was hardly premeditated.

"Was the whole thing planned?" Chris had asked his sister.

"No, not at all," Brittany had said.

McCarthy agreed with what Ayres was saying. And he knew that if they didn't play the video recording of a defendant, the rules of evidence meant Wood and Griffiths couldn't introduce it. McCarthy made his decision. They'd try the case with no motive.

Days later, on October 24, 2011, around 150 juror prospects were summoned to the largest courtroom in Montgomery County, used for high-profile cases. Judge Greenberg warmly greeted the prospective jurors, asking each preliminary questions before describing the case. He asked everyone who had heard or read about it to rise. One hundred and thirty-one people stood up.

Greenberg didn't want to rule any of them out in advance, and knew he'd have to ask if they could keep open minds while they listened to the evidence and arguments. In the meantime, though, he moved on to other questions, seeking factors that could color their views.

"Is there any prospective juror, or member of your immediate family, or a close friend who has been an employee in the legal profession, such as a lawyer, a law clerk, a legal secretary, or a paralegal?"

Eighty-six people stood up.

"Welcome to Montgomery County," Greenberg cracked.

Among those standing was an ambitious young defense attorney, Donny Knepper, who on most days toiled across the street at a courthouse devoted to misdemeanor and traffic offenses. Knepper, thirty-six years old, didn't know much about the case, but wanted to be selected so he could have a front-row seat for the skilled performances of attorneys Doug Wood, Chris Griffiths, John McCarthy, and Marybeth Ayres. He told Greenberg his juror number, 3, fairly sure the judge recognized him, then sat down and returned to his novel, *Life of Pi*.

Greenberg continued asking additional, broad-brush questions of the jurors, then relocated the proceedings to a private office behind a rear door in the courtroom. He took the attorneys back there, asking them to sit on either side of a conference table. He wanted the jurors to come in one by one in a setting where they could candidly answer personal questions.

Knepper knew his low juror number would have him going into the office early. He figured he'd make it through this "qualification" stage, when prospects could be disqualified only for obvious conflicts. His goal was to impress both prosecutors and defense attorneys so that at the next stage—probably a day or two away—they wouldn't use their more subjective "strikes" to eliminate him. Knepper tried to think of it as a job interview.

His path to the defense bar hadn't been a direct one. The son of a cop and a nurse in Erie, Pennsylvania, he spent two years at Penn State University, grew worried about drinking too much beer and drifting without much direction, so he dropped out and joined the U.S. Marine Corps, where he spent four years. Back at Penn State, he got a degree in human development, thought about becoming a family therapist, but decided to enroll in law school.

Shortly after 3:00 P.M., Knepper was told to go see the judge.

"I know you," Greenberg said. "Would you close the door please, Juror Number 3."

McCarthy also recognized Knepper as a defense attorney he'd seen around the courthouse. As a rule, the prosecutor hated having defense lawyers on juries, part of his vocation-avoidance list that included psychiatrists, social workers, and members of the clergy. "I'm not in the redemption business," he liked to joke.

Greenberg looked over Knepper's answers to earlier questions, noting that he had disclosed personal ties to someone in McCarthy's office. "Tell us about that," Greenberg asked.

"Vlatka Tomazic," Knepper said, catching McCarthy's full attention with the name of a prosecutor in his office, "is my girlfriend now of—I don't know exactly when it became official—about nine months."

McCarthy considered Tomazic one of the brighter young prosecutors in his office, and he figured if she was hanging out with this guy Knepper, there must be something to him. He was also intrigued to hear Knepper mention that his dad was a retired police officer.

Wood asked about his practice.

Criminal, traffic, juvenile crime, Knepper told him.

"Do you have any expectation of how your girlfriend wants this case resolved, in terms of what she thinks the outcome should be?" Wood asked.

"No, sir," Knepper said. They wrapped things up, and he headed back to the courtroom.

As the trial lawyers waited for prospective jurors to come and go, a tone of informality quickly grew among the courtroom combatants, and Judge Greenberg encouraged it. He called Brittany's lawyers by their first names, Doug and Chris. He asked McCarthy how his son was doing in his freshman year at Guilford College, in North Carolina, where he played guard on the basketball team.

"Scored thirty points in his first scrimmage," McCarthy

said. "Got diagnosed with mono yesterday. He's out for six weeks. We play Davidson in two weeks."

"Oh, that's a shame," Greenberg said as a new juror entered the room.

The informality spilled over to the attorneys' interactions with prospective jurors, a tactical move they used to try to get jurors to like them. When one consultant said he worked in "business analytics and optimization," McCarthy and Wood each vied to appear more humble than the other.

"Do you want me to ask what that is?" McCarthy asked his counterpart.

"No," Wood said. "I'm going to pretend I know."

The individual questioning lasted the rest of the afternoon and through the next day.

Greenberg and the attorneys returned to the back office to talk to individual juror prospects. The judge said it was becoming increasingly clear they wouldn't find twelve people who didn't know about the case.

"While I was lying awake last night, I thought about this issue, because, you know, it's going to arise time and again," he told the lawyers, saying they would just have to find people who could halt any preconceptions they'd formed. "I can't remove what these people have read about the case."

By Tuesday, word spread around the courthouse that Knepper was still in the running. Colleagues of McCarthy's told him that Knepper could be aggressive when defending clients and urged McCarthy to use one of his strikes to bounce him. The prosecutor figured he probably would.

Wednesday morning, Greenberg had culled the 150 names down to 65 qualified candidates. He moved to the next phase, where the qualified jurors would be asked to stand in the jury box so prosecutors and defense attorneys could begin eliminating some of them. Under Maryland rules, prosecutors McCarthy and Ayres got ten strikes, while defense attorneys Wood and Griffiths got twenty.

Again, because of his low jury number, Knepper knew he'd be among the first in the box. He figured either side had about thirty to forty minutes to strike him as the process would unfold. At his table, McCarthy scanned his list of culled candidates, noting several who'd made bad impressions on him in the back office. He realized he might have to keep Knepper, whispering as much to Ayres, who wheeled around and whispered to their intern, Ashley Inderfurth, to hustle upstairs to their office to see Tomazic. "Go find out what kind of guy he is," she said. Inderfurth rode the elevator up two floors and marched into Tomazic's office. "John wants to know if your boyfriend will make a good juror," she said.

McCarthy was starting to issue his strikes.

At the defense table, Wood sensed an opening. McCarthy had used three of his strikes on African Americans. Wood stood and asked for a private huddle in front of Greenberg's bench, where he issued a "Batson challenge," asserting McCarthy was eliminating jurors based solely on race.

McCarthy countered, giving his reasons for the three strikes. One of the prospects had been irate over juror responsibilities; another had seemed to downplay some trouble her attorney husband had gotten into; an older woman talked about lynchings of a century ago and said that another prospective juror had talked to her about the case.

"She was just very bizarre," McCarthy said. "Her head was jiggling."

The judge tended to agree, even if *bizarre* wasn't the right word: "She was a loose cannon, in my view."

McCarthy advanced his argument: although he was about to strike two more African Americans, including a twenty-year-old he considered an "airhead," he also planned to keep the forty-seven-year-old African American human-resources worker with the British accent. "I want smart, intelligent people that are mature, that have made life decisions on this jury versus a twenty-year-old young girl who is unemployed, who appeared to be ditzy."

Greenberg was swayed, agreeing that McCarthy was making "racially neutral" decisions in keeping five African Americans off the jury.

As for prospective juror Knepper, Wood and Griffiths seemed satisfied that his professional leanings—he'd previously worked in public defender's offices and a legal-aid center before opening a private practice—outweighed his relationship with the prosecutors. McCarthy also had to figure out what to do with Knepper. Inderfurth had returned and delivered Tomazic's reply, which was that although she was hardly unbiased, she thought Knepper would be fair and thoughtful throughout the process.

McCarthy and Ayres quickly and quietly discussed what to do.

"I think we can live with this guy," McCarthy said.

CHAPTER TWENTY-NINE

Losing It

Prosecutors John McCarthy and Marybeth Ayres knew they were about to present a powerful case. Forensic evidence alone would allow them to paint a detailed picture of how Brittany Norwood had killed Jayna Murray. And the prosecutors had hours of video and audio records of Brittany they could play for jurors, convinced that doing so would brand Brittany a pathological liar in their eyes.

But as McCarthy readied himself to deliver his opening statement on October 26, 2011, he knew he had to leave out one important detail that might prey on jurors' minds: he couldn't tell them *why* Brittany killed Jayna.

But the prosecutor was a gifted orator, the result of having spoken in courtrooms for thirty years, and classrooms for thirty-five. He and Ayres had written a detailed statement covering nineteen key points, and they expected it to take an hour. McCarthy used all the tools of good storytelling—short sentences, varied pacing, foreshadowing—building to the end, when McCarthy would reveal two of the bloodied murder weapons, and he opened with a cliff-hanger.

"The story is tragic," he began. "One young woman brutally murdered, allegedly sexually assaulted, a surviving victim left behind, and two unknown assailants loose in our community. The details are breathless, and they are brutal—most supplied by the surviving victim herself. The law enforcement community gathered around this case because those men who did this to these young women had to be found, and had to be held accountable for their crimes. One problem—the concocted boogeymen did not exist."

The front of the courtroom where McCarthy spoke had an odd layout, the result of well-intentioned architects from three decades earlier who prized acoustics over right angles. The resulting courtroom "well" was a circle, defined by the judge's bench, the defense attorneys' table, the prosecutors' table, and a two-tiered section of large, dark-green leather juror chairs. Everything felt squeezed together, and when attorneys delivered opening statements, they did so with jurors pressed close to them—at the best of times, it increased the attorneys' feeling of connection with the jury; at the worst, it was oppressive.

McCarthy quickly identified the person who'd invented the boogeymen, pointing to the defense table behind him. "Jayna Murray's killer is in this courtroom," he said.

Jurors looked at Brittany, as did the more than 200 spectators who attended the trial, as well as members of both her and Jayna's families, seated in the same row up front, though separated by the middle aisle. Brittany was dressed in civilian clothes—on this day a grayish-tan

sweater—in contrast to the prison clothes she'd worn in
pretrial hearings. Her hair was pulled back in a bun. She
looked young and sad, displaying no reaction to what was
being said, and for the most part looked downward.

McCarthy continued, punctuating his opening statement with a PowerPoint presentation and photographs.
By law, he had to limit himself to walking jurors through
the evidence they would hear, without arguing how it was
connected or what it meant. But McCarthy knew how to
make his opening statements vivid and real, not complicated and wordy.

He pushed a button on the wireless PowerPoint con-
troller in his hand. Suddenly displayed across a large pro-
jection screen—across from the jurors and above the
defense table—was a striking blonde, her broad smile illu-
minating the courtroom. "If I could spend a couple of
minutes introducing Jayna Murray to you," McCarthy
said. "At the time of her death, this extraordinary young
woman was working her way towards two additional master's degrees at Johns Hopkins."

Brittany's lead defense attorney, Doug Wood, didn't
like where McCarthy was going. He stood up and asked
Judge Greenberg if he and his partner, Chris Griffiths,
could approach with the prosecutors for a bench conference. With all the evidence against his client, Wood wanted
to keep McCarthy on a tight leash, and knew he'd have to
work for every little victory. Wood whispered to the judge:
"What she did three years ago, how many degrees she had,
isn't relevant to the manner of her death or what caused
her death."

McCarthy agreed to move on. He'd made his point.

He clicked to a new photograph, this one of a serious,

exhausted-looking woman, a photo he'd recently selected over the sunny, smiling photograph of the same person that had initially been part of the PowerPoint. "The defendant in this case is Brittany Norwood," McCarthy said. "This is a photograph that was taken of her on March the 16th, during one of the multiple police interviews of her the week following the homicide."

With the contrast between the two women cemented less than five minutes into his opening, McCarthy dialed back and began talking to the jurors as if he was in their living rooms. The prosecutor clicked to a large, photographic map of downtown Bethesda. He pointed to lululemon athletica, where both women worked, and oriented it among other familiar retailers. "Directly next door, and this will become relevant during the course of the trial, there's an Apple Store that has adjoining walls to lululemon. They are directly next door. For some of you who might like cupcakes, Georgetown Cupcake is a couple of doors down. That's where we are."

He clicked to a diagram of the lululemon store itself, pointing out the different sections of the store—from the cash registers in the front to the stockroom in the back. "There also is a sink in the back," McCarthy said, "where kitchen utensils and things like knives are kept." The word *knives*, mentioned almost casually, hung in the air for a moment.

The prosecutor then spun a narrative that started with the morning the murder was discovered, a day with lots of buzz and foot traffic along Bethesda Avenue because of a hot new product Apple was introducing. Gradually, his relaxed, conversational manner gave way to stark details about what happened, illustrated by a crime-scene photo of a woman facedown in a narrow hallway, surrounded by blood-spattered walls, her pants obviously cut open. "This is Jayna Murray," McCarthy said, adding, "There actually is some staging here by the defendant to make it look like she's been sexually assaulted." From there, he disclosed the autopsy results: more than 300 injuries to Jayna, including 107 wounds to her hands and arms as she tried to shield herself.

McCarthy used other PowerPoint slides to present a timeline of Brittany's and Jayna's movements on the night of the murder: how Jayna and Brittany left the store, went their separate ways, then returned to look for Brittany's wallet. He said the attack started quickly and that Brittany used "seven, eight different weapons" retrieved from different parts of the store, including a hammer, a knife, and a wrench. He keyed in on one weapon in particular—something called a "merch peg," or merchandise peg. The metal bars, about a foot long, have plates at one end that can be affixed to walls so garments can be hung from them. McCarthy noted that the merch pegs were stored in a bucket near where employees keep their personal belongings, a "logical" area to have gone to search for Brittany's wallet.

McCarthy placed a cardboard evidence box on a table in front of the jurors, put on a rubber glove, and pulled out one of the bars in question, raising it to eye level. "You can see up there, there's blood spatter on that merch peg," McCarthy said, lowering his voice and setting up for a pause. "There are—catastrophic—injuries to Jayna's head, where her skull is cracked time and time again, cracked with this and crushed with something else."

McCarthy had planned to put the peg back in the box,

but it occurred to him that the jury should hear something. He slammed the peg on the box. *Whack! Whack! Whack!*

In the jury box, Ron Harrington, a thirty-five-year-old nuclear engineer, leaned forward, gripped by what McCarthy was saying and how he said it. *This guy's going to be colorful,* Harrington thought.

The prosecutor returned the peg to its box and reached for a new exhibit, pulling it out of a brown paper bag. "Jayna, when she was found, had a rope around her neck," he said. He clicked to another PowerPoint slide, which showed four photographs: a differently shaped peg, a wrench, Jayna's battered right hand, and something in the bottom-right corner that wasn't immediately recognizable. Wood had had enough.

"Can we approach, your honor?" he asked.

"All right. Let's take that down for a moment," the judge said, indicating the photograph on the screen.

Too quietly for the jurors to hear, the defense attorney suggested McCarthy was going too far. "Your honor, it gets to a certain point where it's not a statement, it's a closing argument."

Greenberg saw his point, turning to McCarthy. "A couple of times you said: 'We already know such and such,' as though it had already been proven." He told McCarthy to stick to laying out what he believed his evidence would show, not whether it had been proved or what it meant.

The attorneys walked back to their tables. McCarthy was moving to wrap things up, but not before he had made his point about the fourth image, which reappeared on the screen. He said that different weapons left specific wound patterns, such as those in the image on the lower right. "This is a portion of Jayna's skull," McCarthy said.

It looked to be the top of Jayna's head, with the hair shaved to reveal a series of deep gashes.

Leaving jurors with that final image, McCarthy had only one more point to make to complete his case. He said the state's evidence would show that all the injuries, all the weapons, amounted to premeditation on Brittany's part. "Think about how many times," McCarthy said, "she could have chosen a different course of conduct."

As if reflexively, several of the jurors turned their heads toward Brittany to observe her reaction—and they saw none, only a sad face cast toward the floor. *She looks so sweet,* juror Greg Lloyd told himself. The thirty-nine-year-old software engineer worked about ten blocks from the lululemon store. As a young man, he'd scraped with the law and didn't think the system was always fair to defendants. He told himself not to be swayed by dramatic statements. And he wondered what Brittany's lawyers would say.

"Good morning, ladies and gentlemen," defense attorney Doug Wood began, thanking the jurors for enduring the long selection process. "As you can only imagine in a case like this, with the press notoriety, the sensationalism, it is so important to find people who are going to be fair."

He spoke briefly about Brittany, how she was one of nine children, had been raised in Washington State, had played soccer in college. She had sisters living in the Washington area, one of them a doctor. At lululemon, she was called an "educator," not a salesperson. He was beginning slowly, conversationally, outlining a perfectly normal life as he worked to reestablish the rapport he had developed with jurors during their selection.

From there, he built his statement on the very thing McCarthy had been forced to sidestep, taking full advantage of the fact McCarthy had not been able to offer a motive. When Wood described the evening of March 11, 2011, he noted that Brittany and Jayna had earlier worked in the store together with no problems. "There was no conflict between the two of them," Wood said. "Nothing, nothing."

Brittany left the store, Wood said, but she realized she forgot her wallet and called Jayna. Back in the store, something was said between the two that quickly escalated into a loud argument. Wood stressed that it was equally hot on both sides. "Two women's voices were going back and forth, mutually, back and forth, back and forth. It caught the attention of the people inside the Apple Store."

It seemed clear Wood wasn't going back to the masked-men story. He had no choice but to connect Brittany to the murder.

"That's when the fight ensued," Wood told the jurors. "There was a fight between Brittany and Jayna."

Wood used the legal term *mutual affray* to describe the fight, which conveyed that two people squared off with equal animosity. "It was during this mutual affray that Jayna was killed. Jayna was killed by Brittany—not with premeditation, not with deliberation, not with willfulness or malice. It occurred in a fight, ladies and gentlemen. It was a fight that occurred between the two of them. And during that fight, ladies and gentlemen, Brittany Norwood lost it. There's no doubt about that. She lost it. She lost control."

It was so unplanned, in fact, that in her rage Brittany made do with whatever implements she could find.

"There was a horrific argument that occurred between the two of them in that store, and there was a horrific fight that occurred. And Brittany Norwood, not bringing any weapons to the store, she grabbed the stuff that was within her reach and, unfortunately and stupidly, caused the death of Jayna Murray. And she lost it during that period of time. And there's no question about that, ladies and gentlemen."

Wood had to work with what he had, which meant not downplaying Brittany's cover-up, but embracing the more foolish components of it and asserting they were the actions of someone who had temporarily lost her mind. The skilled lawyer found himself having to reach for words and phrases. The actions, he said, "actually show someone who is the exact opposite of someone who had cunning and guile. It shows someone who, in fact, ladies and gentlemen, we submit, got involved in a nightmarish situation, a nightmare, a nightmarish situation and had this sort of imagination or this explanation of what happened."

Brittany's story was consequently full of holes and wrong turns, he said. "These were a series of inept steps taken by Brittany Norwood, because she knew there had been a nightmare, and she was lost. She was lost, ladies and gentlemen."

Wood was not basing his case on an insanity plea, but this was a way to bring what he termed Brittany's confused state into play. In conceding that she had killed Jayna, he had three goals. The first was gaining credibility with the jurors, and the second was stealing thunder from some of McCarthy's upcoming forensic evidence. ("Of course," Wood could say to the jury, "we've already acknowledged this.") The third and most important was eventually to earn her a lighter sentence that could make Brittany eligible for parole in as little as fifteen years.

But Wood was paying a price for his strategy. The jurors would immediately see Brittany as a killer, and they would see everything in the trial through that prism.

In the middle of the trial's second day, Detective Deana Mackie took the stand. Prosecutors played an audio recording of her interview with Brittany, who lay on a hospital bed less than three hours after she had been found tied up in the yoga store. The interview lasted forty-eight minutes—and everyone in the courtroom heard Brittany tell lie upon lie. It started with Brittany asking Mackie how her friend Jayna was doing. The detective deflected the question, and jurors heard Brittany slowly start telling her cover story about two men coming in and attacking her and Jayna. Audibly crying on the recording, Brittany said she tried to help. "I remember trying to help her. I tried to get away from him and tried to help Jayna, and, like, she was bleeding so much," Brittany said.

On some level, Wood did make the kind of headway he had earlier hoped for. Juror Donny Knepper, the defense attorney, could hear obvious holes in Brittany's story. For one thing, she didn't appear to be badly injured, even as Jayna had been massacred. For another, Brittany couldn't remember important details. "Maybe I am biased because I know that Brittany is lying," Knepper would later write in a journal he kept at home. "But to me it sounds so obvious that she is lying . . . How was the detective not suspicious?"

By the third day, McCarthy's case developed a rhythm. He interspersed dry testimony about crime-scene evidence collection with mesmerizing accounts from the two Apple managers, Jana Svrzo and Ricardo Rios. Jana testified first, describing the sounds she heard just after 10:00 P.M. on Friday, March 11. "Something sounded like something heavy was being hit or dragged, some grunting, some thudding, some kind of high-pitched squealing, yelling, perhaps," Jana said.

She told the jury she and Ricardo eventually approached the common wall between the stores, and she recalled hearing two voices at that point, one to her left, one to her right. "It sounded like hysterical noises, and then followed by a different female voice that was saying, 'Talk to me. Don't do this. Talk to me. What's going on?' At that point, there was some more sounds, kind of screams, yelps, yells. It's hard to distinguish. And then the initial, the other voice or another voice saying, in a very low quiet tone saying, 'God, help me. Please help me.'"

Again, the jurors found themselves glued to the testimony. Lloyd, the software engineer, felt for the managers having to live with their decision not to call 911. Harrington, the nuclear engineer, wondered if that decision said something broader about society. Both jurors had objective reactions as well—exactly the kind McCarthy was hoping to evoke. In Lloyd's view, the conversation from inside the yoga store that the Apple managers heard indicated that Brittany had time to think about what she was doing, to stop what she was doing—both pointing to first-degree murder. Harrington factored in the interior Apple Store surveillance video that was played for the jurors, with its little time stamps, and thought the assault lasted a long time. *Even on the short end*, he thought, *it was ten minutes.*

McCarthy had timed the Apple witnesses well for Friday afternoon, giving jurors something to think about all weekend. "I have not been sleeping well," Knepper wrote in his journal. "I do not usually let such disturbing things into my headspace."

Despite all the blood he had seen and all the rest of the damning evidence against Brittany, Knepper was willing to hear a plausible defense from Wood. Maybe Brittany thought that Jayna had stolen her wallet, giving her justification at least to start a fight. "The general public usually presumes that if you get arrested and charged with a crime that you are guilty. I am not doing that," he wrote. "I have not made my decision regarding this girl's guilt."

McCarthy wanted to start off the week with a bang. After a brief fingerprint witness, who was on the stand for less than three minutes, McCarthy called William Vosburgh, the blood-spatter expert whom he'd asked to examine the crime scene. The prosecutor had used him as a witness before and figured his scientific bearing would play well to what was a well-educated jury panel. McCarthy led him through questions about the discipline of bloodstain-pattern analysis. By using "very simple trigonometry," Vosburgh told the jurors, "one can calculate backwards from the shape of the droplet what the point of origin was."

Juror Lloyd took detailed notes, feeling on some level like he was back in a physics lecture at Virginia Tech University. Knepper was also impressed. "He is the guy who really gave us the picture of how this crime occurred. Disturbing stuff," the attorney wrote in his journal. Knepper was further impressed by Detective Dimitry Ruvin, who testified that detectives had wanted to believe and help Brittany, and that there were too many moving parts at the outset to know exactly what was going on. "I trust this guy," Knepper wrote.

As the trial entered its fifth day, Brittany's defense strategy was taking an increased toll on both families. The Norwoods had long wondered about—hoped for—the possibility of a provocation that could help explain what Brittany had done. "Tell me what she did to get you to fight her?" Chris had asked his sister that afternoon in the interrogation room.

To the Murrays, the idea of a fight was offensive, and there was no forensic evidence to support it. *Easy to pick on the dead person*, Jayna's brother Dirk said to himself during the trial. In the Murrays' minds, it was an ambush, not a fight.

Neither family spoke to the other, aside from one accidental encounter during a break. Phyllis Murray walked into a courthouse women's room and ran into two of Brittany's sisters. It was awkward and tense. "We're sorry for the loss of Jayna," one of them told Phyllis. She also asked Phyllis how Jayna's nephews were doing, saying they had two nephews in their family about the same age. "We are working with them," Phyllis replied.

Phyllis was scheduled to take the witness stand late on the fifth day. McCarthy needed someone to formally identify Jayna Murray in photographs, and assert that she didn't have a twin sister, which would have altered the conclusions of DNA testing. McCarthy also knew the emotional impact that seeing Jayna's mother would have on jurors. Judge Greenberg called the attorneys up to his bench for a huddle and told McCarthy he'd be on a tight clock. "Let me be really candid with you," Greenberg whispered to him. "She's been through enough."

Phyllis walked to the witness stand and spelled her

name, speaking in a slightly singsong, upper-midwestern accent. McCarthy asked her how long she'd lived in Texas.

"Off and on for, jeepers, thirty years," she said.

At the sound of her voice, sadness shot through juror Ron Harrington. His mother had a similar small-town air about her. She said "jeepers" all the time. Harrington thought about how his mother would have felt, how she would have coped, if one of her children had been murdered. Tears welled in his eyes. And the more he listened, the more Phyllis strengthened the case against Brittany for him. She said her daughter played volleyball and was athletic. If it had been a fight, Harrington told himself, Jayna would have better defended herself.

As effective as Jayna's mother was, McCarthy saved his best witness for last: Dr. Mary Ripple, the medical examiner. He'd met with her three times during the case, most recently to figure out how they would explain all the injuries without being so repetitive that they risked losing the jurors' attention. Ripple suggested they do it not by injury type, but by areas on Jayna's body. "Let's do it regionally," she said.

Before her testimony, McCarthy and Wood had sparred over whether jurors would be allowed to see autopsy photos and, if so, how many. McCarthy told Greenberg the photos explained the injuries, while Wood countered that their brutality would make it difficult for jurors to remain objective. In the end, Greenberg said he would allow McCarthy to show nine of them, projected from a large video monitor, and the attorneys warned the family members seated behind them what was coming. As Ripple took the stand, the second row was almost empty. Of all the family members, only Earl Norwood remained in the courtroom to see it through with his daughter.

The images were beyond ghastly. Jayna's shaved head looked as if it had been run over by a lawn mower. Greenberg tried not to keep the images projected any longer than necessary. But they truly helped explain how Jayna was killed.

Ripple created the impression that she was speaking only to the jurors and saw no one else in the courtroom. Her words were horrifying but delivered in a style that was both clinical and understandable. She walked them through injuries on different parts of Jayna's body, eventually reaching a gaping wound that was depicted by one of the autopsy photographs projected for jurors. The killer, Ripple said, had first fractured the area in seven places, making it susceptible to a subsequent crushing injury. "These areas are now more fragile because of these defects," she said. "Lots of internal brain injury with regard to that. Do you want me to explain that now, Mr. McCarthy?"

"Yes, why don't you do that."

"Okay, so there's bleeding on the—there's the skull fractures that you can see—and there's bleeding on the surface of the brain that we call 'subarachnoid hemorrhage.'"

McCarthy questioned Ripple for more than two hours. She told jurors how the linear and L-shaped wounds in Jayna's head were consistent with the shape of the merchandise peg. She said the knife wound at the base of Jayna's brain came late in the attack, and likely killed her within a minute. And she explained how Jayna's heart had continued to pump blood into the final wound, meaning she was alive until the end.

When his turn came at last, Wood cross-examined Ripple as best he could and even scored a few minor points. He got Ripple to say that although Jayna's heart was pumping, that didn't mean she was conscious. He also got her to acknowledge that some of the "defensive injuries" to Jayna's hands could have been "offensive injuries," and that some of the injuries could have occurred when she fell into the metal shelving near the spot where her body was discovered. But Wood could do little to overcome the grim power of Ripple's testimony and the enormous contrast between Jayna's autopsy photographs and Brittany's insignificant injuries. The doctor left the stand, and the family members who'd stayed away from the autopsy photographs came back into the courtroom.

McCarthy rested his case.

By then, it was pretty much over for Greg Lloyd, the juror who didn't always think that system was fair, who'd been willing to give Brittany every benefit of the doubt. Even at 331 injuries, he'd told himself, if they'd somehow been part of a long fight, and if Brittany had been acting without thinking, he could at least entertain a verdict of second-degree murder. But Brittany simply didn't have any serious injuries. And now it was clear to Lloyd that she had halted her attack, retrieved a knife, and went back at it.

Wood had signaled for weeks that he would call just a few witnesses—no forensic experts, no psychiatrists. He certainly didn't want his client to testify on the stand and face McCarthy's marathon cross-examination of her five, fiction-filled interviews with detectives. Hoping he'd counterpunched effectively in his own cross-examinations, Wood told Greenberg that his side was done as well. The defense would call no witnesses.

All that was left now were the closing arguments. For seven months, McCarthy had been building to this. He wouldn't get his chance here to say *why* the murder had happened—that would come later, he figured, at sentencing. But he could certainly paint a vivid picture of *what* had happened.

His many forensic experts—in blood spatter, shoe prints, pathology, DNA, fingerprints—gave him data points throughout the store. He had a timeline from cell-phone records, store alarm reports, and the Apple managers' testimony about the screams they'd overheard. The detectives' testimony had stitched together, and then unraveled, Brittany's cover-up.

"This was a difficult case," McCarthy began softly, mindful of the tears some jurors had shed over the autopsy photographs.

And then he laid it out for them. How, after Jayna and Brittany left the store, Brittany had tricked Jayna into coming back with the story about her forgotten wallet. How Brittany lured Jayna back to the stockroom, where employees typically left their belongings. There were no windows back there, no view to the remaining pedestrians on Bethesda Avenue. He reminded the jurors that the steel bars used for garment displays were kept in a bin near the chairs. "The merch pegs are back there," McCarthy said, standing in the circular well without notes, using his hands for expression. His legal pad was on a table in front of him, highlighting key points he wanted to make. But he found himself hardly having to check it.

The prosecutor resisted the urges to fill in blanks—the likely conversation between Brittany and Jayna; in fact, he had never learned for sure how the attack began. Did Brittany sneak up from behind? Were they face-to-face? One thing seemed certain—however it started, Brittany quickly got the best of Jayna, who was too stunned to defend herself. These were not two women grappling—this was an assault.

"It's on," McCarthy told the jury of the attack, "and it's not fair."

He walked them through how evidence showed that Jayna grabbed the back of her bleeding head, staggered forward into the fitting-room area, and reached up to catch herself on a wall near the television set, leaving a bloody palm print and causing the TV to crash to the floor. Jayna now was in escape mode. She probably didn't run for the front door because she knew the two had locked it behind them, and she wanted something quicker—the rear exit that could be pushed open. Maybe the emergency alarm would even sound. Jayna broke away, literally wrestling out of her coat, which Brittany was grabbing. "This was her last mad dash to try to save her life," McCarthy said.

Jayna burst through the purple door to the rear hallway, but Brittany was right behind her. Jayna made it to the back door, McCarthy told the jurors, close enough to get her blood on the push bar. "She doesn't get out," McCarthy said. "She's pulled back." Brittany then pushed Jayna back down the narrow hallway to the corner—still armed with the merch peg. In his mind, McCarthy had decided it was Brittany speaking those clear words in the rear hallway—the phrases asking "What's going on?" and saying "Talk to me." McCarthy figured that Brittany had been trying to determine if Jayna had told their manager about the theft, but he couldn't tell the jurors this, because he hadn't introduced evidence of the alleged theft. So the prosecutor went as far as he could.

"She hadn't 'lost it,'" McCarthy told the jurors, "but

she was demanding that she talk to her: 'Tell me what's going on.' "

McCarthy told jurors how Jayna sank to the floor, eventually so helpless that Brittany was free to search for more weapons—some she thought might be more effective, like the hammer or the rope, and some she wielded for mutilation, like the box cutters. "This was a long, brutal, slow attack," McCarthy said.

At the end of it, McCarthy told the jurors, Jayna began to make loud gasping noises—known as "agonal breathing"—that people emit as they die. He didn't dwell on the autopsy photographs, but he used them as he described the fatal blow to the base of Jayna's skull. The Murrays had been warned the images would be shown, but they remained in the courtroom to support Jayna's memory during the most crucial part of the trial.

"This is the area of the back of her head," McCarthy told the jury.

Jayna's father, David, who had seen terrible violence in combat, looked away but not quickly enough. What he viewed was the worst thing ever—a full-color depiction of what had happened to his only daughter. He kept his head down, shaking and sobbing next to his wife, Phyllis. McCarthy continued, telling jurors how Brittany had retrieved a knife from the kitchen and plunged it into the base of Jayna's skull. "The stab wound that kills her. This is the one that enters her brain. This is the one that mercifully ends it all."

Brittany had been watching McCarthy, but turned her head away from the projected photo. It was one of her few visible reactions during the trial. Her parents, Earl and Larkita, sat still, their arms intertwined.

Legally, it had been a terrible day for Brittany's side as well. The medical examiner's testimony about the length and brutality of the attack made it nearly impossible to argue that Brittany didn't have time to stop and think about what she was doing. Three hundred and thirty-one times. At least five different weapons. As Wood rose to speak, he knew he couldn't erase the images of those autopsy pictures. So he tried to turn it around, to argue instead that no clear-thinking person could have produced such devastation.

"This shows that someone lost control," he said, holding up part of the autopsy documents. "This shows that someone wasn't in their right mind when this occurred. There is no other explanation."

He keyed in on his two strongest points. First, he said, McCarthy's assertion that Brittany lured Jayna back to the store, intending to kill her, made little sense. If Brittany intended to kill her all along, why did she call a friend to get Jayna's number, leaving behind such a trail? If she planned to kill Jayna all along, why didn't she do it before they left the store? And Wood hammered home the fact McCarthy had not given a specific motive for the crime. "The absence of a motive is an indication it's not premeditated," Wood said.

Wood said it started as a fight, and reminded jurors about the cut on Brittany's forehead. "There's only one other person in the world who could have caused that injury: Jayna Murray."

And Wood argued that Brittany's cover-up was delusional, doing so in a way that didn't come across as criticizing the police for not sniffing it out sooner. "They've got different people working on it at the same time. Somebody hears this, somebody hears that, and later on they put it all together. But that does not mean that the story that she is spinning out from the inception [wasn't] ridiculous, *ridiculous*."

Under Maryland rules, the prosecution got the last word, a rebuttal after the defense attorney's closing. Assistant State's Attorney Marybeth Ayres got up to give the rebuttal. She had been on the case since the beginning, going down to the yoga store the day the two women were discovered. She had watched the interrogations live on the closed-circuit monitor at police headquarters. In her quest to understand Brittany, Ayres had read books on psychopaths. Now, she focused on Brittany's "cold and calculating" cover-up.

While Brittany was still dripping with Jayna's blood, Ayres told the jury, she walked to the cash registers to stage the robbery. This was evident, Ayres said, because drops of Jayna's blood were found up front. Then Brittany walked to the sink, cleaned her shoes, cleaned her hands, and cleaned the blood off her forehead, which Ayres told the jurors came from a wound Brittany gave herself while attacking Jayna. From there, Brittany grabbed Jayna's car keys—she had to move Jayna's car from out front so that Rachel Oertli, the manager who lived in an apartment across the street, wouldn't see it—donned a lululemon cap, drove the car three blocks away, parked it, and walked back to the store. Ayres had always thought that at this point, Brittany probably used her fingernails or a box cutter to re-open the cut on her forehead and make her own injuries look worse. The prosecutor now asserted so to the jury: "After she came back from the car, she did something to that, to her forehead, to make it have blood come all the way down her face."

Ayres implored the jurors to put emotions aside and look at the evidence. "As humans, we want to believe it's the masked men. We want that. That makes us feel better," Ayres said. "You don't want to believe that it's the articulate, educated, attractive girl next door. You don't want to believe that, because that's someone you might trust."

Once Ayres finished, the jurors were escorted into their deliberation room, where they sat around a twelve-foot-long table, antsy to talk, but Greenberg's law clerk forbid them to discuss the case until all the boxes and bags of evidence had been carted in. Finally, after ten minutes, the evidence came in, the clerk left, and several simultaneous conversations broke out. For a minute or so, the jurors talked among themselves about how rough the case was. It was attorney Donny Knepper who spoke up first. As he knew, the printed jury form given to them had limited options to consider:

1. *As to the crime of First-Degree Murder, we, the jury, find the Defendant:*
   ___ *Not Guilty* ___ *Guilty.*
   If your answer to Number 1 is Guilty, your deliberations are concluded. If your answer to Number 1 is Not Guilty, proceed to Number 2.
2. *As to the crime of Second-Degree Murder, we, the jury, find the Defendant:*
   ___ *Not Guilty* ___ *Guilty.*

"Hey, hey," Knepper said, "let's do an initial vote to see who would vote for first-degree murder, to see if there are any issues around that."

All twelve jurors raised their hands. Nobody seemed surprised.

But Knepper thought he should at least create a conversation about second-degree murder. He defined the classic scenario: man comes home, finds wife in bed with other man, picks up nearest heavy object, kills wife without really thinking about it. "Somebody make an argument for how this could be second-degree murder," Knepper said.

Greg Lloyd gave it the best shot, figuring it was their duty to at least play devil's advocate. But after several minutes, he realized he wasn't making any sense. *This is ridiculous,* he thought to himself. Someone voiced the question that was bugging them all—Why did Brittany do it?—and silence ensued. Eventually, Ron Harrington wondered aloud if Brittany and Jayna liked the same guy, whether somehow their ties to Seattle played into that. Another juror suggested that perhaps Jayna had accused Brittany of shoplifting, but Knepper found the idea so outrageous that he didn't even respond to it. Finally, he spoke. "You know what? Maybe in ten or fifteen years, Brittany Norwood will come out and explain why she did this. But the fact of the matter is we don't have to know."

Harrington wanted to talk about what had saddened him since the previous afternoon. "Who else had a hard time when Jayna's mother was on the stand?" he asked. Several other jurors agreed.

Harrington knew their work was essentially done, but he wanted to examine one piece of evidence, though. He put on a pair of rubber gloves and pulled the bloodstained merchandise peg out of its box, noting the sharp flange on the end and hefting its one-pound weight. Heavy enough to have good mass, the engineer thought, but light enough to swing rapidly. "Holy crap, this is a perfect weapon," he said, saddened it was such an easy thing to say.

Knepper led another vote. It was unanimous for first-degree murder. Everyone got ready to go back into the courtroom. "Does anybody have any doubt whatsoever?" Knepper asked. "This is a very important decision." Nobody did.

A block and a half way, at a brew pub called Gordon Biersch, McCarthy had just ordered a round: draft beer for him, a Sprite for Ayres, and a rum and Coke for Detective Dimitry Ruvin. Ayres's phone rang. The jury was ready. She smiled. "They wouldn't walk her that quickly." The three hustled back to the courthouse, which they had left just ten minutes before.

By 6:56 P.M., everyone was seated. The jurors filed in to their two tiers of chairs. Not including the time they'd spent waiting for the exhibits to arrive, and for everyone to reassemble in the courtroom, they'd only deliberated for twenty-one minutes.

A juror seated to the far right on the front row—the official foreman—stood. The clerk spoke to him in the official script used for verdicts:

"As to the crime of first-degree murder, we, the jury, find the defendant?"

"Guilty."

Brittany displayed no emotion.

Her family cried. So did Jayna's.

Minutes later, Greg Lloyd, the juror who had started the trial willing to step in if he thought Brittany was being unfairly prosecuted, started to walk out of the courtroom. As he had for the past six days, he saw Jayna's father, David

Murray, near the middle aisle of the second row. Lloyd had tried to remain objective during the trial, but his emotions had overwhelmed him that morning during presentation of the autopsy photos, and he'd wept. The feelings hadn't ebbed all day. He stopped to shake David's hand, each man looking into the wet eyes of the other. "I am so sorry for your loss," Lloyd said.

Moments later, in the vestibule outside the front entrance to the courtroom, Detective Jim Drewry was looking for someone. A sheriff's deputy he knew led him into a small room near the entrance, where witnesses typically wait. There sat Earl Norwood, the man who had invited him fishing, even as Drewry was dead set on locking up his daughter for the rest of her life. "None of this was personal," Drewry told him.

CHAPTER THIRTY

More Than Three Hundred Blows

Brittany Norwood's sentencing hearing was scheduled for 1:30 P.M. on an overcast Friday afternoon, January 27, 2012, with winds whipping to thirty miles per hour. For weeks Montgomery Circuit Court Judge Robert Greenberg had weighed whether to impose a life sentence that offered Brittany a chance at parole in the distant future, or impose a sentence of life with no chance at parole.

Expecting hundreds in the gallery, Greenberg had again reserved the county's largest courtroom. By 1:15 P.M., more than 150 people had already taken their seats. Three minutes later, sheriff's deputies escorted in Jayna Murray's family, leading them down a center aisle and seating them in the second row on the left side. Then came Brittany Norwood's family, escorted down the aisle to the second row on the right. On both sides of the aisle, the occupants of the second rows leaned on each other, held hands in their laps, and for the most part stared straight ahead.

By the time Judge Greenberg called the hearing to order, at 1:36 P.M., there were more than 200 spectators.

He would hear first from both families, then their attorneys, and then—if she chose to speak—from Brittany. He had already read filings submitted by the prosecution and the defense, which offered a preview of how each side would try to define Brittany and how each side hoped she would be punished.

Prosecutors John McCarthy and Marybeth Ayres, supported by more than sixty letters from Jayna's family and friends, strongly urged a sentence of life without parole. They labeled Brittany "evil"—someone who'd attacked Jayna with as many as ten weapons, who could then shift into cover-up mode and slice open Jayna's pants and underwear to stage a rape, who'd lied to her own family about phantom attackers knowing the address of the home where they were staying. Brittany "showed no regard, nor empathy, for anyone," the prosecutors wrote.

On the other side, Brittany's attorneys Doug Wood and Chris Griffiths, backed by letters from Brittany's eight siblings and others, urged Greenberg to look decades into the future, when Brittany might at least have a chance to convince a parole board to release her. They described their client as "neither a calculating killer nor a deranged psychopath" but someone who'd "become overwhelmed with emotion" and "committed the unthinkable." They attached a report by Dr. David Williamson, the head-trauma expert who visited Brittany at the jail three times and whose credentials had worried McCarthy. But his report said nothing about concussion-related problems from the soccer field. Instead, it dealt with moodiness and depression. "Over the past five years, Ms. Norwood developed phases of depressed mood or moodiness," Williamson wrote. "During exacerbations, she would become socially isolative, experience emotional disturbances, have changes in her appetite, her sleep patterns and at times contemplate her own death and even develop fleeting suicidal ideas. She had trouble during those phases keeping up with her everyday responsibilities, fell behind on her bills. She often neglected her hygiene and appearance. She noted that she was forgetful and had concentration problems."

Before the hearing, McCarthy and Wood had done some horse-trading. The prosecutor wanted to allow eight people to speak about Jayna and the murder's impact on them and why Brittany should receive the maximum sentence. Wood could have insisted on only one speaker, but what he really wanted was a chance to speak last. Deal, McCarthy said.

Jayna's father, David Murray, rose and walked to the podium in the well of the courtroom, facing the judge. His hands shook as he steadied a prepared statement before him. Twenty feet away sat Brittany, her hair pulled back, her head bent, her legs twitching. She wore a black cardigan sweater over a light pink shirt and white necklace.

"I miss Jayna more than can be expressed in words," David said, trying somehow to capture what he'd been through for ten months—the bottomless grief, the crushing guilt of an ex-soldier who hadn't been able to protect his child. "She was more than a daughter," David said, his voice breaking as he spoke about how close his family was. "She was one of my four best friends."

David paused for a video of Jayna bungee jumping off of a bridge in Washington State on her thirtieth birthday, her smile beaming into the courtroom to the music of Tom Petty's "Learning to Fly." Behind David, Brittany's mother, Larkita, sat with tears streaming down her face.

Jayna's mother, her two brothers, her two sisters-in-law, her longtime boyfriend, and one of her closest friends spoke as well. "I wake up every day and set the intention to build the strength to be happy," Marisa Connaughton told Greenberg, "even if it is just for one minute."

McCarthy then described what Brittany had inflicted on Jayna: not only brutal strikes and stabs that crushed Jayna's skull and damaged her brain, but also the slicing and cutting wounds that amounted to mutilation. "They're torture," he said of the cuts. "They're sadistic."

Freed from the trial's restrictive rules of evidence, McCarthy now had his chance to explain Brittany's motive. It was a question to which he'd been assembling his answer since March, interviewing those who knew Brittany, studying the crime and the cover-up, talking to Ayres about her research into psychopathy. Only one thing engendered any compassion in him for Brittany: she seemed to have been born miswired. The section of her brain where a conscience should be simply hadn't developed fully. And apparently what Brittany had done was expand that gap in her brain, feed it for her own thrills. She stole from close friends just to see their reactions; she led a dark, secret life, uninhibited by any sense that it was wrong; she knew how to stay one step ahead of trouble, or talk her way out of trouble when it caught up to her. That only gave her more confidence to do as she pleased. It was here that Ayres's views on psychopathy came into play, suggesting that Brittany was on a contradictory path of self-destruction. The more secrets Brittany kept, the worse she felt about herself as people all around her succeeded—and succeeded without deceit and subterfuge. "Anyone who is like this lacks self-esteem and self-worth," Ayres had told McCarthy. The two had talked about Brittany's affection for her family, which seemed genuine. "I think that side was real," Ayres said.

McCarthy wanted to offer Greenberg—and everyone else in the courtroom—a sense of the Brittany he'd come to know. He started off talking about her family.

"Your honor has been doing this for more than thirty years," he said. "I've been doing it for thirty years. Mr. Wood's been doing it for thirty years. We always hear about these terrible families that the defendants that come before us come from—they didn't really ever have a chance, they were never given a real opportunity." That was hardly the case for Brittany. "This is a lovely family," McCarthy said. "Supportive of her. Even here today."

The opportunities they gave her led to a college scholarship, he said. Yet she stole, she got thrown off the soccer team, she moved to Washington, D.C., and she continued to steal. She made a mess of her job at the first lululemon store where she worked, in Georgetown.

McCarthy knew he couldn't reveal too much about Brittany's most shameful secrets—he'd long concluded she was into prostitution, but it hadn't been part of the trial—so he worked the edges. He told Greenberg that Brittany had accidentally dropped a subway card on the floor of the store the night of the murder. The card came from a "prostitution self-help group in the District of Columbia," McCarthy said. Later, he told the judge about Brittany's text messages involving "providing personal services," prompting Wood to object, and Greenberg to put a halt to it.

But McCarthy was on solid ground when he recounted what he'd learned about the events leading to the murder.

He described how Jayna and Brittany had checked each other's bags, how Jayna had confronted Brittany about trying to steal a pair of pants, how Brittany couldn't explain herself, how the two left the store and Jayna called her manager.

"Brittany Norwood was about to be fired the next day," McCarthy said.

And it wouldn't have been just a firing. It would have resurrected the Georgetown suspicions, and it would have cost her the personal-trainer job she had lined up at the fancy health club where she really wanted to work.

"She was on her way," McCarthy said. "It was more than a pair of pants. It was an unraveling of the life she had set for herself." So Brittany came up with a ruse about forgetting her wallet and called Jayna. "She lured Jayna back to the place where this killing began," he said.

McCarthy couldn't know exactly what happened immediately after the two returned to the store, but he had his assumptions. Brittany probably asked Jayna not to report the theft to the store manager, Rachel Oertli. Jayna probably responded in one of two ways: *"It's too late. I already have,"* or *"I can't do that. It's between you and Rachel."* Within seconds, McCarthy concluded, Brittany attacked. Was she enraged? Was she trying to silence the witness? McCarthy had always thought it was a combination of the two—and he'd come to believe something else. At some point after the murder—maybe during the staging, or after she'd started talking to the detectives, or after the lululemon athletica company had reached out to lend her support—Brittany actually thought she'd come out of the whole thing ahead. She'd have her job at Equinox. She'd have the sympathy of all those around her. It wouldn't be that big a deal, really. But who really knew what happened in those critical seconds? Only Brittany. Maybe not even Brittany.

For McCarthy, it was enough to have walked the judge through her complicated past, the bag check, the attack, and the cover-up. "There was cunning and guile involved in this," he said, and he urged Greenberg not to give Brittany a chance at parole.

As they waited to ask Greenberg for leniency instead, Brittany's family had heard a horrible new word—*torture*—added to the description of what Brittany had done. Her oldest brother, Sandré, stepped forward first. He told the Murrays how sorry his family was for their loss. It was a crime so brutal, he acknowledged, that he and other family members could have turned their backs on Brittany.

But they didn't, Sandré said, because of all the things she had done for her parents and siblings and nephews before March 11, 2011. "One is not given this type of love and support, not even from family," he said. "It can only be earned."

He urged the judge to give Brittany a chance at parole. "Brittany is a person worthy of rehabilitation and, maybe, at some point, redemption."

Not until Sandré spoke his final words did Brittany raise her head briefly and look his way, wearing the same blank expression she had throughout the proceedings. "Please, your honor, at least give her some hope," he said. "If you leave her with hope, you leave our family with hope."

Brittany's lead attorney, Wood, got up to speak, talking about the devastation not just to the Murrays, but to the Norwoods as well. "Every time they think it's healing, the wound will be opened by regret," Wood said. "It will be opened by looking around and not seeing Brittany and realizing what she had done. Her absence will always be there and will always torture that family. What I would say to that family, though, your honor, is that it's not their fault . . . They did everything they could. But they're always going to wonder about that regret. And that's a punishment that their daughter has inflicted on them."

Wood ended as Sandré had: even a distant, remote chance at parole would give the family some hope, he said.

But it was the next moment that so many in the courtroom had waited for since Jayna's death, among them Chasity Wilson, Jayna's close friend from their days at Halliburton in Houston. Chasity had been in the United Arab Emirates on business and had come home through Washington so she could be at this hearing. She sat just behind the Murray family. She'd tried to get a look at Brittany when she'd arrived, but couldn't see her. Now, however, Brittany stood up. She hardly looked look like a monster, Chasity thought.

"May I address the Murray family and my family first?" Brittany asked.

"Yes," Greenberg said.

"During the break, I really considered if I wanted to say anything because I figured, 'What was the point?'" Brittany began, her head cocked and body slouched.

Most people in the courtroom were hearing her soft and steady voice for the very first time. In Chasity's mind, and in the minds of many of Jayna's supporters, the substance of those first words created the immediate impression that Brittany didn't care. But Brittany's supporters heard something else: the weight of her crime bearing down on her more than ever.

"But for the Murray family," she continued, "what do I honestly say to your family when your daughter is gone and I'm the one who has been convicted of her murder? I know whatever I say to you today won't take the pain away over your loss of Jayna." Brittany's voice shook.

"But before I go to prison, I needed for you to hear me tell you just how deeply sorry I am. My hope for your family is that someday you will be able to find the forgiveness in your heart and peace. And I am truly sorry. For my family," she said, sniffling and pausing, "as you know, I couldn't have asked for a better family. Mom and Dad, you've been the most loving and supportive parents I could have ever hoped for. To my brothers and sisters, I have always shared such a special bond with each of you. And that will never change no matter the circumstances. I am truly blessed to have all of you as my family. I don't want any of you to think that I am here today because of anything you did or did not do. I truly love you all very much, and thank you for the tremendous amount of love I feel from you every day."

She reached for a tissue to wipe her nose. With his arm around his wife's shoulders, Earl Norwood watched his daughter and subtly mouthed words of support to her. "Your honor, I understand I'll be severely punished for the crime I have been convicted of. And now I face a possible lifetime in prison. I also know there are many people who want for me to have a sentence without hope. But I am asking you today to leave me with some. I don't even ask you this for myself. I truly ask you this for my family, that is, especially my mom and dad. Thank you."

She sat down, having spoken for less than three minutes, not admitting to killing Jayna but referring only to "the crime I have been convicted of," carefully chosen words that could not be used against her when she appealed the verdict. Legal niceties aside, the passive words were a kick in the gut to Jayna's family and friends. Brittany had made no admission. She did not explain.

Greenberg had said little during the three-hour hearing. He'd presided over this case for months, including the pretrial hearings, rendering decisions based on law and evidence. Now, the husband and father of three children spoke directly to the Murrays and Norwoods, choking over his words as he thanked them for sending him letters to review. "I want to assure each and every one of you I read those letters. I felt your pain on both sides, and I understand the emotions that you expressed."

Within several minutes, though, he had moved on to describing the brutality and cold-blooded nature of Brittany's actions.

"I guess we'll never know, Ms. Norwood, whether, when you went back to that lululemon store, you intended to kill Ms. Murray. And to be candid with you, I'm not 100 percent sure that when you went back there that was your intention. But once you started your assault, you reveled in the gore. What has struck me as most remarkable about this case, ma'am, especially in light of the fact that I'm being told that you wanted a career as a physical trainer, is the incredible physical condition in which you found yourself on that day—to be able to rain down more than three hundred blows with a variety of lethal instruments that I think were not immediately available to you is nothing short of astounding to me, ma'am. I confess to you, I once sat and just went like this"—here Greenberg made a pounding motion—"three hundred times. It took me about eight minutes to do that."

Greenberg continued. "With adrenaline coursing through your body, you mutilated this woman. And after every blow, you had a chance to think about what you were doing. The lies that you told afterward were incredible. You're one hell of a liar, ma'am."

Nothing about Brittany had impressed him. But her family had.

"I watched your family during this trial, and I wanted to cry for them, because they appear to be the personification of the American dream," Greenberg said, turning his head to the second row. He spoke of raising children and how they eventually leave home. "You know at some point, we who are parents, we send our children off into the world. I have three children I sent off into the world. And they're either off to college, or they're off to the workplace, and all we can do is hope that we instilled in them the values that we had, that they're good citizens. But sometimes things go wrong, terribly wrong."

Next he spoke about Jayna's family, and what Brittany had done to them.

"No parent should ever have to bury their child. Sometimes things happen. We lose a child to accident, disease. And while as parents we may not accept that, at least we understand it. We understand why our loved one was taken away. But when a murder so horrific occurs, ma'am, there isn't any such acceptance."

Thirty feet away, from his second-row seat, Jayna's

brother Dirk started to feel that the sentence he and his family wanted was coming. When Greenberg first began to speak, Dirk had whispered to his wife, April, that the judge wasn't going to issue a no-parole sentence. "He's not going to do it. He's not going to do it," he'd said. But now, to Dirk's ears, Greenberg had stripped Brittany of her identity. He kept calling her "ma'am."

Greenberg spoke about how she had no drug problem, no deep psychiatric illness. "The information that I have— provided from your family and from your attorneys— expresses complete bewilderment as to how this could have occurred."

He said how reluctant he was to give her even the slightest chance at freedom.

"Stand up, please," the judge told her. Brittany did as requested, void of expression. "It's the sentence of this court that you be confined to the Maryland Division of Correction for the balance of your natural life without the possibility of parole."

Clapping and cheers erupted. Chasity said "Yes!" as did others.

"Please!" Greenberg said, silencing the crowd.

Brittany showed little reaction. Her father, Earl, looked down, his arm around his wife.

Greenberg dryly went through Brittany's right to appeal. Then he looked up at the attorneys, and it was over. "Thank you, counsel. That will conclude the matter."

In the crowd, Jayna's mother, Phyllis, shook as she hugged first her husband and then Fraser Bocell, Jayna's longtime boyfriend. Up front, sheriff's deputies put Brittany back in handcuffs and led her away. She looked only at the door in front of her. Earl Norwood kept his arm around his wife as he spoke to one of his sons.

The two lead detectives in the case, Dimitry Ruvin and Jim Drewry, stood up and stretched their legs. They knew Brittany was headed to the Maryland Correctional Institution for Women, about twenty-five miles away, in Jessup, and each planned to eventually pay her a call. Ruvin figured he'd wait five years. Drewry thought he'd go sooner, maybe 2014. But both of them intended to ask the same question: why?

In all the commotion, Wood asked Greenberg for one last bench conference. When the attorneys approached, Wood told the judge that Brittany's parents were staying in town until the end of the weekend. Given that it was Friday, he asked the judge to recommend that Brittany be kept temporarily at the local jail so they could see her before they left. As everyone knew, the transfer to Jessup would delay visits until she was fully processed there.

"I don't feel I have the power to do that, Mr. Wood," Greenberg said. "I'm sorry."

Epilogue

LULULEMON ATHLETICA

The murder of Jayna Murray inside the lululemon athletica store in Bethesda, Maryland, pushed grief 2,900 miles to the company's headquarters, in Vancouver, Canada. When executives there heard the tragic news that Jayna and her coworker, Brittany Norwood, had been attacked, they reached out to both families and offered to help. A week later, however, when police pinned the murder on Brittany, the company suddenly faced new concerns—over both liability and public image. Executives made the decision to not publicly discuss Brittany's tenure.

On a concrete level, lululemon had to decide what to do with its store in Bethesda once the police completed their forensic testing. Retain the store's marquee location, next to the Apple Store and across from the cobble-stoned pedestrian avenue called Bethesda Lane, and risk upsetting customers, who'd be asked not to dwell on the fact that they were shopping in a former crime scene? Ultimately, yes. As spring turned to summer in 2011, lululemon executives revealed their plans in a carefully worded statement:

"It is with warm and grateful hearts that we are announcing the reopening of our newly renovated Bethesda store on Friday, June 24. The reopening will embrace the theme of 'love' in honor of Jayna Murray. More than ever, we remain committed to the people of Bethesda and look forward to continuing to share with this community the same love, passion and grace with which Jayna lived her life."

The renovation featured a new stained-glass window across the top of the storefront, which spelled *love* in cursive script. The next day—with traffic blocked outside the store along Bethesda Avenue—lululemon held a community yoga class. Loyal customers showed up with mats, rolled them out, and struck poses for an hour.

Not everyone was thrilled. Employees returned to a store that had been renovated but not overhauled. The location of bathrooms—in one of which Brittany had staged her own attack—were the same, as was the layout of the fitting area where Brittany had laid down bloody, size-14 shoe prints in an effort to implicate intruders who had never existed. A door led to a small closet where Jayna had been beaten and slashed and stabbed to death.

Customers who followed the case closely could look around and see the similarities. Some asked saleswomen questions about the case: "Where are the shoes? You had shoes at the store that day."

These days, Saturday mornings along Bethesda Avenue look very much the same as they did before the murder. Couples stroll the sidewalks, holding their children's hands and their dogs' leashes. Shoppers walk in and out of the Apple store and Georgetown Cupcake. Most customers no longer view the lululemon store as a crime scene. Many support the company's decision to reopen it, even those like labor attorney Ellen Silver, who had misgivings the first time she returned. But speaking outside the store recently, she wondered aloud what good it would have done to have the space now playing host to a restaurant. That would have meant pretending the murder didn't happen. "This is somehow reaffirming of life," she said.

Lululemon executives consistently declined reporters' requests for interviews about the case. Margaret Wheeler, the company's top human-resources executive—or, in lulu parlance, the "Senior Vice President of People Potential"—agreed to speak by phone for thirty minutes only on the condition that the questions broadly covered the company's culture and what it looked for in employees. Wheeler said lululemon looks for sales workers who are outgoing, smart, lead a healthy lifestyle, and are committed to setting and achieving goals. "Even though we teach it," she said of goal setting, "we actually look for people who are predisposed to being goal setters and being up to really big things in their lives in lots of different things."

Regarding the murder case, although Wheeler was the company's point person after the tragedy—she attended the trial and got to know the Murrays and the workers at the Bethesda store—she deferred to remarks by then-lululemon CEO Christine Day after the verdict. That 217-word statement remains the most detailed from the company about the case. "We have all been deeply affected by the loss of Jayna Murray and the violation of our safe and loving store environment," Day said. "The actions of Brittany Norwood that night are the antithesis of the values of our company and are not reflective of the outstanding people who work for lululemon."

As for its business, lululemon is facing furious competition from companies such as Gap and Nike, which have both spread into yoga-apparel sales, and recently endured a controversial recall of thousands of pairs of yoga pants that were mistakenly made of see-through fabric. But lulu's money-making magic has remained intact, as has its aura of meeting more intangible goals. "Reaching a billion dollars in revenue is clearly an important milestone that as a company we can all be very proud of," Day said in 2012 as she announced record-setting sales. "But far more important than the number itself are the beliefs, values, culture and people that achieved it. We really are so much more than our numbers; it is the everyday actions of our dedicated team that translates into an unparalleled guest experience and allows us to achieve our ultimate goal of elevating the world."

THE APPLE MANAGERS

The Apple Store managers and security guards in Bethesda took a public flogging for not calling 911 the night they heard screams coming from the adjacent lululemon athletica store. On November 3, 2011, the day after Brittany Norwood was convicted of murder, someone placed white flowers on the sidewalk outside Apple that were arranged into the number "331," the number of injuries Jayna Murray had suffered, according to a report on Washington's NBC-4 television station. Commentators and bloggers wrote that their inaction raised broader questions about society, or even reflected poorly on their parents.

As of this writing, the only public remarks that Jana Svrzo and Ricardo Rios have made about that night were those from the witness stand during the trial. Svrzo declined to comment for this book, and Rios did not respond to messages. Apple's corporate public-relations officials declined to talk about the case or make the managers available for interviews. In discussions with detectives and prosecutors, Jana broke down over what had happened; although Ricardo showed less emotion, those who interviewed him couldn't tell if that was his natural disposition or his feelings about what happened. Ricardo still works at the Bethesda Apple Store next to lululemon. Jana transferred to Apple's store in Georgetown, where she is a senior manager.

The murder also weighed on security guard Wilbert Hawkins, who no longer works at the Bethesda Apple Store. "I feel sad that happened on my shift, right next door," he said. Wilbert described the noises from the lululemon store as yells and crashing sounds, and he remembered telling Ricardo not to worry because he'd heard noises there before. He said his sense of danger had been shaped by his past: growing up in a rough neighborhood in Washington, D.C., then working a series of security jobs in office buildings, construction sites, and housing projects before his Apple posting in Bethesda. Had he been working somewhere else, Wilbert said he wouldn't have dismissed what he was hearing. "I would have done something different, much different," he said. "I would have been expecting it."

The lack of action by the Apple managers and security guards bore hallmarks of what scientists have long called the "Bystander Effect," which holds that a person is less apt to call 911 when others are around. "The key phrase is 'diffusion of responsibility,'" said Joel Lieberman, a psychologist who chairs the Criminal Justice Department at the University of Nevada, Las Vegas. "It's a pretty powerful effect. It's robust."

Lieberman has studied group behavior for decades. He

and others believe that people's brains often work against them in such situations, telling them that if someone is truly in trouble, someone else will call 911. "That really shocks the layperson. But these situations don't surprise me," says Lieberman. "The more observers there are, the less likely people are to get involved." People also are more apt to call 911, he said, when specifically asked to do so.

Several factors conspired to invoke the Bystander Effect that night: the calm and safety of downtown Bethesda, creating the mind-set that even harsh screams didn't mean violence; the terrible fact that Jayna Murray couldn't point to one person and ask for help; the diffusion of responsibility, in which the Apple managers looked to the security guards for guidance, and the guards deferred to the managers; and the fact that lots of people were still out and about at 10:10 P.M. on a Friday in downtown Bethesda.

"It almost sounds like a perfect recipe," Lieberman said.

Of course, he and other bystander experts are quick to add, other factors could also have been at play—such as an individual's character, or his or her sense of empathy, or level of "self-efficacy," a psychology term describing a person's belief that he or she can complete a goal. In the end, though, Lieberman came back to this: "When things like this happen, the people who don't call 911 seem like monsters. How can people be that cold? But time and time again, we've seen this happen to people who are not monsters."

THE DETECTIVES

Detectives Jim Drewry and Dimitry Ruvin still work murders for the Montgomery County Police Department.

Drewry has moved to the cold-case squad, giving him regular hours and Fridays off ahead of his planned retirement in late 2013. The job has other rewards as well. In April of 2013, Drewry sat in a courtroom as sixty-four-year-old Richard E. Ricketts was sentenced to life in prison for a vicious rape he'd committed more than thirty years earlier. The squad had found Ricketts in Florida after testing old evidence in the case for DNA and matching the results against a database of known offenders. "You are a wretched and warped man," Montgomery Judge Terrence McGann said during the sentencing, an opinion Drewry had no quarrel with. Because so much of cold-case work is based on forensics, Drewry rarely interviews suspects anymore, but he hopes to get one last chance—with Brittany Norwood—before he retires. But he remains pessimistic about what the interview will bring, even if he manages to see her. "Can anybody really figure out someone like Brittany?" he says.

Ruvin and the other Montgomery County detectives have moved into more spacious, more modern headquarters, but the space doesn't yet feel right to Ruvin. Maybe it's the higher cubicles, making each detective feel more isolated. Maybe it's the size of their floor, which allows officers and civilians from other departments to wander through. Maybe it is the interrogation rooms—new and improved, sure—but too far from their computers to enable them to go check something quickly. Maybe it's none of that. "We're cops. We bitch about everything," Ruvin deadpans, sitting inside his high-walled cubicle and fielding a call about a long-running case he is working. The detective still sees evil erupt out of nowhere in his county. On June 10, 2013, Ruvin also found himself at a sentencing hearing—watching forty-seven-year-old Curtis Lopez get sent away for life for crushing his estranged wife's skull with a thirty-pound dumbbell and her eleven-year-old son's skull with a baseball bat. Ruvin has stayed in touch with Jayna Murray's family, and, like Drewry, he plans to pay Brittany a call in prison. But he wants to wait a few more years—until Brittany has exhausted her appeals, until she feels she has nothing to lose by being candid with him. "I think her mind has to get used to the fact she's not getting out," the detective says.

Sergeant Craig Wittenberger, who supervised the lululemon investigation, retired from the Montgomery force after thirty-one years, and took a job with the federal government. "There were no winners in this case," Wittenberger said shortly before he retired. "Jayna was brutally murdered. Both Jayna's and Brittany's families have been torn apart. Brittany's probably just been conniving people her whole life."

Another person dragged into the case was Keith Lockett, the homeless Bethesda man who had the misfortune of showing up in an emergency room after the murder while talking about having just been in a fight. Wittenberger, Drewry, and Ruvin had no choice but to go full-tilt at him, even as they could never really get comfortable with the idea of him unleashing such brutality. Keith has largely stayed out of trouble since being questioned in the investigation, picking up a minor trespassing charge and two drinking-in-public citations, according to court records. Reached on a cell phone he keeps, Keith declined to talk about the case.

THE LAWYERS

Marybeth Ayres, the Montgomery County Assistant State's Attorney who helped prosecute Brittany Norwood, was promoted to head the office's gang unit, taking on crimes often committed in the county's middle- to lower-class neighborhoods. These areas aren't as rough as those in inner-city Baltimore or Queens, where Ayres worked before she came to Montgomery, but among some residents, there is a parallel: violence, particularly in the form of protection or retribution, is a way of life. Ayres often thinks that Brittany should have been different, given how she was raised and the opportunities she had. "True evil," she says these days from behind her desk, "comes from a complete lack of empathy."

In the summer of 2012, State's Attorney John McCarthy considered a run for Maryland attorney general, but as he found himself weighing his family life against the eighty-hour weeks that would come with a new and bigger office—and when a political ally and popular state senator decided to run for attorney general—McCarthy had his answer. He'd remain Montgomery County's State's Attorney.

The public's fascination with the lululemon case continues to amaze him. He speaks regularly about the trial to civic groups and other attorneys, and even, on May 10, 2013, to about forty Maryland judges at their annual training conference. "We don't have many murders in Montgomery," he began, "but the ones we have are often completely bizarre." He clicked through a PowerPoint presentation, projecting evidence photographs. He played video shot from inside the Apple Store, showing the managers approaching the wall to better hear the screams and thuds—as McCarthy himself moved closer to his audience. "The murder is happening closer than Judge Salmon is to me," he said, indicating a distance of eight feet.

Brittany's defense lawyers, Doug Wood and Chris Griffiths, returned to their winning ways after the trial. On November 15, 2012, their client Alexis Simpson was acquitted on all charges after being accused of stabbing her college roommate to death in the throat. "Clearly, the jury felt she acted in self-defense," Griffiths told reporters after the verdict. He and Wood still maintain a public silence about the lululemon case, in part, they say, because Brittany is still pursuing her appeal, and also out of the wishes of the Norwood family.

THE MURRAYS

On the eleventh day of every month, Chasity Wilson, one of Jayna Murray's close friends from Halliburton, helps organize a lunch or happy hour for those who knew Jayna in Houston. They share stories and remember how Jayna made them laugh, trying to redefine the day of the month on which Jayna was murdered. In May 2013, the eleventh fell on a Saturday when the Murray family was gathering at a cemetery north of the city, where days earlier a nine-foot custom-chiseled Celtic cross had been erected over their cemetery plot. Chasity spoke to Jayna's parents, altered her group's typical plans, and invited everyone to the gravesite. The mourning is always there, and on this day this was the place to go.

Jayna's friends and parents—David and Phyllis Murray— were joined by her brother Hugh and his wife, Kate, in town from North Carolina with their first child, and by Jayna's brother Dirk, his wife, April, and their two young sons. The boys, who had called Jayna "Tia T," helped their grandmother place flowers in two stone vases at the base of the cross. About thirty minutes after everyone had arrived, David and Phyllis gathered them all around him to read a poem that captured what they feel Jayna tries to tell them every day. "So live your life, laugh again, enjoy yourself and be free. Then I know with every breath you take, you'll be taking one for me," David recited, choking up over the words.

Jayna's family tries to live out that philosophy but can't always pull it off. For Dirk Murray, the nightmares have become less frequent, but they still occur: he is outside a locked store, desperate but unable to get in to his sister as she is being brutally murdered. By day, he works to shield his sons from learning details of Jayna's death, at least until they're older; already, though, there have been challenges, things the boys have picked up on from overheard conversations among adults, the way kids do. Dirk and April know that the day is coming when they'll have to carefully explain to the boys what really happened.

Hugh Murray remains a captain and attorney in the U.S. Army. He is stationed at Fort Bragg, where he prosecutes cases as part of the army's legal arm, the JAG Corps. As the lululemon case unfolded in 2011, Hugh and Kate, also an attorney, explored three possible lawsuits. One was a wrongful death case against Brittany. But she had no money. The second was a claim against Apple. But what legal responsibility did the company have outside its stores? The most compelling case seemed to be a negligence claim against lululemon athletica, which knew it had a questionable employee on its hands. Countering that were several factors: Hugh, Kate, and the rest of the Murrays didn't want to drag out the case any longer; they didn't want to see themselves as victims; Jayna had been so fond of lululemon; and lululemon had been so good to them after the tragedy. In the end, the Murray family decided not to sue.

David Murray returned to overseas oil and gas work, managing a project in Israel when he wasn't in Texas. The memories of his daughter are constant. "Not too many minutes of the day go by when I don't think about Jayna." He thinks less and less about Brittany Norwood, even as he yearns for answers. "I still want to know why."

Phyllis Murray received from the police the jewelry Jayna had been wearing on the night she was killed, including a pinkie ring, which she wears all the time and constantly finds herself touching. She takes pride in a nonprofit started by her sons and her daughter's friends, the Jayna Murray Foundation, which soon will begin awarding scholarship money from more than $80,000 raised so far. She looks at scrapbooks of her daughter and tries to remember her laugh. "But there are days," she says, "when nothing will make you happy."

THE NORWOODS

Earl Norwood still runs an upholstery shop on a stretch of industrial parks in Kent, Washington, about twenty miles south of Seattle. The shop sells foam to other businesses, makes mattresses, and repairs upholstery on home furniture, car seats, RV seats, and boat seats. The inside of the shop looks as one might expect: sofas here, fabric swatches there, large pieces of foam over there. When approached in person, Earl politely declines to comment on the case. "I don't know what I'd say," he says, adding only that nothing he could say would change anything.

Neither his wife, Larkita, nor any of their sons and daughters returned calls or letters to discuss what Brittany was like before March 11, 2011. Doug Wood, one of Brittany's attorneys, said that the family did not want to be interviewed. Brittany's parents and eight siblings did however write letters to Judge Robert Greenberg ahead of Brittany's sentencing hearings. The letters expressed deep sorrow to the Murray family, but were carefully scripted, in deference to Brittany's pending legal appeal, stating nothing about the murder and acknowledging only that Brittany had been convicted of it or, even more vaguely, that she had done something that warranted prison time. They also described Brittany as a good person who eventually deserved a chance at parole.

"I want the world to have a chance to know Brittany for more than what took place on one extremely unfortunate day and know her the same way I do," her younger brother Zachary wrote.

"Brittany is from a family of kindhearted people, a family that has been through thick and thin," another younger brother, Josh, wrote. "A family with two loving parents that have worked as hard as they possibly could to do anything for their children, no matter what."

Larkita wrote that her heart was broken for Jayna's family: "Seeing them hurting in court was very difficult for me. I live with this sadness every single day."

The families' suffering was all too familiar to Russell Butler, executive director for the Maryland Crime Victims'

Resource Center, who spent seventeen years as a criminal defense attorney. Time and time again, he has seen murder cases tear through the families of victims and killers. "It's the same event, but the trauma manifests in different ways," Butler said.

The victim's family members often find themselves dwelling on the way he or she died. The more gruesome the death, the harder it is not to think about. "It's vicarious trauma. They relive it," he said. "They visualize it in their head, over and over and over."

The defendant's family members also dwell on what happened, but from a different point of view: the fact that their flesh and blood inflicted pain can cause them to feel responsible. Did they miss something? Should they have gotten help for their loved one? "They can't separate themselves from it," Butler said.

BRITTANY NORWOOD

Until Brittany Norwood speaks about the case, her mindset and motives won't be known.

In court papers submitted prior to her sentencing, Brittany's attorneys, Doug Wood and Chris Griffiths, said that she did not suffer from any mental disorder that met the legal definition of insanity. "Ms. Norwood is neither a calculating killer nor a deranged psychopath," they wrote, arguing that she was amenable to rehabilitation and deserved a chance at parole. "Ms. Norwood became overwhelmed with emotion during a confrontation, and before she could regain her composure, she committed the unthinkable. It is understandable why the jury rejected that characterization of Ms. Norwood's state of mind, but her defense was honest. Ms. Norwood committed a crime of passion."

But experts who study psychopaths say that Brittany's personality and actions bear at least some of the hallmarks of the condition—which is not so much a mental illness as a personality disorder, and is marked by superficial charm, pathological lying, and a stunning lack of remorse and guilt. As for what made Brittany turn so violent, the experts say it's important to think about why murders happen in the first place. On one extreme are killers who strike from reaction and emotion, just as Brittany's attorneys described. On the other extreme are killers who see a solution to a problem. It is the latter end of the spectrum where psychopaths—even those who've never been in a fistfight—are more apt to be.

"Their threshold for becoming violent is lower," says J. Reid Meloy, a forensic psychologist and author of *The Psychopathic Mind*. "They don't have things that inhibit the rest of us, like conscience, empathy, sympathy."

In Brittany's case, detectives could never determine exactly how the crime started. Did Brittany strike from behind as the two were walking through the store? Did it start off as a face-to-face confrontation? Either way, Brittany seems to have concluded that her only way out of the mess—being caught shoplifting, not getting the personal trainer job she wanted—was to eliminate Jayna. Under such a scenario, she switched into murder mode not because she snapped, but because it was such an easy segue to make. "For psychopaths, the emotional brakes aren't there," says Robert Hare, author of *Without Conscience*, the book that Jayna's brother Hugh found so revealing after the murder.

"It probably seemed like the right thing to do at the time," says Matthew Logan, a longtime criminal investigator and psychologist who has interviewed more than two hundred psychopaths in prisons. "They think, 'I don't like this situation. I don't like what this person is doing to me. I am going to take the person out.'"

Brittany did so, struggling to find the right weapon as she delivered blow after blow. But what about the nonlethal slashings to Jayna's face—the notion, as Judge Robert Greenberg put it, that Brittany "reveled in the gore"?

They're all part of the package, according to Meloy, Hare, and Logan, who along with ten other psychopath experts wrote about the disorder in a 2012 FBI training publication devoted to the subject. Psychopaths, they wrote, are threats not only because they con and manipulate, but also because they seek thrills and control. "If psychopaths commit a homicide, their killing likely will be planned and purposeful, not the result of a loss of emotional control," the experts wrote. "Their motive more commonly will involve sadistic gratification. When faced with overwhelming evidence of their guilt, they frequently will claim they lost control or were in a rage when committing the act of violence. In fact, their violence often is emotionless, calculated, and completely controlled."

Brittany is now Inmate Number 401149 at Maryland's only female prison, the Maryland Correctional Institution for Women. Originally built in 1939, the facility has an interior courtyard bordered by a mix of old red-brick support buildings and modern living quarters—all surrounded by fences, razor wire, and guard towers. The prison is known for its sewing shop, and in particular the shop's production of giant American flags. Most inmates share a double-cell. As of the spring of 2013, Brittany was one of 765 inmates there, and one of 54 serving life sentences, according to a Maryland prison spokesman. Citing confidentiality rules for inmates, he declined to comment on Brittany's conduct in prison or what kind of programs she might be participating in.

Those who know Brittany, and those involved with investigating and prosecuting her, wonder how she is doing there—a suburban girl who'd never been locked up among hardened and larger inmates from the streets of Baltimore and other rough spots in Maryland. Detective Dimitry Ruvin, for one, thinks Brittany will not be pushed around in prison. All her life, he thinks, she fooled people about who she really was, owing to her ability to put on whatever persona she needed to get by. "It will serve her well up there," he said. As to whether Brittany really knows what she did or why she did it, even her supporters have wondered how long it will take for that to sink in. After her sentencing hearing, one of her defense attorneys, Doug Wood, addressed the subject during a press conference. Giving Brittany a chance at parole, even a remote one, would have helped guide her rehabilitation, he said. "She could come to terms with what she did," Wood said, "and try to figure out why it happened."

On May 31, 2013, Brittany's appellant attorneys filed another request to delay their legal brief outlining why her conviction should be reversed and a new trial ordered. It is unclear what argument they can or will advance. Their brief is due in late 2013.

Author's Note

I learned that the body of an apparent murder victim had just been found inside an upscale yoga store called lululemon athletica in Bethesda, Maryland, minutes after the police did—not from some trusted informant deep inside the local police department, but because a colleague of mine from the *Washington Post*, Eric Athas, happened to be standing fifteen feet from the store when patrolmen and paramedics rushed into the place. He'd come to Bethesda that morning—March 12, 2011—to get an early spot in line for the latest gizmo from Apple.

Deep Throat . . . CIA moles . . . or a colleague waiting to buy a new iPad? You take what you can get.

So I arrived, notebook in hand, and was standing outside the freshly strung yellow crime-scene tape as Detectives Jim Drewry and Dimitry Ruvin and Sergeant Craig Wittenberger put on their evidence gloves and booties, opened the door of the yoga store, and slipped inside. It was one of those moments in journalism, repeated countless times, when you realize just how little you know about what's going on. Over the next eleven months, as the *Post*'s police reporter for Montgomery County, Maryland, I wrote stories about the investigation, the trial, and its aftermath. But many of the details of the case and its conclusions remained a mystery: How and why was Jayna murdered? What exactly had led detectives to her killer? What behind-the-scenes maneuvers did the lawyers make? And who were Jayna Murray and Brittany Norwood, the principals at the heart of the story?

The *Post* granted me a six-month leave of absence to try to find out. I assembled a trove of records, which quickly filled three deep file drawers in my basement office. Under the Maryland Public Information Act, I obtained more than 2,000 pages of documents and electronic files related to the case. I interviewed approximately 154 people—from autopsy technicians to retailing experts to cops to longtime Bethesda residents. I am grateful for the time that many of the case's key players afforded me, in some cases sitting down for multiple, recorded interviews that stretched on for hours. Among them were the three detectives I'd seen going into the store—Drewry, Ruvin, and Wittenberger—as well as prosecutors John McCarthy and Marybeth Ayres, and forensic experts Mary Ripple, William Vosburgh, and David McGill. Jayna Murray's parents, David and Phyllis, and her brothers, Hugh and Dirk, also spent more than twenty hours in interviews with me.

Several key figures declined to be interviewed, most notably Brittany Norwood, as well as her family and her attorneys—just as they had declined all interviews from any reporters after the story broke. Their reasons were understandable: as of this writing, Brittany is still appealing her conviction. Neither she nor her supporters wanted to jeopardize that effort or bring more attention to the case. Instead, I studied letters her family members wrote to the presiding judge. I quoted every word Brittany spoke at her sentencing hearing, which remain her only public comments about the case. Most fruitfully, I read 11,000 text messages that Brittany sent and received from 2008 to 2011. These days, communiqués like these offer a direct view into not only what a person is probably doing, but also what she is likely thinking. To make the texts easier to read, I sometimes spelled out text shorthand, but never in a way to change the texts' meaning. When Brittany texted a friend thanking her for setting up an interview for a fitness trainer job, for instance, she wrote, "I owe u big time," which I changed to "I owe you big time." I also interviewed as many of Brittany's former friends, coworkers, coaches, and neighbors as I could.

I studied other written and electronic records, most of which have never been made public, including contemporaneous notes kept by detectives; audio and video recordings of law enforcement interviews with witnesses and suspects; evidence logs; diagrams sketched by crime-scene investigators; approximately 1,500 photographs from the investigation; 359 pages of analysis of citizen tips that poured in to detectives; and internal police reports summarizing all stages of the case. Montgomery County's chief prosecutor, State's Attorney John McCarthy, allowed me to read notes and outlines he wrote as he compiled his case and tried it in court. Donny Knepper, the defense attorney who served on the jury, also shared with me the journal he wrote at night and early in the morning as the trial took place. I reviewed my own notes from covering the trial, and read the 2,878-page official transcript of all the proceedings, which revealed conversations that had taken place out of earshot of the public and the jury. I also reviewed all the documents, electronic files, and physical evidence entered into the court record for the case. They included legal motions leading up to the trial; reports on DNA, blood spatter, and shoe prints; Jayna Murray's autopsy report; 79 pages of Brittany Norwood's medical records; and a brief psychological evaluation submitted for her sentencing hearing. I listened to tapes of the 911 calls, studied internal Apple Store video recordings, and watched and listened to more than six hours of interviews that detectives conducted with Brittany. I first learned about a piece of dialogue spoken by Jayna Murray—"We caught the bitch."—from the reporting of Washington, D.C., journalist and writer Peter Ross Rauge, which I was able to confirm from sources. I learned about Jayna sending her brother, Hugh, a package to Iraq from the reporting of Erin Donaghue at Bethesda-Chevy Chase Patch, which I then spoke to Hugh about. I poked through boxes of physical evidence from the trial, still stored on shelves on the third floor of the Montgomery County Circuit Court-house. I examined the red Buddha statue, the size-14 Reebok sneakers, and the black lululemon cap with the small bloodstain on the inside band, which had been found in the back of Jayna's car. I lifted the bloodstained, metal merchandise peg, just as two of the jurors had during deliberations. At nearly a pound, with its sharp, flanged edge, the bar is a horrendously perfect weapon.

In the book, I tried to present this material as a narrative account of what characters said and thought as events unfolded. I was aided by detectives' notes and, in certain cases, digital recordings. The investigators also testified under oath—during pretrial hearings and during the trial—about conversations that had taken place. From the witness stand, they recalled many of the most striking

scenes of the case. Witnesses, like the Apple Store managers, also testified about what they said to each other during
the events described.

Even so, much of the dialogue relies on people's memories of what they said or what they heard, and readers
would be well-served to remember that recollections are
just that. When writing about a conversation, I tried to
collect the memories of as many of the people present as
possible, in some cases as many as five people who were in
the room. When their memories of exact words differed,
I presented the dialogue that best reflected the consensus.
In hundreds of cases, I was able to use notes and reports
to support when and where and how something was said.
So when Detective Ruvin remembered the comments he
made inside the police department's evidence garage, I
had reports from crime-scene investigators confirming that
Ruvin was there at the moment he remembered saying,
"Oh yeah, we got blood. We got blood."

No one in this book read the entire manuscript before
it was published. Nor was anyone promised they'd get a
chance to review any sections. For the sake of accuracy, I
showed key characters whom I interviewed sections in
which they were quoted. I did this to check that I had
accurately captured what they said or what they were
thinking. No substantial changes or deletions resulted
from this process.

A note about privacy. Cases such as this one inevitably
drag the lives of private people into the public eye. In telling this story, I have delved into the lives of people who'd
rather I had not done so—principally, Brittany Norwood's
family, friends, and roommates. I tried to make those
names and materials public only when it added to an

understanding of who Brittany Norwood was or what she did. In one case, I used a pseudonym—to protect the identity of Brittany's roommate at the time of the murder. She spoke freely to detectives and prosecutors prior to the trial, even as her life was being turned upside down by the revelation that she had shared a roof with someone whom she, in retrospect, didn't know at all.

I thank colleagues at the *Post* who encouraged me to step out from the comforting chaos of daily newspaper work to tackle this project, namely Greg Jaffe, Craig Timberg, Maria Glod, Mike Semel, and Vernon Loeb. Thanks also to those who read early drafts of my manuscript and offered valuable encouragement and criticism: Greg, Craig, and Maria, as well as Alison Howard, Dominic Preziosi, Pam Feigenbaum, Patrick Hickerson, Katharine Weymouth, Mike Wilson, and Stephen Merelman. My parents also weighed in on early drafts, including my dad, who was never less than candid: "This chapter was better than the one before it, which was kind of boring" was among his memorable reports. Thanks also to the fact-checking and research excellence of Jennifer Jenkins. The best reader of all was also the best part of my life, my wife and *Post* colleague Dana Hedgpeth. Another round of thanks are due to all of my family members who helped with so many home duties that I allowed to take a backseat to this project—Jet, Valerie, Lee, Margie, Morris, Emily, Mark, Nancy, David, Claire, and, again, Dana.

I also want to thank my agent, David Patterson at Foundry Literary + Media, who not only sold this book for me, but was essential in walking a first-time book writer through such a new and unfamiliar world. At Berkley Books, Shannon Jamieson Vazquez was the best kind of editor—someone who writes better than the author she is reading, and uses those skills to tighten, clarify, and simplify without changing meaning.

Jayna's parents and brothers—David, Phyllis, Hugh, and Dirk—gave me almost endless time and insights, even when I asked the difficult questions. As the Murrays said from the beginning, they wanted me to learn as much as I could about their daughter and sister, flaws and all. Jayna wasn't perfect, which to the Murrays made her all the more cherished.

Although the Norwoods chose not to speak with me, the family remains highly respected by those who do know them, and who shared their thoughts with me.

The accomplishments and demeanor of the members of both families—who all sat in the second row throughout the trial—were hardly lost on Judge Robert Greenberg. Moments before he sentenced Brittany, he looked at them and said, in a voice choked with emotion, "We don't pick our families. But, frankly, if I had to pick a family, I'd want either the Norwoods or the Murrays."

For years I have written about tragedies visited on parents. They always told me I'd never understand until I had kids myself. During the time I wrote this book, our first daughter approached her first birthday. I can't pretend to know exactly how the Murrays or Norwoods feel, but I certainly understand it better.

The story of one of the most bizarre mass murders ever recorded—and the girl who escaped with her life.

From national bestselling author

ROBERT SCOTT

with Sarah Maynard and Larry Maynard

The GIRL *in the* LEAVES

In the fall of 2010, in the all-American town of Apple Valley, Ohio, four people disappeared without a trace: Stephanie Sprang; her friend Tina Maynard; and Tina's two children, thirteen-year-old Sarah and eleven-year-old Kody. Investigators began scouring the area, yet despite an extensive search, no signs of the missing people were discovered.

On the fourth day of the search, evidence trickled in about neighborhood "weirdo" Matthew Hoffman. A police SWAT team raided his home and found an extremely disturbing sight: every square inch of the place was filled with leaves, and a terrified Sarah Maynard was bound up in the middle of it like some sort of perverted autumn tableau. But there was no trace of the others...

INCLUDES PHOTOGRAPHS

Praise for Robert Scott and his books:

"Compelling and shocking...[A] ground-breaking book."
—Robert K. Tanenbaum

"Fascinating and fresh...[A] fast-paced informative read."
—Sue Russell

RobertScottTrueCrime.com | penguin.com